Norm and Ideology in Spoken French

David Hornsby

Norm and Ideology in Spoken French

A Sociolinguistic History of Liaison

palgrave
macmillan

David Hornsby
School of European Culture and Languages
University of Kent School of European Culture and Languages
Canterbury, Kent, UK

ISBN 978-3-030-49302-8 ISBN 978-3-030-49300-4 (eBook)
https://doi.org/10.1007/978-3-030-49300-4

Cover illustration: Alex Linch shutterstock.com

This Palgrave Macmillan imprint is published by the registered company Springer Nature Switzerland AG.
The registered company address is: Gewerbestrasse 11, 6330 Cham, Switzerland

For Elizabeth and Meli

Preface

While one might question the wisdom of adding to the already copious literature on liaison in French, I was drawn to the subject as a sociolinguist for three reasons. Firstly, as the title suggests, a variable phenomenon subject to highly complex prescriptive rules, and mastered only by a minority of speakers, offered an ideal case study for Anthony Kroch's ideological model of variation and change, as outlined in Part I. Secondly, although it is generally accepted that liaison occurs most frequently in scripted styles, the relationship between liaison and literacy remained under-explored, and called for a diachronic examination as provided in Part II. Finally, liaison provides a striking example of French sociolinguistic data failing to fit established theoretical models. This *exception française* has become something of an 'elephant in the room': frequently observed, but rarely addressed or discussed. I attempt to shed some light on this broader question in Parts III and IV.

Completion of this book would not have been possible without the help and advice I have been given at various stages. I am grateful to the British Academy for Small Grant SG40599, which greatly facilitated transcription and data analysis for the 'Four Cities' project, and to the University of Kent Modern Languages Research Committee for financial support during the fieldwork period. A University of Kent internal research award was enormously helpful in the latter stages of manuscript preparation, and I should also like warmly to thank three Kent colleagues,

Vikki Janke, Shane Weller, and Ibi Reichl, for their support during this period.

I am indebted to Tom Baldwin, Tony Bex, Zoe Boughton, Aidan Coveney, Jacques Durand, Julien Eychenne, Bernard Laks, Ian Mackenzie, Elissa Pustka, Peter Trudgill and especially Nigel Armstrong for advice and comment on earlier drafts; any remaining errors and misunderstandings are entirely my own. The debt this book owes more widely to the *Phonologie du Français Contemporain* project, launched by Jacques Durand, Bernard Laks and Chantal Lyche, will be evident from even a cursory look at these pages. I am grateful to Rhiannon Chappell, Rachel Dickinson and Emma Furderer at the University of Kent Templeman Library, all of whom went out of their way to help me locate obscure but invaluable source material. Elizabeth Hornsby, Jayne Hornsby, Marie-Louise Jackson, Martin Kane, Jon Kasstan and David Stalley all kindly proofread draft chapters and made perceptive and helpful comments. Thanks are due too to the Language and Linguistics editorial team at Palgrave Macmillan, and particularly to Alice Green for her unfailing support. Finally, thank you to my long-suffering family for their forbearance as the project came to fruition, and to Amelia Holmes, who has waited a very long time to see this book in print.

Canterbury, UK David Hornsby

Contents

List of Figures

List of Tables

Part I

Models

1

Ideology and Language Change

1.1 Kroch's Model of Language Variation

In a seminal article published in *Language and Society* in 1978, Anthony Kroch appeared to question one of the core tenets of linguistics. The axiom 'Linguistics is descriptive, not prescriptive' had become as much a *raison d'être* as a guiding principle for a discipline determined to challenge language-related prejudice. Linguists generally, and sociolinguists in particular, had been at pains to stress the equality of all varieties, and reject folk-linguistic stereotypes associated with regionally or socially defined speaker groups. So when Kroch observed, citing evidence from Labov's famous (1966) New York City survey, that 'prestige dialects require special attention to speech' and 'non-prestige dialects tend to be articulatorily more economical than the prestige dialect' (1978: 19–20), he was acutely aware that his views could be characterised as reviving prescriptive stereotypes of 'lazy' working-class usage.

As he made clear, however, Kroch's intention was not in any way to be judgmental or prescriptive. In claiming that 'working-class speech is more susceptible to the processes of phonetic conditioning than the prestige dialect' (p.18), Kroch was simply arguing that language change has an ideological component which, however inconvenient it might be, could no longer be ignored. While working-class speech follows 'natural' phonetic conditioning processes,[1] higher status groups, he claimed, actively

[1] For a definition of 'natural' he cites principles of 'naturalness' presented by Miller (1972) and Stampe (1972); on 'naturalness' in non-standard varieties see also Anderwald (2011).

D. Hornsby, *Norm and Ideology in Spoken French*,
https://doi.org/10.1007/978-3-030-49300-4_1

resist these same processes in order to maintain social distinction (1978: 30):

> Our position, as stated earlier, is that prestige dialects resist phonetically motivated change and inherent variation because prestige speakers seek to mark themselves off as distinct from the common people and because inhibiting phonetic processes is an obvious way to do this. Thus, we are claiming that there is a particular ideological motivation at the origin of social dialect variation. This ideology causes the prestige dialect user to expend more energy in speaking than does the user of the popular vernacular.

Presenting evidence from a range of studies, Kroch cites three examples of phonetic change, namely (i) consonantal simplification (ii) vocalic processes of chain shifting and (iii) assimilation of foreign phonemes to a native pattern, all of which, he argues, are further advanced in non-standard varieties. Among higher status groups, by contrast, resistance to such linguistic processes demands a particular effort 'motivated not by the needs of communication but by status consciousness' (p. 19), which procures social advantage for the user. Linguistic conservatism on the part of elite groups, viewed by Kroch as the embodiment of their ideological value-system, had also been observed by Bloomfield (1964 [1927]: 393–94) half a century earlier:

> These dialects are maintained by social elites and such elites are by and large conservative. The use of conservative linguistic forms is for them a symbol of their whole value system. From this standpoint the conservatism of the literary language has basically the same source as that of the spoken prestige dialect, since the standards of the literary language are set by the elite.

Kroch's emphasis on the ideological dimension has been challenged in recent years by commentators who associate linguistic conservatism not with ideology, but with isolation (see especially Trudgill 1992, 2011). Isolation may even promote the very opposite of the simplifying changes Kroch associates with low-status speakers. Milroy and Margrain (1980), for example, highlight the exceptional phonological complexity of the working-class vowel system of English in Belfast, a relatively peripheral city within the United Kingdom in which close-knit communities inhabit what Milroy (1980) describes as 'urban villages'. Andersen (1988) has noted the prevalence of 'exorbitant phonetic developments' in isolated communities, such as *kugv* ('cow') /ku:/ > /kigv/ in Faroese (see Trudgill 2011: 153), which again appear to run counter to the expectations of Kroch's model. One can also, moreover, point to counter-examples within the evidence which Kroch himself cites. He notes, for example, that /r/-deletion in New York is a simplifying change which, according to Labov's (1966) evidence, is both further advanced among working-class speakers and stigmatised by elite groups. Within England, however, the pattern is reversed: the prestige accent RP (Received Pronunciation) is notably non-rhotic, while some low-status varieties retain non-prevocalic /r/; similar remarks apply to 'HAPPY-tensing' in many British English varieties, where replacement of a lax unstressed final vowel by a tense one results in increased articulatory effort. But Kroch is careful not to claim that 'regular phonological processes can all be reduced to simplification of some sort' (p.23, fn. 9), and among the 'established prestige dialects' to which he restricts his remarks, his model has a clear and obvious relevance to the case of standard French, a language which has probably seen more rigid top-down codification than any other.

1.2 The 'Least Effort' Principle

Similar observations had certainly not been lost on French commentators. Kroch himself (p.18, fn.4) cites Schogt (1961: 91), who had drawn attention to class-based differences in speech, and notably the conservatism of upper-class varieties, contrasting 'la langue populaire riche en innovations, qui a pour elle le grand nombre, et la langue des classes aisées, qui est plus conservatrice et qui s'impose par son prestige'. In similar vein, simplifying tendencies in working-class speech had been subsumed in a broad 'principe du moindre effort' or 'least effort principle',[2]

[2] The term 'loi du moindre effort' in the context of the French language appears to have been first used in a little-known article by Léon Bollack (1903; see Hornsby and Jones 2006), who identifies

which had been central to at least two descriptive works (Bauche 1920; Guiraud 1965) on *français populaire* (broadly conceived as the working-class speech of Paris),[3] as well as strongly influencing Frei's (1993 [1929]) *La Grammaire des Fautes*. The least effort principle in these works is not restricted to phonetic processes as for Kroch, and includes for example the elimination of inflectional redundancy which distinguishes spoken French from the formal written code: *les petites princesses arrivent* for example has four suffixal plural markers (underlined) in writing, but only one marker *les* [le] in speech. Informal deletion of the negative particle *ne* (e.g. 'je sais pas' for 'je ne sais pas') is known to be more common in working-class than in middle-class speech (see Ashby 1981; Coveney 2002: 55–90), and can be understood again in terms of the least effort principle, in that it reduces the number of explicit markers of negation from two (*ne* and *pas*) to one (*pas*). The same principle can be seen to have been extended further in the colloquial, and still highly stigmatised, *t'inquiète !* for *ne t'inquiète pas !*, where both *ne* and *pas* can be deleted because word order in the case of the negative imperative is itself a marker of negation (contrast the positive imperative *inquiète-toi !*, where the pronoun follows rather than precedes the verb).

Echoes of Kroch's claims regarding the conservatism of elite groups are also to be found in prescriptive works. The *Avant-Propos* (p.V) to Fouché's (1959) *Traité de prononciation française* (which, the author notes, is based on investigations 'dans divers milieux cultivés de la capitale'), for example, recalls Kroch's comments on ideology and the phonetic assimilation of loan words:

> Mais déjà pour certains exemples, la prononciation à la française a provoqué chez plusieurs de nos informateurs un léger sourire et parfois davantage. Nous pensons en particulier au nom propre anglais *Southampton*, prononcé à la française *Sou-tan-pton* ou *Sou-tan-pton(e)*. C'est qu'un nou-

---

simplifying tendencies with 'éléments transformistes' destined to overcome the conservatism of standard French (in similar vein, Frei 1929 would see non-standard French as 'français avancé', heralding the standard language of the future). Bollack's focus, however, was on writing rather than speech, and his use of the term is not linked to social class or ideology.

[3] And, by extension, francophone France more generally: 'le français populaire de Paris est, avec quelques différences sans grande importance, le français populaire de toute la France, de la France, du moins, qui parle français' (Bauche 1920: 183).

> veau courant s'est fait jour. En effet, on répugne de plus en plus dans les milieux cultivés à prononcer les noms propres étrangers d'introduction récente comme s'ils étaient français. Seule la masse continue l'ancienne mode.

Whether or not this represented an innovation as the author suggests (we will see evidence in Part II that this trend was in fact far from new), the evident disdain in *milieux cultivés* for regular processes of assimilation practised by *la masse* is laid bare in Fouché's account and is entirely consistent with Kroch's claims. In fact, Fouché's example neatly illustrates the way elite groups maintain social advantage through language. By resisting phonetic assimilation of loan words, members of privileged groups are able to signal a degree of familiarity with the donor languages, and thereby possession of a cultural capital unavailable to those without access to high-level education. As Bourdieu observes (1982: 51–52), the linguistic capital enjoyed by elite groups can only be procured at significant cost in terms of time, effort and (by implication) money:

> La langue légitime doit sa *constance (relative) dans le temps* (comme dans l'espace) au fait qu'elle est continûment protégée par un travail prolongé d'inculcation contre l'inclination à l'*économie* d'effort et de tension qui porte par exemple à la simplification analogique (*vous faisez* et *vous disez* pour *vous faites* et *vous dites*). (Author's emphasis.)

1.3 The Ideology of the Standard

Bourdieu's conception of *la langue légitime*, a totemised prescriptive standard imposed by state sanctioned elites, is best viewed in terms of what James and Lesley Milroy (2012) have termed 'the ideology of the standard'. Lesley Milroy (2003: 161; cited by Armstrong and Mackenzie 2012: 26) has defined a language ideology as 'a system for making sense of the indexicality inherent in language, given that languages and language forms index speakers' social identities fairly reliably in communities'. Like all ideologies, it is largely unconscious and represents an internalised set of beliefs which are perceived by those who hold them as 'received wisdom' or simply 'common sense'. As Armstrong and

Mackenzie (2012: 6) point out, the ideology of the standard in particular legitimises a hierarchical ordering of society and contains a normative element, directing the way speakers ought to behave. The standard itself 'borrows prestige from the power of its users' (*ibid.*), who have an interest in its maintenance and therefore generally oppose change as Kroch suggests. This ideology is extraordinarily powerful and pervasive in France, where, as Brunot (1966: III, 4) famously observed, 'le règne de la grammaire.. a été plus tyrannique et plus long qu'en aucun pays'.[4] In his seminal sociolinguistic account of standardisation in France, Lodge (1993: 156) sets out its three core tenets, which we summarise below:

1. The ideal state of a language is uniformity: non-standard language is improper and change is to be deplored.
2. The most valid form of the language is to be found in writing; speaking is considered to be 'less grammatical' than the written form and the purest form of the language is to be found in the work of the best authors.
3. The standard language, which happens to be used by those with most power and status, is inherently better than other varieties. Other sociolects, which happen to be used by those with little status and power, are seen as debased forms of the standard and can be dismissed as 'sloppy' or 'slovenly' ways of expressing oneself.

The first of these beliefs demonstrates why standardisation should be seen as an ideology rather than simply a process. As language is always subject to variation and change, the ideal of uniformity, manifested in a one-to-one relationship between correct form and meaning, can never fully be realised, even with the support of purist institutions, which attempt to eliminate variability from the legitimised variety. The most iconic of these institutions is the *Académie Française*, founded by Richelieu in 1635, the conservatism of which drew this stinging rebuke from Fénelon in an open letter in 1714: 'On a appauvri, desséché et gêné notre

[4] Cf. Klinkenberg (1992: 42) 'le français offre sans doute l'exemple le plus poussé qui soit de centralisme et d'institutionalisation linguistique'. The opening chapter of L.C. Harmer's *The French Language* (1954) is appropriately entitled 'A Nation of Grammarians', a label attributed to Duhamel (1944: 50).

langue.' In more recent times this conservatism has found expression in opposition to loan words from English, and resistance to feminisation of professional titles. The second core belief in particular, that the written language is inherently superior,[5] is especially deep-rooted in France, and has notably hampered many an attempt to reform the orthographic system. In a culture which identifies French with its written form, reform proposals are not infrequently pilloried as attacks on the language itself (see Désirat and Hordé 1976: 218–20)[6] and indeed the complexities of French spelling which make it so difficult to learn are held up as something of a virtue.[7] Standard forms are seen not merely as correct, but also as inherently more beautiful than low-status variants. As we will see repeatedly below in respect of liaison, purist strictures are often defended in terms of the *harmonie* of the favoured forms, or the *cacophonie* of those proscribed, without any need being felt to explain how *harmonie* or *cacophonie* are defined.

The most steadfast defenders of the status quo tend, of course, to be those who have had the means, time and resources to master the complexities of the standard written norm. The minority who do so secure

---

[5] Cf. Kroch (1978: 30):

> The influence of the literary language on the spoken standard is one manifestation among others of a socially motivated inhibition of linguistic change. This conclusion is reinforced by the fact that prestige dialects not only inhibit changes that violate written forms but also resist changes in such features as vowel quality long before those changes would cause noticeable contradictions between the written and the spoken forms.

[6] The widely-held belief that 'correct' French is to be equated with its written form is neatly illustrated by a hypercorrection, and a purist response to it. In Etiemble's famous (1964) broadside against Anglo-American loanwords, *Parlez-vous franglais?*, the singer Dalida is quoted as having said 'je n'ẹn ai pas prises [pʁiz]' during a television interview, in what appears to have been an unsuccessful attempt to make a past participle agreement. Rather than comment on the inappropriateness to speech of what is essentially an arcane orthographical rule, formally inculcated through years of daily school *dictées* but rarely mastered by French native speakers, Etiemble (p. 282) excoriates this non-native French speaker for 'une belle grosse faute contre notre syntaxe'. That a man of the left, and a champion of French independence from US capitalism, should find himself judging a relatively uneducated immigrant by the exacting orthographic standards of a privileged class does not appear to have been viewed at the time as in any way incongruous.

[7] Ball (1997: 191-92) lists some of the more vitriolic responses to the proposed 1990 spelling reforms, which included the following from Yves Berger in the November 1990 edition of *Lire*: 'Stupide, inutile, dangeureuse : c'est une entreprise qui relève de la pure démagogie, de l'esprit de Saddam Hussein'.

the considerable social advantages which accrue from the third core belief, that the standard variety is inherently superior. These include improved educational outcomes, enhanced employment opportunities, professional success, and even favourable treatment from medical professionals, who pay greater attention and offer more positive diagnoses to middle-class patients (see Bourdieu 1982: 45 fn.21). By contrast, those who do not are left in a state of linguistic insecurity which hampers their self-esteem and restricts life chances,[8] and are subject to sanction by a normative establishment, whose primary purpose, for Bourdieu, is to maintain the value of the linguistic capital monopolised by elites (1982: 49):

> La dépossession objective des classes dominées (…) n'est pas sans rapport avec l'existence d'un corps de professionnels objectivement investis du monopole de l'usage légitime de la langue légitime qui produisent pour leur propre usage une langue spéciale, prédisposée à remplir *par surcroît* une fonction sociale de distinction dans les rapports entre les classes et dans les luttes qui les opposent sur le terrain de la langue. Elle n'est pas sans rapport non plus avec l'existence d'une institution comme le système d'enseignement qui, mandaté pour sanctionner, au nom de la grammaire, les produits hérétiques et pour inculquer la norme explicite qui contrecarre les effets des lois d'évolution, contribue fortement à constituer comme tels les usages dominés de la langue en consacrant l'usage dominant comme seul légitime, par le seul fait de l'inculquer.

Central to Kroch's thinking is what Bourdieu above and elsewhere refers to as *distinction* (see especially Bourdieu 1979), that is the

---

[8] Gueunier et al. (1978) contrast attitudes among speakers in Tours, a city traditionally associated with 'good' French, with those observed in areas of linguistic insecurity such as Lille, where a working-class male informant bemoaned his own perceived inability to speak his native language (p.157):

> Nous, les gars du Nord, on fout des coups de pied à la France … s'appliquer, on peut y arriver, mais..on arrivera jamais à parler français, c'est pas vrai! … Je pourrais aller à l'école pendant dix ans, ben j'arriverais jamais à parler le français.

maintenance and regular use by elite groups of various symbols of cultural capital, in this case prestige linguistic forms, which enable them to distance themselves socially from the majority of the population. Their capacity to do so depends on the inaccessibility to all but a privileged few of certain elements of the prestige norm. This in turn raises the question of what 'inaccessible' might mean in this context, to which thus far we have offered only a partial answer. For Kroch, elite groups are schooled to use variants associated with careful or prepared speech which are not subject to what he considers normal phonetic conditioning, and which therefore require greater thought and articulatory effort. Linguistic forms can, however, also be inaccessible to low-status groups because they can only be learned through formal education, to which they have restricted access.[9] This is particularly true of those which (a) do not occur, or no longer occur, in speech and therefore are not acquired as part of mother-tongue competence and (b) require detailed knowledge of complex prescriptive rules, both of which are present in abundance in written standard French. In fact, such is the distance between informal spoken and formal written French that some scholars (e.g Massot 2005, 2006; Hamlaoui 2011; Zribi-Hertz 2006, 2011) have proposed a diglossic model for modern French in which the L functions are fulfilled by a mother-tongue variety which Massot labels *français démotique* (FD), and the H functions by *français classique tardif* (FCT), an archaic variety which has to be learned via formal education. While the diglossia hypothesis remains controversial (see Coveney 2011 for critique),[10] the maintenance in writing of moribund tense and mood forms (e.g. the past historic, past ante-

---

[9] Citing the example of the French vowel system, which has undergone significant simplification from twelve to seven oral vowels, Armstrong and Mackenzie (2012: 19) link social distinction to maintenance of a conservative written standard, a theme we develop below:

> The elements in the maximal twelve-vowel system, redundant in this linguistically functional view, continue however to serve a sociolinguistic purpose, as indeed is typical generally of 'conservative' elements in a linguistic system. This is facilitated in part by the fact that the functionally redundant elements in the twelve-vowel system have orthographic correlates, which are not equally accessible to all speakers.

[10] For a discussion of the diglossia hypothesis with respect to variable liaison, see Hornsby (2019).

rior and imperfect subjunctive) which have long since been lost from the spoken language, together with a complex system of agreements and verb endings which are for the most part not realised in speech, is certainly consistent with Bourdieu's characterisation of standard French as 'une langue semi-artificielle' (1982: 51).

Bourdieu paints a picture of a linguistic marketplace in which the highest values accrue to the most inaccessible 'goods', namely those associated with a highly codified standard, against which all others are viewed as defective or devalued. This engenders a perpetual scramble for prestige in which the dominated seek desperately to increase their market value through acquisition of linguistic capital, while the dominant elites seek constantly to distance themselves from them by using forms to which only they have access. There are clear echoes here of Fischer's (1964: 286) views on the mechanism of language change, as quoted by Kroch (1978: 21):

> Martin Joos (1952) (…) speaks of 'the phonetic drift, which was kept going in the usual way: that is, the dialects and idiolects of higher prestige were more advanced in this direction, and their speakers carried the drift further along so as to maintain the prestige-marking differences against their pursuers. The vanity factor is needed to explain why phonetic drifts tend to continue in the same direction; the "inertia" sometimes invoked is a label not an argument'. This protracted pursuit of an elite by an envious mass and the consequent 'flight' of the elite is in my opinion the most important mechanism in linguistic drift, not only in the phonetic drift which Joos discusses, but in syntactic and lexical drifting as well.

Within this 'marketplace', values are protected by a court of linguistic arbiters whose decisions are not to be questioned:

> Nul n'est censé ignorer la loi linguistique qui a son corps de juristes, les grammairiens, et ses agents de contrôle, les maîtres de l'enseignement, investis du pouvoir de soumettre universellement à l'examen et à la sanction juridique du titre scolaire la performance linguistique des sujets parlants. (Bourdieu 1982: 27)

This 'corps de juristes' is, of course, rarely open about its role in maintaining social distinction, though the subjective social basis of judgement in Vaugelas' (1970 [1647]) *Remarques sur la langue française* is set out clearly in the *Préface*, which links notions of *bon usage* both to a social elite, setting 'la plus saine partie de la cour' against 'la lie du peuple de Paris'. There is, moreover, a disarming frankness about the Academy's 1673 rejection of modest spelling reform proposals (see Chap. 3): 'Généralement parlant, la Compagnie préfère l'ancienne orthographe, qui distingue les gens de Lettres d'avec les Ignorants et les simples femmes.'[11] Indeed, as seventeenth-century grammarians attempted to provide for French the fixity and prestige which would establish the language as a legitimate heir to Latin, the need for a complex set of rules accessible only to the few was never far from their minds. As Poplack et al. (2015: 16) observe, if French were to be taken seriously as a prestige language then, bluntly, it had to be difficult to master: 'To achieve the required legitimacy, the language would need rules; apparently, the more intricate and dogmatic, the better.'

It would be hard to imagine an area of the prescriptive norm more subject to intricate and dogmatic rules than liaison, which makes it an ideal testing ground for Kroch's model of variation and change. As we shall see in Chap. 3, liaison consonants recall a period when final consonants were generally pronounced: their variable retention in a limited range of environments would therefore seem to reflect linguistic conservatism. Non-realisation of final consonants, on the other hand, is consistent in at least two respects with simplifying processes associated with lower-status groups in Kroch's model: the loss of a consonant in coda position firstly represents an overall reduction in articulatory effort, and secondly, by generalising the zero final consonant form to all contexts, it offers allomorphic regularisation. As the orthographic residue from a former pronunciation, liaison consonants are particularly favoured in styles which involve reading aloud (e.g. poetry recital), and elsewhere can be used by skilled speakers, for example in set-piece political speeches, to invoke the authority of the written word, which exerts inordinate power

[11] Cited in 'L'orthographe : histoire d'une longue querelle': http://www.academie-francaise.fr/lorthographe-histoire-dune-longue-querelle (accessed 22.2.2020).

in the francophone world. The intricacies of liaison are generally mastered only by a highly literate elite, while presenting numerous pitfalls for the unwary or inexperienced. Mindful of these dangers, Passy (1906: 130), in his *Les Sons du Français*, a non-prescriptive work intended to further the cause of orthographic reform, references in a footnote a comment by a protagonist in Eugène Labiche's 1867 one-act vaudeville comedy *La Grammaire*: 'J'évite les liaisons. C'est prétentieux… et dangereux.'

It is worth recalling the original context of the play, which would have been familiar to much of Passy's audience. A relatively ill-educated former shopkeeper, François Caboussat, finds his social and political ambitions hampered by his problems with spelling. This was not the only Labiche play in which orthography figured prominently for comedic or satirical purposes (see Portebois 2006: 45–56), but it was the first to make spelling its central theme. Caboussat bemoans his own inability to form past participle agreements correctly, associating liaison very clearly both with elevated speech and the written word:

> Je suis riche, considéré, adoré… et une chose s'oppose à mes projets… la grammaire française !… Je ne sais pas l'orthographe ! Les participes surtout, on ne sait par quel bout les prendre… tantôt ils s'accordent, tantôt ils ne s'accordent pas… quels fichus caractères ! Quand je suis embarrassé, je fais un pâté… mais ce n'est pas de l'orthographe ! Lorsque je parle, ça va très bien, ça ne se voit pas… j'évite les liaisons… À la campagne, c'est prétentieux… et dangereux… je dis : "Je suis allé… " (Il prononce sans lier l's avec l'a.) Ah ! dame, de mon temps, on ne moisissait pas dans les écoles… j'ai appris à écrire en vingt-six leçons, et à lire… je ne sais pas comment.

Caboussat perfectly exemplifies the *petit bourgeois* identified by Bourdieu, whose desperate attempts at social advancement are thwarted by a lack of linguistic or cultural capital. He also illustrates the ideological power of the written word in a country which still views writing as the norm and speech a poor deviation from it. Grammar in the mind of this socially aspirant individual is associated with writing and his perceived inability to speak correctly—not knowing for example how to form 'dangerous' linguistic liaisons or observe the rules of preceding direct object agreement—derives primarily from his difficulties with spelling. Its links to an arcane orthographic system and complex set of prescriptive rules make variable liaison a prime locus of social distinction, strewn with traps for the unwary Caboussats of this world.[12]

As important as knowing the social rules is having the social confidence to know how and when to break them and thereby avoid 'l'hypercorrection d'un parler trop châtié, immédiatement dévalué par une ambition trop évidente, qui est la marque de la petite-bourgeoisie de promotion' (Bourdieu 1982: 56). Liaison is therefore as much of interest for the complexity of its prescriptive rules as for the social sanction associated with applying them too rigidly, a danger of which Passy (1906: 130) warns his readers:

> L'emploi des liaisons varie considérablement selon le style et selon les personnes. Dans le langage littéraire on lie beaucoup plus que dans le style familier; mais ce sont surtout les instituteurs, les professeurs de diction, et encore plus les personnes peu instruites essayant de 'parler bien', qui introduisent des liaisons en masse. Parfois alors elles se trompent et emploient mal à propos (z) ou (t) comme son de liaison [*des cuirs, des velours*][13]

1.4 Plan of This Book

By virtue of its complexity and opacity to outsiders, liaison merits examination in the context of the ideological model of Kroch and Bourdieu as outlined above. In the remainder of Part I we will present an established model of liaison and examine some of the theoretical and practical questions it raises, before considering some comparable phenomena in

---

[12] Cf. Bourdieu (1982: 42; fn. 18):

> Seul le facultatif peut donner lieu à des effets de distinction. Comme le montre Pierre Encrevé, dans le cas des liaisons catégoriques, qui sont toujours observées par tous, y compris dans les classes populaires, il n'y a pas de place pour le jeu. Lorsque les contraintes structurales de la langue se trouvent suspendues, avec les liaisons facultatives, le jeu réapparaît, avec les effets de distinction corrélatifs.

[13] Passy appears to suggest here that *cuir* and *velours* refer to false liaison involving [z] and [t] respectively. General usage has, however, settled on *velours* for [z] and *cuir* for [t].

contemporary English (Chap. 2). In Part II, we will offer a diachronic perspective, focusing in Chap. 3 on the loss of final consonants from the Late Latin period onwards, before examining in Chap. 4 the views of prescriptive grammarians, whose resistance to phonetic change created conditions in which, in Armstrong's (2001: 202) words:

> The situation was ready for the imposition or consolidation by upper-class speakers of a linguistically arbitrary system; one that is not transparently rule-governed, but can only be learned through long immersion in the appropriate milieu. Clearly, the motivation for developing or maintaining such a system is to be able to distinguish members of the group from non-members. We can draw a parallel between variable liaison and any in-group code whose function is to mystify non-initiates.

Attention turns in Part III to the way in which speakers negotiate the complexities of variable liaison, drawing on research from over four decades. Chapter 5 considers liaison from a geographical perspective, while Chap. 6 examines some surprising and often contradictory findings from variationist studies which have explored its relationship with familiar extralinguistic factors such as class and gender. Chapter 7 reports on our own findings from the 'Four Cities' project, focusing particularly on differences between scripted and unscripted speech, before investigation in Chap. 8 of a very particular group of speakers, the so-called *professionnels de la parole publique*, whose use of liaison has long been known to diverge significantly from that of the general population. We will see throughout Part III that the complex and multi-faceted nature of liaison as a variable phenomenon makes broad brush generalisations dangerous, and forces the researcher to construct the bigger picture from small and often in themselves statistically insignificant pieces of data. In Part IV, we attempt to draw some general conclusions from the findings available, notably concerning the relationship between liaison and literacy, and in doing so lay the foundations for a twenty-first-century style model.

References

Andersen, H. (1988). Center and Periphery: Adoption, Diffusion, and Spread. In J. Fisiak (Ed.), *Historical Dialectology: Regional and Social* (pp. 39–84). Berlin: Mouton de Gruyter.

Anderwald, L. (2011). Are Non-Standard Dialects More 'Natural' Than the Standard? A Test Case from English Verb Morphology. *Journal of Linguistics, 47*, 251–274.

Armstrong, N. (2001). *Social and Stylistic Variation in Spoken French: A Comparative Approach*. Amsterdam, Netherlands: John Benjamins.

Armstrong, N., & Mackenzie, I. (2012). *Standardization, Ideology and Linguistics*. Basingstoke: Palgrave Macmillan.

Ashby, W. J. (1981). The Loss of the Negative Particle *Ne* in French: A Syntactic Change in Progress. *Language, 57*, 674–687.

Ball, R. (1997). *The French-Speaking World: An Introduction to Sociolinguistic Issues*. London; New York: Routledge.

Bauche, H. (1920). *Le langage populaire: Grammaire, syntaxe et dictionnaire du français tel qu'on le parle dans le peuple de Paris*. Paris: Payot.

Bloomfield, L. (1964 [1927]). Literate and Illiterate Speech. *American Speech, 2*(10), 432–439. Reprinted in D. Hymes (Ed.), *Language in Culture and Society* (pp. 391–396). New York: Harper and Row.

Bollack, L. (1903). La Langue française en l'an 2003. *La Revue, 15 July*, 5–24.

Bourdieu, P. (1979). *La Distinction*. Paris: Minuit.

Bourdieu, P. (1982). *Ce que parler veut dire: L'Economie des échanges linguistiques*. Paris: Fayard.

Brunot, F. (1966). *Histoire de la langue française: des origines à 1900* (13 Vols.). Paris: Colin.

Coveney, A. (2002). *Variability in Spoken French: A Sociolinguistic Study of Interrogation and Negation*. Bristol: Elm Bank Publications.

Coveney, A. (2011). A Language Divided Against Itself? Diglossia, Code-Switching and Variation in French. In F. Martineau & T. Nadasdi (Eds.), *Le français en contact: Hommages à Raymond Mougeon* (pp. 51–85). Québec: Presses de l'Université Laval.

Désirat, C., & Hordé, T. (1976). *La Langue française au 20ᵉ siècle*. Paris: Bordas.

Duhamel, G. (1944). *Civilisation Française*. Paris: Hachette.

Étiemble, R. (1964). *Parlez-vous franglais?* Paris: Gallimard.

Fischer, J. (1964 [1958]). Social Influences on the Choice of a Linguistic Variant. *Word, 14*, 47–56. Reprinted in D. Hymes (Ed.), *Language in Culture and Society* (pp. 483–489). New York: Harper and Row.
Fouché, P. (1959). *Traité de prononciation française* (2nd ed.). Paris: Klincksieck.
Frei, H. (1993 [1929]). *La Grammaire des Fautes*. Geneva, Paris: Slatkine Reprints.
Gueunier, N., Genouvrier, E., Khomsi, A., Carayol, M., & Chaudenson, R. (1978). *Les Français devant la norme*. Paris: Champion.
Guiraud. (1965). *Le Français populaire (Que sais-je?)*. Paris: Presses Universitaires de France.
Hamlaoui, F. (2011). On the Role of Phonology and Discourse in Francilian French Wh-Questions. *Journal of Linguistics, 47*(1), 129–162.
Harmer, L. C. (1954). *The French Language Today: Its Characteristics and Tendencies*. London: Hutchinson.
Hornsby, D. (2019). Variable Liaison, Diglossia, and the Style Dimension in Spoken French. *French Studies, 73*(4), 578–597.
Hornsby, D., & Jones, M. (2006). Blue-Sky Thinking? Léon Bollack and 'La Langue française en l'an 2003'. *Language Planning and Language Issues, 30*(3), 215–238.
Joos, M. (1952). The Medieval Sibilants. *Language, 28*, 222–231.
Klinkenberg, J.-M. (1992). Le français, une langue en crise? In M. Wilmet, J.-M. Klinkenberg, B. Cerquiglini, & R. Dehaybe (Eds.), *Le français en débat* (pp. 25–44). Brussels: Duculot.
Kroch, A. (1978). Toward a Theory of Social Dialect Variation. *Language in Society, 7*, 17–36.
Labiche, E. (1867). *La Grammaire*. Retrieved from http://www.corpusetampois.com/cle-19-labiche1867lagrammaire.html.
Labov, W. (1966). *The Social Stratification of English in New York City*. Washington, DC: Center for Applied Linguistics.
Lodge, R. A. (1993). *French: From Dialect to Standard*. London: Routledge.
Massot, B. (2005). *Français et diglossie: Décrire la situation linguistique française contemporaine comme une diglossie: arguments morphosyntactiques*. Thèse de doctorat, Université de Paris 8. Retrieved from http://inferno.philosophie.uni-stuttgart.de/~benjamin/pdf/these-benjamin-massot-version-soutenance.pdf.
Massot, B. (2006). *Corpus-Based Ungrammaticality in French: A Pilot-Study*. Unpublished paper. Retrieved from http://inferno.philosophie.uni-stuttgart.de/~benjamin/recherche.html.

Miller, P. (1972). Vowel Neutralization and Vowel Reduction. In P. Petanteau, J. Levi, & G. Phares (Eds.), *Papers from the Eighth Regional Meeting of the Chicago Linguistic Society* (pp. 482–489). Chicago: Chicago Linguistic Society.

Milroy, L. (1980). *Language and Social Networks*. Oxford: Blackwell.

Milroy, L. (2003). Social and Linguistic Dimensions of Phonological Change. Fitting the Pieces of the Puzzle Together. In D. Britain & J. Cheshire (Eds.), *Social Dialectology: In Honour of Peter Trudgill* (pp. 155–172). Amsterdam: John Benjamins.

Milroy, L., & Margrain, S. (1980). Vernacular Language Loyalty and Social Network. *Language in Society, 9*, 43–70.

Milroy, J., & Milroy, L. (2012). *Authority in Language: Investigating Standard English* (4th ed.). London: Routledge.

Passy, P. (1906). *Les Sons du Français: leur formation, leur combinaison, leur représentation*. Paris: Firmin-Didot.

Poplack, S., Jarmasz, L.-G., Dion, N., & Rosen, N. (2015). Searching for Standard French: The Construction and Mining of the *Recueil historique des grammaires du français*. *Journal of Historical Sociolinguistics, 1*(1), 13–55.

Portebois, Y. (2006). *Les Arrhes de la Douairière: Histoire de la dictée de Mérimée ou l'orthographe sous le Second Empire*. Geneva; Paris: Droz.

Schogt, H. G. (1961). La notion de loi dans la phonétique historique. *Lingua, 10*, 72–92.

Stampe, D. (1972). On the Natural History of Diphthongs. In P. Petanteau, J. Levi, & G. Phares (Eds.), *Papers from the Eighth Regional Meeting of the Chicago Linguistic Society* (pp. 578–590). Chicago: Chicago Linguistic Society.

Trudgill, P. (1992). Dialect Typology and Social Structure. In E. Jahr (Ed.), *Language Contact and Language Change* (pp. 195–212). Berlin: Mouton de Gruyter.

Trudgill, P. (2011). *Sociolinguistic Typology: Social Determinants of Linguistic Complexity*. Oxford: Oxford University Press.

Vaugelas, C. F. de (1970 [1647]). *Remarques sur la langue françoise* (J. Streicher, Ed.). Geneva: Slatkine Reprints.

Zribi-Hertz, A. (2006). Français standard et francilien commun: conséquences du phénomène diglossique pour la description et l'enseignement du français. Retrieved from www.soc.nii.ac.jp/sjllf/archives/taikai/2006a/2006a.conference.hertz.pdf.

Zribi-Hertz, A. (2011). Pour un modèle diglossique de description du français: quelques implications théoriques, didactiques et méthodologiques. *Journal of French Language Studies, 21*, 231–256.

2

What Is Liaison?

2.1 Definitions

Liaison is an external sandhi[1] or 'joining' phenomenon which involves the pronunciation of a normally silent word-final consonant before a vowel. It bears some similarities, both historically and synchronically, to such English phenomena as 'linking *r*' in non-rhotic dialects (e.g. *a pair /r/ of trousers*) and indefinite article allomorphy (***a** pear/**an** apple*). It is of particular interest in French because of the complex conditions under which it may/may not be realised.

It should first be noted that French final consonants may be stable or unstable, and are not as uncommon as is sometimes supposed: Tranel (1987: 154–55), citing Juilland's *Dictionnaire inverse de la langue française* (1965: 437–56), claims that consonant-final words in fact slightly outnumber those which end in a vowel. Stable consonants fall into two categories, the first of which emerged from the loss of final unstressed or 'mute' *e* (*e-muet*) in most varieties of French, including reference French (RF).[2] As Posner observes (1997: 263), this vestigial orthographic final

[1] 'A general term, originating from the work of Sanskrit grammarians, for the phonological modifications that occur between juxtaposed forms.' (Brown and Miller 2013: 393).

[2] Detey et al. (2016: 56):

> Over the last ten years, the expression *Reference French* (RF) has spread in the literature and often replaces *Standard French*. This label is often preferred for its ability to allow for a

D. Hornsby, *Norm and Ideology in Spoken French*,
https://doi.org/10.1007/978-3-030-49300-4_2

vowel, still realised as schwa [ə] in some meridional French varieties, has been seen historically to 'protect' preceding consonants from the elision which might otherwise have taken place, as can be seen for example in *vase* [vaz], *bonne* [bɔn], *ingrate* [ɛ̃gʁat] (compare *vas* [va], *bon* [bɔ̃], *ingrat* [ɛ̃gʁa]). A second stable group comprises word-final consonants which either survived the large-scale erosion which took place between the twelfth and sixteenth centuries or were restored to pronunciation by grammarians at a later date (see Chap. 3), as in *chef* [ʃɛf], *dot* [dɔt] or *tir* [tiʁ]. Unstable consonants are realised either consistently or variably in prevocalic position but not prepausally or before a consonant, for example *les* [lez] *enfants* but *les* [le] *filles* or *mettez-les* [le]. Liaison in French denotes the realisation of these unstable consonants in prevocalic position, and represents a particular case of the wider phenomenon of forward syllabification or enchaînement in French,[3] by which word-final consonants become the onsets of following word-initial ones (e.g. *chef impressionnant* [ʃɛ#fɛ̃#pʁɛ#sjɔ#nɑ̃]), which affects both stable and unstable final consonants.[4] Liaison occurs non-variably in some contexts (e.g. *ils*-[z]-*ont; mon*-[n]-*ami*), and variably in others (e.g. *trop*-[p]/Ø-*aimable; les trains*-[z]/Ø-*arrivent*; see Sect. 2.2 below). For Fagyal et al. (2006: 65) liaison reflects a strong cross-linguistic tendency to avoid hiatus, that is to provide all syllables with an onset,[5] which can even override grammatical considerations in some cases, for example in the suppletive use of masculine possessive adjectives with vowel-initial feminine nouns (*mon amie; son horreur*), or conversely the use of the demonstrative *cet* (homophonous in most varieties with the feminine form *cette*) before vowel-initial

plurality of 'references', thus avoiding the all too frequent focus on hexagonal French. On the other hand, just like Standard French, it remains an abstract set of features that speakers may come close to, depending on a number of social and geographic factors. (Authors' emphasis.)

[3] Delattre (1966a: 39) argues for a qualitative difference between the two in that the increase in articulatory tension in the case of liaison is marginally greater than for *enchaînement*: 'L'union consonne-voyelle est donc plus étroite dans la liaison que dans l'enchaînement'.

[4] Although a marginal phenomenon for most speakers, liaison without enchaînement (e.g. *j'avais un rêve* [ʒa.vez.ʔɛ.ʁɛv]) is possible and was a particularly common feature of political discourse in the late 1970s and early 1980s (see Encrevé 1988 and 8.4 below).

[5] For an excellent discussion of syllabification in French, based on the maximum onset principle (see McMahon 2002: 111–12) and the sonority hierarchy, see Fagyal et al. (2006: 54).

masculine nouns (*cet homme*). But an explanation for liaison based solely or even largely on hiatus avoidance seems implausible given both the wide range of environments in which liaison does not occur, and evidence of an apparent decline in liaison in familiar usage (see Sect. 6.6 below).

Historically, liaison consonants represent vestigial realisations of word-final segments which have been lost in all but prevocalic environments. Liaison is blocked for a small, unproductive group of lexemes known inappropriately (for aspiration of orthographical *h* is no longer involved) as the *h-aspiré* set, consisting of fifth to eighth century CE Germanic borrowings which retained initial /h/. This consonant was later lost, leaving what amounts to an inaudible barrier to elision and liaison, setting this group apart from other orthographically *h*-initial lexemes, which follow the pattern of vowel-initial lexemes in these two respects (Table 2.1).

Liaison in contemporary French is traditionally seen to affect 6 consonants: /z/, /t/, /n/, /ʁ/, /p/, and /k/, as in the following examples (Table 2.2).

Liaison in contemporary French with /p/ is essentially limited to two adverbs *beaucoup* and *trop*, while liaison with /g/ is listed as a possibility only with *long* by Tranel (1987: 174) as an alternative to the canonical /k/[6] in this context, which is seen as archaic. Voiceless /k/ has traditionally been preferred here in prescriptive works, recalling the position in Old French where, as in Germanic, final oral stops were devoiced (hence *grand* [t] *homme* in spite of a general tendency for masculine adjectives in liaison to correspond to the feminine form (here *grande* [gʁɑ̃d]). Devoicing affects the stops /d/ and /g/, but not /b/, which generally occurs either before mute *e* (see above) or in recent borrowings with a stable final consonant (*club, toubib*). No liaison occurs after final *–mb* sequences (e.g. *plomb*). Conversely, voiceless fricatives such as /s/ became voiced intervocalically, hence [z] not [s] in liaison contexts, giving potentially three forms: zero, voiced and voiceless consonant. This pattern can still be observed for the numerals *six* and *dix*, and until recently also for *neuf*,

[6] Tranel (1987: 174) recommends /k/ only in the context of *sang impur* in the French national anthem *la Marseillaise*, but notes that even here it is unnatural for most speakers as liaison after singular nouns is generally very rare in modern French.

Table 2.1 Liaison and elision with *h-aspiré* and non *h-aspiré* lexemes

h-initial	*h-aspiré* initial
l'homme	le hibou
l'haleine	la hache
les [lez] hirondelles	les [Ø] hiboux
cet hélicoptère	ce [Ø] héros

Table 2.2 Canonical RF liaison consonants

Liaison consonant	Examples	Liaison context
/z/	bons [z] amis	plural adjective + noun
	soldats [z] américains	plural noun + adjective
	les [z] enfants	plural determiner + noun
/t/	veut [t] -il?	verb + clitic
	grand [t] homme	adjective + noun
	ils arrivent [t] à l'heure	verb + complement
/n/	un/mon [n] accueil	article/possessive adjective + noun
	bien [n] aimable	adverb + adjective
/ʁ/	léger [ʁ] accent	adjective + noun
	aimer [ʁ] un enfant	infinitive + complement
/p/	beaucoup [p] aimé	adverb + complement
	trop [p] aimable	
/k/-/g/	*long* [k/g] *été*	adjective + noun
	sang [k/g] impur	set expression

where [v] is heard prevocalically. Linking with /v/ however represents a case of enchaînement rather than liaison, because the final consonant is now stable and *neuf* [nœf] is preferred preconsonantally to the archaic [nœ]:

j'en ai six/dix/neuf [sis] [dis] [nœf]
six/dix/neuf personnes [si] [di] ([nœ])
six/dix/neuf ans [siz] [diz] [nœv]

The most common liaison consonants are /z/, /n/ and /t/, in this order for the PFC corpus (see Sect. 6.3.1); other researchers have reported a different ordering, but generally /z/ occurs more frequently than /t/ (see Durand et al. 2011: 124).

Liaison is of particular interest to variationists for a number of reasons. Firstly and most obviously it is subject to a highly complex prescriptive norm which even native speakers struggle fully to master. More importantly, it is a variable phenomenon which, as we shall see in Part 3, defies normal sociolinguistic assumptions, not least because it shows greatest variability in the formal usage of higher status groups, rather than in working-class vernacular. This, for Encrevé (1988: 46), makes it a *phénomène sociolinguistique inversé*:

> Toutes les données connues et toute observation directe indiquent, en effet, que ce sont les locuteurs du français les plus scolarisés qui présentent le plus large système de variation sur la liaison. La partition traditionnelle entre liaisons obligatoires, facultatives et interdites, reprise à juste titre par tous les phonologues modernes, témoigne bien que, pour la liaison, même les tenants les plus stricts de l'homogénéité du bon usage n'ont pas pu renvoyer la variation à la ténèbre de la performance ou de l'agrammaticalité [..] la liaison oblige au contraire à chercher dans le « standard » la variation.

2.2 Delattre's Liaison Typology

As noted above, some liaisons are categorically made by all French native speakers, while others are variably realised. In a third set of environments, a final orthographical consonant is never realised in prevocalic position (e.g. after *et*). While these essential facts about liaison have been known at least since the seventeenth century, this tripartite model of what came to be known as *liaisons obligatoires*, *facultatives* and *interdites* respectively was first set out fully and explicitly in the mid-twentieth century by Pierre Delattre, in three articles published in *French Review* (Delattre 1947; 1955; 1956) and reprinted in the same volume (Delattre 1966a, b, and c), to which in-text reference will be made here. Delattre's model remains influential more than seventy years after its initial elaboration, underpinning many later descriptive and prescriptive approaches (e.g. Fouché 1959; Ågren 1973; Malécot 1975b; Léon 1978; Tranel 1987). It is presented in detail in the first of Delattre's articles, and summarised in his *Tableau Simplifié*, which we reproduce below.

While the *obligatoires* and *interdites* sections mirror the familiar *Dites… ne dites pas* columns of contemporary prescriptive works, most of

Delattre's three articles are devoted to the more complex—and sociolinguistically more interesting—question of the determinants of *liaisons facultatives*, where the link consonant may or may not be realised. Delattre outlines 10 *tendances générales* for his *facultative* category (1966a [1947]: 40–42). These include warnings against (2) making liaisons across sense groups (*Le petit/attend sa maman*), or generally with /n/ after nasal vowels (6), except with a small set of adjectives, for example *mon, ancien* (6 and 7), where denasalisation of the vowel is also recommended. Short words (5) favour liaison, as do plurals rather than singulars (4) and transitions generally from grammatical or functional elements to lexemes with full semantic content (3) (*nous arrivons; les amis*).

The second of Delattre's articles (1966b [1955]) sets out in detail the following five key factors affecting liaison generally (pp. 57–62):

1) **Style**

It is noteworthy that Delattre sees this factor as 'de beaucoup le plus fort'. He identifies four styles: *conversation familière, conversation soignée, conférence* (i.e. public lectures or speeches) and *récitation de vers*, the first two of which (although Delattre does not mention this point directly) are presumably unscripted, while the last two imply reading aloud, or recitation of scripted material. By way of illustration, he offers the sentence:

Des (1) hommes (2) illustres (3) ont (4) attendu

and suggests that in *conversation familière* only liaison (1) would be realised, while (1) and (4) would be typical in *conversation soignée*. Liaison (2) would be added in *conférence*, and all four liaisons would be realised in *récitation de vers*.

2) **Syntax**

Delattre underlines a point made by almost all commentators since the seventeenth century, namely that closeness of union between two elements favours liaison, using the now discredited 'potential pause' criterion[7] to determine the degree of union between juxtaposed elements. In

[7] For critique, see Harris (1972).

his example above, he argues that a pause is more likely between the noun phrase *hommes illustres* and the verb phrase *ont attendu* than between *ont* and *attendu*: accordingly the degree of syntactic bonding in the first case is graded at 2 (on a scale from 0 to 10), while the latter is graded at 7. Delattre's gradings are reproduced below (1966b [1955]: 58):

10: Entre le déterminatif et le nom : *des enfants*
10: Entre l'adjectif et le nom : *de beaux enfants*
10: Entre le verbe et le pronom personnel : *ont-ils*
9: Entre l'adverbe et le modifié : *tellement aimable*
8: Entre la préposition et son complément : *pendant un jour*
7: Entre l'auxiliaire et le participe passé : *vous avez aidé*
6: Entre l'auxiliaire et l'infinitif : *vous allez aider*
5: Entre le nom et l'adjectif : *des enfants intelligents*
4: Entre le verbe et son complément : *il désirait un cadeau*
3: Entre le pronom et le verbe : *les miens attendront*
2: Entre le nom et le verbe : *les enfants attendront*
1: Entre la conjonction et ce qui suit : *pourtant il est là*
1: Entre la conjonction et ce qui précède : *il sortait et ne rentrait plus*

3) **Prosody**

Delattre lists three potentially important interactions between syntax and prosodic factors. The first of these is length: generally the longer the linked element, the weaker the syntactic bond and therefore the lower the likelihood of liaison. This is particularly true for subject-verb sequences: thus *les plus petits des enfants attendront* is less likely to show liaison than *les enfants attendront*; a longer second element (e.g. *les enfants attendront longtemps leurs parents*) would similarly tend to inhibit liaison. The importance of the first element in particular is recognised notably in the PFC project, which employs separate codings for mono- and pluri-syllabic words. The second factor is intonation—a declarative, falling intonation favours liaison while a rising, interrogative one blocks it. Finally, *accent d'insistance* on the first syllable may be accompanied either by lengthening the first vowel (e.g. *C'est IMpossible*) with liaison omitted, or by using liaison without enchaînement [sɛt#ɛ̃pɔsibl].

4) **Phonetics**

Four additional factors, argues Delattre, are purely phonetic and not affected by considerations of style or syntactic bonding:

a. Vowel+Consonant sequences (VC) (e.g. *des noms amusants*) liaise more readily than Consonant+Consonant (CC) sequences (*des contes amusants*)
b. Similarly, CC sequences allow liaison more readily than CCC ones (e.g. *des actes historiques*)
c. Liaison is possibly also favoured where the vowels are similar (e.g. *vous avez été*) and disfavoured where they are not (e.g. *tu as été*)

5) **Historical factors**

Delattre identifies three historical phenomena which have been maintained over centuries, continuing to override other factors:

a. Liaison with singular nouns ending in a nasal consonant is absolutely ruled out, even in poetry recital or classical theatre. This is because nasal consonants were absorbed into the preceding vowel, which nasalized, rather than being deleted in preconsonantal and pre-pausal positions. Nasal consonants were maintained after open syllables word-internally, without the preceding vowel undergoing nasalization: a similar pattern is evident in closely bonded sequences (e.g. Adj. + N *bon ami* [bɔnami] or *mon amour* [mɔnamuʁ]), where liaison does occur and the vowel may additionally be denasalized.
b. Liaison is much rarer with singular nouns than with plurals because /s/ was the most resistant of the word-final consonants to phonetic erosion, on account both of its structural importance as a flexional

marker, and of grammarians' efforts to maintain it (see Dauzat 1930: 97).

c. *h aspiré*—see above.

In the last of the three articles (1966c [1956]), Delattre turns to frequency of liaison in the case of his *facultative* category. His evaluations of relative frequencies for different liaison contexts in 'conversation naturelle de la classe cultivée' (1966a [1947]: 49–50) is subjective rather than empirical, and he readily acknowledges a multiplicity of external factors potentially influencing even this style—from the clothes worn by the interlocutor to the time of day or the weather—for which it is impossible to control. But nonetheless he identifies six broad frequency bands, labelled *très fréquente*, *assez fréquente*, *mi-fréquente*, *peu fréquente*, *rare*, and *très rare*, which he applies to five broadly defined liaison environments:

A Following a plural noun

Liaison here ranges from *peu fréquente* (e.g. Plural Noun + Adj.) to *rare* (e.g. Plural Pronoun + Adj., *Les uns aimables, les autres arrogants*).

B After verbs

A full range of frequencies is observed here from 'lie presque toujours' (e.g. *C'est impossible*) to 'lie presque jamais' (e.g. *Il a dit un mot*) via 'lie près de la moitié du temps' (*Il allait à l'école*).

C After invariables

In the category of *invariables* Delattre includes (i) adverbs and prepositions, after which liaison ranges from *très fréquente* to *mi-fréquente* and (ii) conjunctions, for which the corresponding range is *peu fréquente* to *très rare*. For group (i), liaison is seen as obligatory (1966c [1956]: 52) for monosyllables such as *en* and *très*, but *très fréquente* where the noun has a determiner (e.g. *chez un ami*), or before a past participle. Liaison with adverbs of negation falls into the *mi-fréquente* category,[8] while the potential for enchaînement with the fixed consonant /ʁ/ in *vers* puts liaison here in the *rare* category. For polysyllables, liaison is *assez fréquente*, but for adverbs

[8] The case of *plus*, which is ambiguous in meaning between 'more' and 'no more' if *ne* is suppressed, is resolved in favour of liaison for the positive meaning and no liaison for the negative, with the qualification that *plus* in the former case is [plyz] when it qualifies an adjective (*C'est plus* [plyz] *élégant*—it is more elegant) and [plys] before a past participle (*il a plus* [plys] *étudié*—he has studied more). See Delattre (1966c: 52).

preceding infinitives the nature of the bond with the infinitive is important: liaison is *assez fréquente* where the adverb qualifies the infinitive (e.g. *Vous devriez/ mieux étudier*) but *peu fréquente* where it qualifies a preceding verb (e.g. *J'aimerais mieux/ étudier*). For conjunctions generally 'on lie peu', and even less ('la liaison est rare') where the conjunction is polysyllablic (e.g. *assez, horriblement*).

D After singular nouns ending in *s* or *t*

Delattre advises that liaison in this context is *très rare*, to the point of being to all intents and purposes *interdite* for the purposes of instruction, but concedes that the title 'Prisunic' (from *prix unique*) reflects that fact that such liaisons are possible. He adds, somewhat censoriously (1966c: 53): 'Tel recteur d'université, ayant, nous supposons, le sentiment de son importance, nous disait (en conversation intime) il y a quelques mois: *C'est un droit tindéniable!*'. Though such liaisons are very rare, they are more common, Delattre claims, with [z] than with [t].

E Liaison with dates

In cases such as *Le deux avril*, hesitation between liaison and non-liaison is attributed to the indeterminate status of the numeral between adjective (which favours liaison) and noun (which does not). Liaisons with *premier* (clearly an adjective) are seen as *très fréquentes* while liaisons with *deux* or *trois* are *peu fréquentes*. Monosyllabic *août* is seen to be slightly more receptive to liaison than *avril*.

2.2.1 The Delattre Model: A Retrospective Critique

Delattre's model represents the first serious attempt to categorise different kinds of liaison and to weight variable liaison probabilities, and it has stood the test of time in so far as its essential tripartite structure remains unchallenged, even if the basic terminology of *obligatoire*, *facultative* and *interdite* environments has largely given way to the less prescriptive terms *invariable, variable*, and *erratique* respectively (Encrevé 1988: 46). Delattre was ahead of his time in identifying a wide range of linguistic and stylistic factors affecting liaison, and his insights remain pertinent and influential more than six decades after they were first published.

The main drawback for a model conceived before the advent of modern sociolinguistic survey techniques, however, is that his observations are based on his own expert intuitions rather than on empirical data. Many of these intuitions have indeed stood up to experimental scrutiny: the link between length of conjoined elements and liaison, for example, has been borne out by a succession of empirical studies, including the PFC, while the group percentage liaison scores for relevant sequences in the 'Four Cities' Project reading exercise (see Chap. 7) were found by Hornsby (2019) to align perfectly with Delattre's frequency bands referred to above.

There are, nonetheless, some internal inconsistencies and contradictions. Delattre hesitates for example over the status (*interdite* or *très rare*) of liaison after singular nouns ending in <s> or <t> (1966a: 52–53), and his coefficient of 3 (from a maximum 10) for Pronoun + Verb sequences seems difficult to square with his inclusion of the category *pronom personnel + verbe* in the *obligatoire* column of his *Tableau Simplifié* (see Table 2.3 above). But more importantly, as a number of subsequent commentators working with empirical data have demonstrated, many of his supposedly 'obligatory' liaisons in fact have proved to be highly variable, even in scripted styles (see Hornsby 2019: 585–87), and indeed the very basis for determining liaison frequency on the basis of grammatical categories has been questioned in the light of empirical findings. Recent empirical research (see in particular Côté 2017) has suggested that non-variable liaison is in fact restricted to a rather narrower hard core (*noyau dur*: see Ch. 5.1) of tightly bound elements for which liaison is consistently realised throughout the francophone world. With no reliable baseline data being available for the period in which Delattre was writing, we cannot be certain whether Delattre's intuitions were simply unreliable, or whether some items have moved from the invariable to the variable category in the intervening period.

While Delattre was ahead of his time in attempting to quantify syntactic cohesion as a key determinant of liaison frequency, his measure seems rather makeshift and the basis for determining the coefficients is less than clear: why are Auxiliary + Infinitive sequences assigned as score of 6, for

Table 2.3 Delattre's *Tableau Simplifié* (after Delattre 1947: 152)

	OBLIGATOIRES	FACULTATIVES	INTERDITES
NOM	*déterminatif* + { *nom* / *nopronom* / *adjectif* } vos enfants deux autres un ancien ami	*nom pluriel* + des soldats anglais ses plans ont réussi	*nom singulier* + un soldat anglais son plan a réussi
VERBE	*pronom personnel* + *verbe* ils ont compris nous en avons *verbe* + *pronom personnel* ont-ils compris allons-y	*verbe* + je vais essayer j'avais entendu dire vous êtes invité il commençait à lire	
INVARIABLES	*invariables monosyllabiques* + en une journée très intéressant	*invariables polysyllabiques* + pendant un jour toujours utile	*et* + et on l'a fait
SPÉCIALES	*formes figées* comment allez-vous les Etats-Unis accent aigu tout à coup de temps en temps		*h aspiré* des héros en haut + *un, huit, onze et dérivés* la cent huitième en onze jours

example, while Pronoun + Verb sequences score 3? The measure is also confusing in that it mixes syntactic and non-syntactic criteria. Delattre suggests, for example, that for Noun + Adjective sequences the bonding coefficient of 5 reduces to 1 when the noun is singular, while in the case of Determiner + Noun sequences the coefficient falls from 10 to 0 when *h-aspiré* nouns are involved, in spite of the fact that in neither case is the essential syntactic relationship between the conjoined elements affected. Delattre's schema therefore appears to fall awkwardly between a measure of internal syntactic cohesion on the one hand and a general rule of thumb for determining liaison probabilities on the other.

Delattre's rather rough and ready measure of cohesion reflects the fact that, while there is general agreement that the rhythmic group or in Grammont's (1914: 130) terms *le mot phonologique* is the domain of liaison, the notion of internal cohesion on which it depends proves surprisingly elusive. For Bybee (2005), syntactic cohesion is linked not to grammatical categories per se as Delattre assumes but to frequency of co-occurrence. Liaisons which in her terms are 'établies', which we can interpret as meaning obligatory, are those which historically have occurred frequently enough to be easily memorable, irrespective of grammatical category. She cites, for example, data from Ågren (1973; see below Ch.8.2) which suggest that two syntactically similar frames *est* [t] + *un* + Noun and *suis* [z] + *un* + Noun have similar syntax but very different rates of liaison: 98.7% and 47% respectively. In terms of constructions, she suggests a continuum ranging from common fixed expressions such as *c'est*-[t]-*à-dire*, where co-occurrence is regular and frequent, and liaison occurs categorically as if word-internally, to constructions which combine frequently used closed class grammatical material (such as prepositions) with open class items (e.g. *dans* + NP) and finally at the other end of the spectrum, plural constructions of the form N + [z] + Adj which include two elements from open classes, where liaison is least likely and most restricted to frequently co-occurring items (e.g. *Champs-Élysées*).

Liaisons are more likely to persist, she argues, in high-frequency contexts, for the same reason as very common irregular verb forms are generally maintained. Thus, in sequences of the form Det + Noun + Adj non-liaison is more common than liaison, because vowel-initial adjectives in this schema constitute a minority and the default selection is for the liaison consonant not to be realised. Note that it is frequency of co-occurrence of different elements, rather than the frequency of individual linking words which is important.[9] Similar arguments can be invoked to explain the pre-nominal linking form in *vieil aveugle*, which binds one of a small group of commonly occurring pre-nominal adjectives to an adjectival noun, while liaison is absent in *vieux aveugle*, where an adjectival noun is followed by a member of the open class of post-nominal adjectives, only a minority of which are vowel-initial, making non-liaison the unmarked choice.

---

[9] Citing Sampson's (2001) failure to get native speakers to liaise with /n/ in anything other than the monosyllable contexts *mon, ton, son* etc., Durand and Lyche (2008: 45–46) go so far as to suggest that native speakers may actively avoid unfamiliar potential liaison sequences in spontaneous speech.

Data from the PFC lend support to Bybee's frequency-based model. Liaison proves more frequent with *être* than with other verbs, but is considerably more common after *est* than after *était*, both of which show higher incidence of liaison than *étais*. Similarly, liaison with the prenominal adjective *grand* proves not to be invariable as one might expect of a prenominal adjective, showing a much higher incidence in the semi-lexicalised sequence *grand honneur* than in the less commonly occurring *grand émoi* (Durand et al. 2011: 116). Overall, Durand et al. (2011: 121) note that, of 111 broad construction types observed in the PFC database at the time of writing, just 21 very high-frequency constructions account for over 90% of the liaisons in the corpus (see Table 2.4 below). Of these, the vast majority involve liaison with /z/, /n/ and /t/ (23648/23953 tokens = 98.7%), with small contributions from /ʁ/ and /p/, which only occur in variable environments, in stark contrast to /n/, which only occurs in non-variable ones. At that point there had been no incidence of liaison /k/ in any of the PFC styles.

The nature of Delattre's four styles, finally, remains an open question. Are they to be envisaged as ranked in quantitative terms (i.e. we see a greater number of liaisons as the style becomes more formal) or in qualitative ones (i.e. a broader range of liaisons is available as the style becomes more formal, as his example sentence would appear to suggest), or some combination of both? Delattre gives us relatively little to work with here, but even with the data now available, we can only offer a partial answer to this question, to which we return in Chap. 9.

2.3 Status of the Liaison Consonant

As Durand and Lyche (2008) point out, the complexities of liaison have long provided a fertile testing ground for phonological theories. Within the generative paradigm alone, Encrevé (1988: 79–135) references seventy-five publications over a twenty-year period (1965–1984) which begins with Schane's (1965) French Truncation Rule,[10] sees its explicit

[10] First proposed by Damourette and Pichon (1911: 27) and developed by Schane (1965: 92), the French Truncation Rule treated final consonant deletion in preconsonantal position and elision of

Table 2.4 Liaison tokens and percentage realisations in high-frequency grammatical contexts in the PFC corpus (after Durand et al. 2011 Tableau 2; p. 122)

Ranking	Grammatical context	Tokens	Percentage of total PFC liaisons	Cumulative percentage of PFC total
1	PRO_L_VERBE	4629	27.5	27.5
2	DET_L_NOM	2086	12.4	40.0
3	PRP_L_NOM	1173	7.0	46.9
4	NUM_L_NOM	1026	6.1	53.0
5	PRP_L_VERBE	860	5.1	58.2
6	KON_L_VERBE	726	4.3	62.5
7	PRP_L_VERBE	712	4.2	66.7
8	KON_L_PRO	532	3.2	69.9
9	PRP_L_DET	482	2.9	72.8
10	DET_L_ADJ	433	2.6	75.3
...	...	...	...	...
21	VERBE_L_PRP	164	1.0	91.1
...	...	...	...	...
111	VERBE_L_NUM	1	0	100

abandonment by Schane himself eight years later, and its resurrection in another guise by Kaye and Lowenstrum (1984). In the absence of reliable empirical data, theoretical edifices have often been built on prescriptive models of French speech. Selkirk's highly influential (1972) work used Fouché's (1959) pronunciation manual as its source while Schane drew, *inter alia*, on Grevisse's *Bon Usage*. Inordinate attention was often paid to examples divorced from actual usage: Durand et al. (2011: 116) cite for example the case of *sot aigle*, a sequence whose frequency in natural speech they describe as 'proche de zéro'. Refinements to existing models have been made, and in some cases their theoretical bases called into question, as more empirical findings, most notably from the *Phonologie du Français Contemporain* project, have become available.

A particular focus of debate has been the status of the liaison consonant. Here generative treatments have generally started from the

final vowels (e.g. in *j'arrive*) in prevocalic position as parallel processes. It drew much criticism on account of the very different morphological and contextual constraints affecting each (see for example Dell 1973: 182).

assumption of an underlying consonant in the phonological representation of the link word W_1, which is subject to deletion under specified conditions. This interpretation has advantages beyond presentational elegance, neatly capturing synchronic and diachronic regularities in the data. Masculine, feminine and liaison forms of an adjective such as *petit*, for example, can be derived by rule from a underlying representation (in this case /pətit/), which also provides the stem for other derivations (e.g. *petitesse*). At the same time, positing an underlying or latent consonant accounts for the historical facts[11] in so far as liaison recalls Old French word-final consonants, retained in the orthography, which have undergone phonetic erosion and survive only in prevocalic environments (see Chap. 3). But for all its attractions, the notion of an underlying final consonant seems counter-intuitive from a synchronic point of view in that it takes realisation of the liaison consonant as the default and specifies a set of conditions under which it is blocked, in the face of abundant evidence both that French copes perfectly well with hiatus at word boundaries and that in many cases of variable liaison it is non-liaison which is the default or unmarked form. What Durand et al. (2011: 123) term a *une compétence ultra liaisonnante* is also inconsistent with a failure by many speakers to identify the appropriate W_1 consonant. In the Four Cities project reading exercise for example (see Chap. 7), there was some liaison with the more common lexical item *long* (though none at all with *sang*), but when it did occur the linking consonant was more likely to be /t/ (50/192 occurrences) than canonical /k/ or /g/ (32/192 occurrences), in spite of an orthographical prompt which might have been expected to favour /g/, casting doubt on the psychological validity of a putative underlying /lɔ̃g/ for all speakers. PFC survey data presented further challenges to the notion of an underlying consonant in W_1 coda position, given that the liaison consonant typically occupies the W_2 onset position. In non-variable environments, we would expect by the *loi de position* under such an analysis that the ensuing closed syllable of the linking word W_1 would require a half-open vowel, for example in *les amis* [lɛzami],

[11] Albeit at the expense of a description based not only on prescriptive sources but also an archaic orthography considerably out of step with modern spoken usage: '[Schane] postulait des formes de base assez proches à la fois de l'orthographe et du latin' (Durand et al. 2011: 103–104).

whereas in fact meridional varieties where the *loi de position* is strongly maintained are found consistently to produce [lezami] with a half-close vowel. This would suggest as Durand and Lyche (2008: 54) indicate that the liaison consonant must be either extra-metrical (/le.z#ami/), epenthetic between W_1 and W_2 (/le#z#ami/), or a prefix of W_2 (/le#z+ami/). Problems such as these lead Durand and Lyche to reject the classical generative position as the only one entirely incompatible with the data. The complexity of the phenomenon and dangers of a 'one size fits all' approach are however underlined by the behaviour of liaison /n/, which as the same authors point out (2008: 55) does form part of W_1 monosyllables *mon, non, ton, son*, for which the half-closed vowel in open syllable predicted by enchaînement in, for example, *mon ami* *[monami] does not occur. Metrical and autosegmental approaches, by contrast, posit a 'floating' consonant available as onset to the following W_2 or, in a refinement introduced by Encrevé (1983, 1988) to handle liaison without enchaînement, as coda to W_1.

Epenthetic approaches reject underlying final consonants in favour of insertion rules in liaison environments, while analyses based on suppletion posit seperate long and short forms of W_1 stored in the mental lexicon, to be realised in the surface under the appropriate rhythmic, syntactic, morphological and stylistic conditions. In both models the liaison consonant would have to be learned on a construction by construction basis, which is compatible with a frequency-based liaison acquisition model such as that presented by Chevrot, Chabanal & Dugua (2007; see also Chevrot et al. 2005), who argue for an initial acquisition stage in which a range of variants, e.g. for *arbre* [naʁbʁ], [zaʁbʁ], [taʁbʁ], are used fairly indiscriminately (e.g. *les arbres* [lenaʁbʁ]). At the second stage, these variants are accurately linked to the correct W_1 (*les arbres* [lezaʁbʁ]), with high-frequency sequences learned first, and finally at the third stage abstract structures (in this case *les* + [z] X) are learned and applied to all relevant sequences. High-frequency constructions are mastered first, and the full range of obligatory liaisons have generally been learned by age 3–5. Variable liaison is acquired later, generally by age 6–8, and shows much greater developmental variability, with children from socially advantaged homes learning at a significantly faster rate than their disadvantaged peers.

2.4 Linking Consonants in English

Before considering liaison in past and present French, it is instructive to examine another language in which hiatus at word boundaries is variably resolved. Parallels can be drawn between liaison in French and the hiatus resolution system of vernacular British English, as investigated by Britain and Fox (2008), in the context of putative vernacular universals (see Chambers 2000, 2004). Their evidence suggests that urban growth and the associated contact between speakers of different varieties is promoting outcomes which are familiar both from other, unrelated dialects of English and from other languages.

Britain and Fox begin by highlighting the complexity of hiatus resolution in traditional vernacular English, identifying five main hiatus blocking strategies:

(a) V +[high] –[front]/+[round] + [ʷ] *Go inside* [gʌuʷɪnsaɪd]
(b) V +[high] +[front],-[round] + [ʲ] *Jellyandice-cream*[dʒɛlijənaɪskɹiːm]
(c) V –[high] + [ɹ] *cider apple* [saɪdəɹæpɫ]]
+ [ɹ] *Vodka and tonic* [vɒdkəɹəntɒnɪk]
(d) *a* + [n] *an apple* [ənæpɫ]
(e) *the* /# V → [ði] + [ʷ], [ʲ] *the apple* [ðiʲæpɫ]

Hiatus glides are inserted after a high vowel (a and b): [ʲ] with front and [ʷ] with back rounded vowels, but (c) and (d), which involve consonants maintained only in prevocalic environments, bear the more obvious historical similarities to French liaison. Insertion of linking /r/ after low vowels notably restores in many cases a word-final consonant which has been lost from non-rhotic varieties in non-prevocalic environments, while in what has become known as 'intrusive *r*', an /r/ is inserted for which there is no etymological justification (e.g. after *vodka* in the example above). Similarly in (d) we see retention of a lost consonant in prevocalic position, /n/ having been lost from unstressed *an* in preconsonantal position during the Middle English period, resulting in the modern *a*/*an* allomorphy and the only orthographical representation of a hiatus-breaking consonant in English. In Delattre's terminology, (c) represents a *liaison facultative*—almost certainly more frequent in the case of linking *r* than intrusive *r*—while (d) has been until recently, for most British English speakers at least, a *liaison obligatoire*. Finally, the definite article *the* is one of a number of items (including *to, my, you*) which have non-high vowels in unstressed preconsonantal position, but a high-vowel final allomorph which triggers the glide [ʷ] or [ʲ] before a vowel.

The hiatus resolution system of traditional vernacular British English is therefore a complex system, involving phonotactic rules, at least four consonants [ʲ ʷ ɹ n][12] and allomorphy in articles and some common function words. Such a system might seem ripe for simplification, and Britain and Fox argue that a reorganisation of this kind is indeed underway, most notably in high-contact urban areas. They cite evidence, firstly, of 'variable lack of allomorphy' in the article system (e.g. *a old chap*) in a range of English dialects from Cambridgeshire to Sussex, and across the south west (2008: 10), and note similar findings in Sydney, New York and in African American Vernacular English. A more radical reorganisation appears to be in progress in East London, where findings from Tower Hamlets, an area closely traditionally associated with Cockney speech, but where 55% of the population now comes from a range of ethnic minority groups, indicate a profound inter-generational shift. While older Cockney English speakers mostly retain the traditional hiatus resolution system intact, adolescents in particular show absence not only of article allomorphy but also of linking /r/, and general tendency to use glottal stops [ʔ] as hiatus breakers. Older boys of Bangladeshi heritage appeared to be leading this change, closely followed by younger Bangladeshi boys. Quoting Lombardi (2002), Britain and Fox suggest that, as pharyngeals, glottal stops have the least marked place of articulation and are therefore to be expected as default epenthetic consonants at word boundaries, as is generally the case in children's English until the adult norm is acquired. The changes seen in East London may, moreover, be indicative of universal vernacular tendencies, and are in line with

[12] And possibly a fifth: [v]. Britain and Fox (2008: 8 fn) note that speakers who use the unstressed [ə] allomorph of *of* retain [və] prevocalically: contrast *cup of tea* [kʌpəti:] with *cup of Earl Grey* [kʌpəvɜɫgɹeɪ]

similar changes observed independently in Singapore, South Africa and New Zealand (2008: 35).

Parallels between hiatus resolution in English and liaison in French should not be overplayed. Glide insertions represent, in Heselwood's (2006: 80) words, 'low level articulatory transitional phenomena' rather than vestigial or latent consonants as in the French case; except in the case of /r/, the phenomena which seem to offer the closest historical similarities to French liaison affect only a restricted range of common function words, and even insertion of linking or intrusive /r/ is governed by language-specific phonotactic rules which do not affect French liaison consonants. The vernacular system, for the most part, is neither subject to a prescriptive norm nor reflected orthographically, as in the French case. Nonetheless, a complex system which presents particular difficulties to post-adolescent learners appears to be undergoing simplification, most notably in areas where non-native L2 English speakers are present in large numbers. In Parts II and III of this book, we shall see how those who find themselves excluded from another highly complex, and in this case prescriptive, norm for hiatus at word boundaries have developed simplifying strategies of their own, and effected a system reorganisation in similar fashion.

References

Ågren, J. (1973). *Etude sur quelques liaisons facultatives dans le français de conversation radiophonique: Fréquences et facteurs*. Uppsala: Acta Universitatis Upsaliensis.

André Malécot, (1975). French Liaison as a Function of Grammatical, Phonetic and Paralinguistic Variables. *Phonetica 32* (3): 161–179.

Britain, D., & Fox, S. (2008). Vernacular Universals and the Regularisation of Hiatus Resolution. *Essex Research Reports in Linguistics, 57*(3).

Brown, K., & Miller, J. (2013). *The Cambridge Dictionary of Linguistics*. Cambridge: Cambridge University Press.

Bybee, J. (2005). La liaison: effets de fréquence et constructions. *Langages, 158*, 24–37.

Chambers, J. (2000). Universal Sources of the Vernacular. In U. Ammon, K. Mattheier, & P. Nelde (Eds.), *The Future of European Sociolinguistics* (Special Issue of *Sociolinguistica: International Yearbook of European Sociolinguistics* 14) (pp. 11–15). Tübingen: Niemeyer.

Chambers, J. (2004). Dynamic Typology and Vernacular Universals. In B. Kortmann (Ed.), *Dialectology Meets Typology* (pp. 127–145). Berlin; New York: Mouton de Gruyter.

Chevrot, J.-P., Dugua, C., & Fayol, M. (2005). Liaison et formation des mots en français: un scénario développemental. *Langages, 158*, 38–52.

Chevrot, J.-P., Chabanal, D., & Dugua, C. (2007). Pour un modèle de l'acquisition des liaisons basé sur l'usage: trois études de cas. *Journal of French Language Studies, 17*, 103–128.

Côté, M.-H. (2017). La liaison en diatopie: esquisse d'une typologie. *Journal of French Language Studies, 27*, 13–25.

Damourette, J., & Pichon, E. (1911–1927). *Des mots à la pensée. Essai de grammaire de la langue française.* Paris: D'Artrey.

Dauzat, A. (1930). *Histoire de la langue française*. Paris: Payot.

Delattre, P. (1966a [1947]). La liaison en français, tendances et classifications. In P. Delattre (Ed.), *Studies in French and Comparative Phonetics: Selected Papers in French and English* (pp. 39–48). The Hague: Mouton. First Published in *French Review, 21*(2), 148–157.

Delattre, P. (1966b [1955]). Les facteurs de la liaison facultative en français. In P. Delattre (Ed.), *Studies in French and Comparative Phonetics: Selected Papers in French and English* (pp. 55–62). The Hague: Mouton. First Published in *French Review, 29*(1), 42–49.

Delattre, P. (1966c [1956]). La fréquence des liaisons facultatives en français. In P. Delattre (Ed.), *Studies in French and Comparative Phonetics: Selected Papers in French and English* (pp. 49–54). The Hague: Mouton. First Published in *French Review, 30*(1), 48–54.

Dell, F. (1973). *Les règles et les sons: introduction à la phonologie générative.* Paris: Hermann.

Detey, S., Lyche, C., Racine, I., Schwab, S., & Le Gac, D. (2016). The Notion of Norm in Spoken French: Production and Perception. In S. Detey, J. Durand, B. Laks, & C. Lyche (Eds.), *Varieties of Spoken French*. Oxford: Oxford University Press.

Durand, J., & Lyche, C. (2008). French Liaison in the Light of Corpus Data. *Journal of French Language Studies, 18*, 33–66.

Durand, J., Laks, B., Calderone, B., & Tchobanov, A. (2011). Que savons-nous de la liaison aujourd'hui? *Langue française, 169*, 103–135.

Encrevé, P. (1983). La Liaison sans enchaînement. *Actes de la Recherche en Sciences Sociales, 46*, 39–66.

Encrevé, P. (1988). *La Liaison avec et sans enchaînement: Phonologie tridimensionnelle et usages du français*. Paris: Seuil.

Fagyal, Z., Kibbee, D., & Jenkins, F. (2006). *French: A Linguistic Introduction*. Cambridge: Cambridge University Press.

Fouché, P. (1959). *Traité de prononciation française* (2nd ed.). Paris: Klincksieck.

Grammont, M. (1914). *Traité pratique de prononciation française*. Paris: Delagrave.

Harris, R. (1972). Words and Word Criteria in French. In F. Barnett et al. (Eds.), *History and Structure of French. Essays in the Honour of Professor T.B.W. Reid* (pp. 117–133). Oxford: Blackwell.

Heselwood, B. (2006). *Final Schwa and R-Sandhi in RP English*. Leeds Working Papers in Linguistics and Phonetics.

Hornsby, D. (2019). Variable Liaison, Diglossia, and the Style Dimension in Spoken French. *French Studies, 73*(4), 578–597.

Juillland. (1965). *Dictionnaire inverse de la langue française*. The Hague: Mouton.

Kaye, J., & Lowenstrum, J. (1984). De la syllabicité. In F. Dell, D. Hirst, & J.-R. Vergnaud (Eds.), *La Forme sonore du langage* (pp. 123–155). Paris: Hermann.

Lombardi, L. (2002). Coronal Epenthesis and Markedness. *Phonology, 19*, 219–251.

McMahon, A. (2002). *An Introduction to English Phonology*. Edinburgh: Edinburgh University Press.

Posner, R. (1997). *Linguistic Change in French*. Oxford: Clarendon Press.

Sampson, R. (2001). Liaison, Nasal Vowels and Productivity. *Journal of French Language Studies, 11*, 241–258.

Schane, S. (1965). *The Phonological and Morphological Structure of French*. Unpublished PhD thesis, MIT.

Selkirk, E. (1972). *The Phrase Phonology of English and French*. Unpublished PhD dissertation, MIT.

Tranel, B. (1987). *The Sounds of French*. Cambridge: Cambridge University Press.

Part II

Diachronic Perspectives on a Prescriptive Norm

3

A Brief History of French Final Consonants

3.1 Introduction

Rebecca Posner (1997: 265) has described liaison in modern French as 'an uneasy half-way house between the regular enchaînement of the sixteenth century and a foreseeable complete disappearance of Old French word-final consonants', the normative complexities of which continue to present, in Bruneau's words (1927: 53), 'un véritable casse-tête' for native speakers. As we shall see in Chap. 4, these complexities owe much to resistance by grammarians from the sixteenth century onwards to change from below in the direction of final-consonant deletion. Our task in this chapter, however, is to consider the causes and consequences of the changes affecting word-final consonants through which this 'half-way house' came about, and to determine how and why the liaison consonants came to be retained in modern standard French. In doing so we will focus on two developments of major long-term significance: the shift from stress-timed to syllable-timed rhythm (see Tranel 1987: 197) which makes French distinct among the Romance languages, and the legacy of Latin as a model for writing and by extension for good speech.[1]

---

[1] Space considerations preclude an exhaustive discussion of developments here: for more detailed accounts, the reader is referred to Darmesteter (1910); Nyrop (1935); Fouché (1952), Pope (1952); Brunot (1966); Ewert (1966); Bourciez and Bourciez (1967); Price (1971), and Posner (1997).

D. Hornsby, *Norm and Ideology in Spoken French*,
https://doi.org/10.1007/978-3-030-49300-4_3

3.2 Final Syllable Erosion in the Post-Roman Period

As Price (1971: 44–48) points out, the evolution of final consonants in French should be seen as a three-stage process affecting: (a) consonants which were final in Vulgar Latin (VL) (b) consonants which either survived into Old French (OFr) in the final position, or became word-final as a result of final syllable erosion and finally (c) consonants subject to changes occurring between the Old and early Modern French periods.[2] A first set of changes was triggered indirectly from the fifth century by incursions from Germanic tribes, notably the Franks, predominantly but not exclusively in northern Gaul (see Lodge 1993: 54–65). In assimilating to the local Gallo-Roman varieties which had evolved from VL in the areas which they had conquered, these settlers applied the strong oxytonic (penultimate syllable) stress pattern of their native Germanic varieties, with far-reaching implications for the later development of French. This would lead ultimately, *inter alia*, to the levelling of diphthongs and loss of word-internal [ə] in hiatus (see Pope 1952: §171). More importantly for our purposes, it would precipitate the loss of unstressed final syllables and subject word-final consonants to the same phonetic developments as internal ones.

Strong oxytonic stress led to a weakening of unstressed final syllables, and the widespread loss of final Latin consonants. Commentators agree that the first VL final consonant to be lost, during the Roman period and probably from around the first century CE, was [m], which has left no trace in any of the Romance languages (e.g. *florem* > Mod. Fr. *fleur*—see Price 1971: 44).[3] Zink (1986: 76) and Ewert (1966: §84) also date the loss of final [k] and [n] (the latter surviving only in monosyllables such as

[2] Time periods in the development of a language are notoriously difficult to define and are at best approximations offered for general guidance. For expository convenience here we follow Ayres-Bennett (1996) in defining the Old French (OFr) period as encompassing the tenth to the thirteenth centuries CE.

[3] Cf. Darmesteter (1910: 118):

> **M** est tombée dès les premiers temps de l'Empire, à la fin de tous les mots, sauf de quelques monosyllabes. Le latin populaire disait **rosa, muru, omine, fructu, die**, en face du latin littéraire **rosam, murum, hominem, fructum, diem.**

non and *en*) to the late Latin period. Post-vocalic final [t] weakened to [θ] (*cantat* > *chantet*[tʃãntəθ]), before being deleted entirely by the early twelfth century (see Pope 1952: §346).

Unstressed final vowels also fell with the exception of [a], which weakened to [ə] before being lost altogether in most varieties: the maintenance of unstressed word-final [ə] in some southern varieties (e.g. VL *vasa* > *vase* [vazə]) is a conservative pronunciation in this respect. [ə] was also introduced to support word-final consonant clusters which emerged from vowel loss, but ultimately suffered the same fate (e.g. *merlu* > *merle*). Reduction of final syllables had implications for morphology, transforming the Latin seven-case system to a two-case system in Old French. As can be seen from the example of *murus* (> *mur*) below, only final *-s* from the flexional system survived into Old French (Table 3.1).

By the OFr period final consonants therefore included some survivors from VL, and others which found themselves in final position as a result of attrition of unstressed syllables (e.g. *partem* > *part*, *campum* > *champ*). Voiced segments in this position were subject to devoicing, as in Germanic, a pronunciation which survives canonically in liaison for orthographical <d> and <g> in *grand* [t] *homme* or *sang* [k] *impur*, and began also to be lost in preconsonantal position in early OFr (see Ayres-Bennett 1996: 278) before consonants, while the voiceless fricatives [f] and [s] were voiced in prevocalic environments, leaving three possible pronunciations in some cases for the same word (see Sect. 2.1 above). Intervocalic consonants [w], [p], [d], [t] and [s] became [v], [v], [ð], [ð] and [z] respectively, undergoing devoicing to [f], [f], [θ], [θ] and [s] in final position, though this was not consistently reflected in writing, which was subject to *rapprochement,* that is signalling of a relationship between words felt to belong together, and/or orthographic alignment with Latin practised by medieval *praticiens* (chancery clerks and civil servants), for example *grant* > *grand*; Lt. *grandem*.

Attrition of unstressed final syllables left French with a considerable number of stressed monosyllabic words, separated only by occasional unstressed pre-tonic syllables (e.g. *ne*). Word-level stress was therefore largely eliminated, leaving only intonational stress in rhythm-group final

Table 3.1 *Murus*: from Latin to Old French

	Latin		OFr	
Sg.	Nom	*murus*	Nom.	**murs**
	Acc	*murum*	Obl.	**mur**
	Gen	*muri*		
	Dat/Abl	*muro*		
Plu.	Nom	*muri*	Nom.	**mur**
	Acc	*muros*	Obl.	**murs**
	Gen	*murorum*		
	Dat/Abl	*muris*		

position (even with normally unstressed clitics, as in *faites-le!*), and a secondary stress rhythm-group initially.[4] The precise timing of this change is uncertain. For Picoche and Marchello-Nizia (1989: 183) it was a 'lente évolution, impossible à dater', but which must have been underway by the ninth century, a position supported by Ewert 1966: §135). Posner (1997: 228–29) however points to ambiguities in the patterns of versification on which such claims are often based, and posits the possible co-existence of two parallel prosodic systems based on word-stress accentuation (nexus) and rhythmic-group accentuation (cursus) during the Old French period, the former associated with a Frankish superstratum and the latter a substratum Celtic influence. What is clear from contemporary metalinguistic comment, however, is that what Pope (1952: §170) calls 'the gradual lessening of the heavy tonic stress that characterised Period I [Fifth-Eleventh Centuries]' and a new tendency to link together words 'closely connected in thought', had been completed by the sixteenth century. Palsgrave (1530: 40), for example, observes:

> And here upon it ryseth why the frenche tong semeth so short and sodayne in pronounsyng; for after they have taken away the consonantes… by reason of the wordes folowyng, they joyne the vowels of the wordes that go before to the consonantes of the words folowynge in redyng and spekyng without any pausyng, save only by kepyng of the accent : as though fyve or

[4] There are some exceptions, for example the *accent d'insistance* (C'est IMpossible!), and as Herzog (quoted by Ewert (1966: §148) observes, in the case of disyllabic words ending in [ə], where stress shifts to the penultimate syllable (e.g. *Vous avez RAIson!*). Ewert, however, writing originally in 1933, sees this pattern as marginal for disyllabic words and not relevant for trisyllables. Certainly in Modern French *A la maiSON* appears at least as natural as *A la MAIson*.

> syx wordes or somtyme mo made but one worde : whiche thyng, though it make that tong more hard to be atteyned, yet it maketh it more pleasant to the eare : for they put away all maner consonantes, as often as they shulde make any harshe sounde, or let theyr sentences to flowe and be full in soundyng.

Thurot p.7 quotes Delamothe (1592), in similar vein, towards the end of the century:

> Nous joignons tellement nos mots ensemble par une mutuelle liaison et proportion de voyelles et consonantes qu'il semble que chasque comma n'est qu'un mot : car encore qu'il y en ait quelquefois sept ou huict, ils sont si bien mariez et enchainez ensemble, qu'on ne les peut desjoindre, sans rompre les reigles de la vraye et naturelle prononciation.

The shift from word-level to rhythm-group level stress, and consequent blurring of the boundaries between words and phrases, had important consequences for final consonants, which were now subject to the same processes as internal ones, notably weakening them in preconsonantal position (see Pope 1952: §209).

There is a general consensus among commentators that those Old French final consonants which had survived attrition of unstressed VL syllables, or become final as a result of attrition, began to be lost in preconsonantal position from the late twelfth century and were mostly lost by the end of the thirteenth (see Price 1971: 46). Unsupported final [t], in spite of its flexional role, began to be deleted along with other final plosives in preconsonantal position from the eleventh century according to Nyrop (1935: §387), but was retained where supported by a preceding consonant until the sixteenth century. The loss of final [s], which also had a flexional role for both verbs and nouns, appears to have begun in the thirteenth century. Orthographical evidence suggests that deletion of final unsupported [l] also began in the thirteenth century, while [r] fared rather better, at least among educated speakers. In the sixteenth century Palsgrave notes that 'R in the frenche tonge shal be sounded as he is in Latyn without any exception', but among uneducated speakers it was already clear that it was generally deleted after high front vowels, most notably in the suffixes *-eur* and infinitival *-ir*, and *-er*. By the late sixteenth century, this practice appears to have extended to high-status speakers too (Pope 1952: §400): De Bèze (1584) condemns rhyming of *Jupiter* (a learned borrowing in which [r] was retained) and *disputer* (Nyrop 1935: §172). In final preconsonantal position at least, Posner (1997: 228) could reasonably claim: '[B]y the early modern period the only syllable-final consonant which survived was *r*, and that was very much under threat.' The status of word-final consonants by the sixteenth century is summarised by Thurot (1881: 3) thus:

> Au XVIe siècle, l'usage sur lequel sont fondées les règles de notre versification subsistait dans toute sa force. Une suite de mots qui n'étaient séparés par aucune pause se prononçait comme un seul mot. Par conséquent, le groupe de consonnes qui étaient formé par la consonne finale d'un mot et la consonne initiale du mot suivant était traité comme un groupe de consonnes médiales; la première consonne, ici la consonne finale du premier mot, était syncopée, excepté l'r. Lorsque le second mot commençait par une voyelle, la consonne finale du mot précédent s'en détachait en quelque sorte, se liait avec la voyelle initiale du mot suivant et formait avec elle une syllabe nouvelle. La consonne finale du dernier mot de la série se prononçait faiblement, et, en général, la consonne finale n'était pas muette devant une pause.

Thurot's allusion to a weakening of final consonants in prepausal environments is supported by evidence, from rhymes and disapproving metalinguistic comment from Tabourot and others (see Pope 1952: §617), which suggests that in popular uneducated speech deletion had started to extend to prepausal position by the end of the sixteenth century. Prevocalic environments were not however significantly affected at this stage and attract little metalinguistic comment. Thurot (1881: 6) concludes: 'La consonne finale se prononçait presque toujours devant un mot commençant par une voyelle', though there are hints from contemporary grammarians that some variability was already evident even here among less educated speakers.

Deletion in prevocalic position does, however, become more and more apparent in the seventeenth century, by which time, in Posner's words

(1997: 264): 'most fixed Old French word-final consonants eventually suffered the same fate as medial coda consonants—attrition and elimination'. Where liaison had been the norm in the sixteenth century, it was now the exception, with only three final consonants [z], [t], and [n] realised with any consistency in this position: [z] and [t] were supported by their role as flexional markers while enchaînement after the unstressed preposed possessive adjectives *mon, ton, son* in particular favoured [n]. The picture which emerges is one of considerable variability, however, with low-status and less educated speakers leading change in the direction of deletion. According to Picoche and Marcello-Nizia (1989: 199), for example, the *p* of *champ* and plural *s* were audible as [p] and [s] throughout the sixteenth and seventeenth centuries; Darmesteter (1910: 154) by contrast claims that final consonants before flexional [s] were deleted as early as the fourteenth century.

3.3 An Etymological Norm for Writing and Speech

While a clear general trend towards deletion was evident, the status of final consonants in the sixteenth and seventeenth centuries was complicated by the abiding presence of Latin as a model for French orthography and therefore, by extension, for good pronunciation. The sixteenth century is widely seen as a period of elaboration of function in Haugen's terms, while the seventeenth is generally viewed as the era of codification, which saw the founding of the *Académie Française* (1635), the publication of Vaugelas' *Remarques sur la Langue Françoise* (1647) and of the first Academy Dictionary (1694). In truth, this division is somewhat simplistic and there is evidence of both processes throughout this period (see Ayres-Bennett 1994). But it is unsurprising that, as French began to replace Latin in its High (H)[5] functions, it drew heavily on its illustrious forebear for both the lexical resources and the prescriptive model its enhanced status required. Aside from its obvious and enduring prestige as a *lingua franca*, the appeal of Latin lay in its fixity, which the as yet uncod-

[5] See Ferguson (1959).

ified French language lacked. In the *Préface* to his *Essais*, first published in 1580, Montaigne (quoted by Lodge 1993: 129) expresses his fears about the instability of French as a medium for writing:

> J'escris mon livre a peu d'homes et a peu d'annees. Si c'eust esté une matiere de duree, il l'eust fallu commettre a un langage plus ferme. Selon la variation continuelle qui a suivy le nostre jusques a cette heure, qui peut esperer que sa forme presente soit en usage, d'icy a cinquante ans? Il escoule tous les jours de nos mains et depuis que je vis s'est alteré de moitié. Nous disons qu'il est a ceste heure parfaict. Autan en dict du sien chaque siecle.

What Nyrop (1935: §51) calls 'l'idôlatrie des langues classiques' was not, however, devoid of ideological considerations. At a time when prestige norms for French were far from firmly established, use of highly Latinised language offered one means of conferring distinction in Bourdieu's sense on literate, high-status individuals,[6] who were increasingly conscious of the need to distance themselves from the lower classes, whose usage begins to attract negative metalinguistic comment from the sixteenth century. Popular speech is roundly condemned for example by Estienne (1578) in *La Précellence du langage françois* (p.170; cited by Pope 1952: 39, fn. 2):

> or ie presuppose, quand ie parle ou de nostre langage Parisien ou de ceux que i'appelle les dialectes, qu'on entende qu'il faut premierement oster toutes les corruptions et depravations que luy fait le menu peuple

Indeed, a conservative pronunciation based on Latinate etymological orthographic conventions largely inherited from the medieval *praticiens* offered, for commentators such as Guillaume des Autelz (quoted by Nyrop 1935: §119), a bulwark against the ravages wrought upon the language by the uneducated lower classes:

> [Contrairement à ceux qui] veulent reigler l'escripture selon la prononciation, il sembleroit plus conuenant reigler la prononciation selon l'escripture:

[6] This could of course be taken too far: the pompous overuse of Latinate terms by individuals seeking to assert status is pilloried for example by Dolet and Rabelais (see Pope 1952: §71).

pource que la prononciation uzurpée de tout le peuple auquel le plus grand nombre est des idiots et des indoctes, est plus facile à corrompre que l'escripture propre aux gens scavants.

As we shall see in the next chapter, the influence of Latin, coupled with increasing sensitivity to social differences in speech, was a major factor which would lead grammarians to resist final consonant deletion as a change led by the lower classes, and in some cases to advocate restoration of orthographical consonants long after most speakers had ceased to pronounce them. We see this influence operating essentially on three levels. Firstly, sixteenth and seventeenth century French commentators depict a language very much in thrall to the Classical languages, turning to Latin in particular for learned borrowing and in some cases a model for prescriptive grammar.[7] Secondly, orthographic convention was already heavily influenced by the Latin of the *praticiens*, and thirdly, writing came to be seen as a model for speech, rather than the other way around, largely because conservative etymological spelling pronunciations enabled literate speakers to distance themselves from 'changes from below' led by their social inferiors. A final consideration was reform of spoken Latin, led notably by Erasmus, which, in an echo of the Carolingian initiatives the early ninth century, sought to steer the Classical language back to its 'pure' form as reflected in the spelling, and away from the vernacular (see Erasmus 1528). Prestige Latin borrowings were thus not subject to final consonant deletion, which in turn promoted a conservative etymological pronunciation more generally in elevated registers. Nyrop (1935: §119), for example, cites the cases of *chirurgie*, and *archevesque*, which had been written *cirurgie* and *arcevesque* and pronounced with an [s] in the Middle Ages, but were realigned with their Latin etyma *chirurgia* and *archiepiscopus* orthographically, leading to a change in pronunciation which persists to this day. Similar considerations prompted restoration of the lost [r] to the infinitival endings *–ir* and *–oir*. Final [r] and final [l] were restored to many other words, and a number of monosyllables regained lost final consonants (e.g. *coq, cinq, joug, serf*) in

[7] See for example Dubois (Sylvius) (1531); Drosai (1544).

high-register speech. Ewert (1966: §110) neatly summarises the changed circumstances of the Renaissance:

> Whereas in the Middle Ages Latin was pronounced as if it were French, the scholars of the sixteenth and seventeenth centuries, having developed the habit of pronouncing Latin as written and sounding each consonant, may be said to have reversed the position: they endeavoured to 'correct' the pronunciation of the vernacular on similar lines. In the case of recent borrowings from Latin, which were essentially book words, they had little difficulty in maintaining intact many consonants and groups of consonants which in the normal course have been modified and brought into line with Popular words.

But if learned vocabulary was subject to the conservative tendencies of reformed spoken Latin, non-learned vocabulary highlighted the clash between upper-class and popular usage which, specifically in the area of final consonant realisation, laid the foundations for the highly complex prescriptive norms governing variable liaison which would later emerge.

Set against the prevailing conservatism of the time, the voices of mid-sixteenth century reformers such as Meigret (1550); Peletier du Mans (1550), Ramée (Ramus) (1562) and Rambaud (1578), who sought in different ways to align French orthography with pronunciation, struggled to be heard.[8] Meigret in particular bemoaned '[une] esthétique de lettres inutiles', but his calls for a complete overhaul of the spelling system, complete with new diacritics and signs such as a barred ɇ to represent [ə], did not find favour with printers, often from conservative dynasties such as Estienne's (1502–1652), which saw them as taking French too far from the one tradition, Latin, which could lay claim to any sort of permanence.[9] Peletier's alternative, and rather less radical, reform proposals only highlighted the extent of regional diversity in

[8] Cf. Pope (1952: §688): 'In France, as in England, despite the bold bid for supremacy made by the phoneticians of the sixteenth century, it was the traditionalists that carried the day, almost all along the line'.

[9] In this connection, Picoche and Marchello-Nizia's (1989: 212) observation that 'Un des grands obstacles à la réforme de l'orthographe est que, limitée, elle est toujours contestable et que, radicale, elle est impossible', remains as pertinent today as it did in the sixteenth and seventeenth centuries.

pronunciation and indirectly made the case for a writing system which stood outside it, as noted by Etienne Pasquier in a letter to Ramus (see Picoche and Marcello-Nizia (1989: 202):

> Ceux qui mettent la main à la plume prennent leur origine de divers païs de la France et il est malaisé qu'en nostre prononciation il ne demeure toujours en nous je ne sçay quoi de ramage de nostre païs.

In similar vein, François Rabelais and others (see Huchon 1981) favoured an etymological spelling system which would retain the primitive 'purity' of the language, a view which would be espoused later by Régnier-Desmarets in his *Grammaire française* of 1706. Phonetic change had left a plethora of monosyllabic homonyms it its wake (e.g. *saint, sain, cinq, sein, ceint, seing*), and the largely etymological orthographic conventions of the *praticiens* were now seen to give volume to such words and thus facilitate readability. Etymological letters which had been lost in the normal course of phonetic change were restored by grammarians, not always successfully. Deletion of initial /h/ in *h-aspiré* words is condemned from the sixteenth century and for example by Lartigaut (1669) in the seventeenth, and is only finally accepted by the eighteenth. In the case of *obscur*, which had been written *oscur* in Old French, an etymological *b* was restored to the orthography initially with a recommendation that it not be pronounced, with opinion among grammarians shifting towards the end of the seventeenth century in favour of the spelling pronunciation [obskyr]. Retention of word-final consonants in spelling, and their later restoration in pronunciation, began to be seen as an important tool in avoiding ambiguity in for example *net, sept, août, porc, oeuf* where there was potential homophony with *né/nez, ses, ou/où,* and *eux.* Final-consonant deletion, which had attracted no comment from Palsgrave, was used in a sixteenth century poem of uncertain authorship entitled *Epistre au Biau Fils de Pazys* (cited by Pope 1952: §74) to parody contemporary vulgar usage. Restoration of final consonants was further aided in the seventeenth century by the loss of vestigial word-final schwa, one effect of which was to reaccustom speakers to hearing consonant sounds in final position.

In what Nyrop (1935: §92) calls 'une décision funeste', the victory of the conservatives was sealed with the publication of the first *Dictionnaire de l'Académie* in 1694, which favoured an etymological orthography as recommended by Estienne.[10] It was certainly true, as Baddeley (1993: 20–26) maintains, that an orthography which recalled its Latin roots facilitated reading (if not writing) for a literate public schooled in Classical language. As well as distinguishing homophones, the retention of etymological *b* in *debuoir* for example (from Latin *debere*) also served to close the syllable by breaking up an <eu> sequence which might otherwise have been interpreted as a diphthong. With the prime function of writing now no longer being for recital or performance, this was spelling as much for the eye as for the ear. But equally the Academy made no secret of ideological motives for preferring a system which was already significantly out of step with usage:

> La Compagnie declare qu'elle desire suiure l'ancienne orthographe qui distingue les gents de lettres davec les ignorants et les simples femmes,[11] et qu'il faut la maintenir partout, hormis dans les mots ou un long et constant usage en aura introduit une contraire. (François Eudes de Mézeray; quoted by Pope 1952: §713)

This was not a system designed with the needs of the relatively uneducated in mind: in Thurot's words (1881: 93). 'Il fallait donc quelque instruction pour ne pas estropier une foule de mots'. Indeed, the Academy's conservative preferences gave further impetus to spelling pronunciations which maintained the social advantages of a literate elite, and favoured restoration of silent etymological letters, e.g *cheptel* [ʃtɛl] →[ʃɛptɛl], *adjugé* [aʒyʒe] →[adʒyʒe]. Restoration of lost final consonants left French with seven liaison consonants in educated usage by the end of the

[10] 'La Compagnie s'est attachée à l'ancienne Orthographe receuë parmi tous les gens de lettres, parce qu'elle ayde à faire connoistre l'Origine des mots.' (quoted by Pope 1952: §713 and Brunot IV/I: 143).

[11] Women were not schooled in Latin in the sixteenth and seventeenth century, and are thus crudely aligned with 'les ignorants' here. As Lodge (2004: 130) points out, the role of Parisian women in leading final consonant deletion both in preconsonantal and in prepausal position draws explicit criticism from Tory (1529: f.57). On women's supposed 'ignorance' and its consequences for language, see Ayres-Bennett (2004: 120–23).

seventeenth century: /p, t, k, z, n, r/ plus /l/, the last of which was restored permanently and would only appear in enchaînement, not liaison (see Pope 1952: §392).

Inconsistency, however, abounded, notably in word-final position. /f/ was reintroduced in the eighteenth century in *suif, juif, neuf, bœuf,* and *œuf* and in words ending *-if*; at the same time final /k/ was restored in *coq, sac, arc, bec* and *bouc* but not in *porc, clerc, jonc,* or *bourg.* /t/ generally remained silent except in *sept* and *huit* and optionally in *fait* and *but*; likewise /s/ was realised word-finally only in learned borrowings such as *cactus, cubitus.* Pressure from printers in particular, however, prompted the Academy to accept modest reforms, some of which had been proposed by Ronsard some two centuries earlier (see Catach 1997: 35), reducing the number of etymological letters in its third and fourth Dictionaries.

There was no consistency either in the general treatment of hiatus. Elision of [ə] as a hiatus resolution strategy, represented orthographically by an apostrophe in the case of *je, ne, que* etc., had been evident since the OFr period, but in many cases hiatus was tolerated or even encouraged, notably before *h-aspiré* nouns (e.g. *le hibou*), proper names (*le roi de Elenie*), numerals (*le onze*), and word-internally with etymological *h* in syllable onset position (*ahuri, dehors*). Other vowels elided inconsistently, or not at all: while contractions of *se* ('if') as in *s'elle*, and *s'on* had occurred in Old French, the form *si* which won out in the sixteenth century continues to elide regularly with *il, ils,* but not with other pronouns; similarly [a] elides with *la*, except before *h-aspiré* words (*l'amie* but *la hache*) or the numeral *une* (*à la une*), but not with *sa, ma,* or *ta* (for which the suppletive masculine forms are used). It was against this idiosyncratic backcloth that the complex prescriptive norms governing variable liaison, as set out notably in the pronunciation manuals of the twentieth century, would emerge.

3.4 Summary

The shift to rhythm-group final stress blurred the boundaries between words and phrases, and subjected final consonants to the same phonetic processes as internal ones. Their loss initially in preconsonantal environments thus mirrored word-internal consonant cluster simplification, and involved precisely the 'articulatory reduction and loss or replacement of perceptually indistinct segments' which Kroch (1978: 23) sees as '[more readily affecting] vernacular dialects than standard ones'. Contemporary metalinguistic observation confirms that this change was led by lower-status speakers, as his model would predict. But while this was a phonetically conditioned development which resulted in reduced articulatory effort, loss of final consonants in preconsonantal position cannot simply be described as a net simplification of the linguistic system, as it produced greater allomorphic complexity, with many lexemes now having two or even three forms rather than just one. We might therefore expect that, over time, this complexity might be reduced to favour the simplified vowel-final allomorph in all environments, and that this change might be favoured by lower-status speakers while encountering resistance from social elites, who would cleave to a conservative norm and stigmatise such changes as 'adulterating' the language. And indeed, this is exactly what we find. Zink's (1986: 78–79) summary of sixteenth- and seventeenth-century developments in particular reads like a textbook example of elite resistance to change as described by Kroch, the two opposing social forces embodied here in 'la langue savante' and 'la langue populaire' battling to a standstill:

> au cours de cette période et, de façon plus franche encore, à partir du XVIe siècle, alors que la langue savante s'en tient à cette distribution, la langue populaire tend à unifier la prononciation en généralisant l'effacement et à finir le mot sur une voyelle. Il faut donc distinguer, à cette date, deux niveaux de langue, d'autant mieux différenciés que les grammariens s'efforcent d'imposer des régressions pour les consonnes les plus exposées et y réussissent parfois. Cependant, aucune tendance ne l'emporte vraiment et, au milieu du XVIIe siècle, la fixation de la langue fige une situation encore anarchique.

The ideological underpinnings of this conflict are evident from the kind of spoken norm which elite groups preferred: one which was heavily influenced by Classical Latin to which only the well educated had access, and based on written norms which enabled the literate to signal their distinction from 'les ignorants'. Those reformers who sought to democratise orthography by realigning it with majority pronunciation were largely ignored. As codification proceeded apace, notably in the seventeenth century, what emerged from Zink's 'situation encore anarchique' was a norm for final consonants which Posner (1997: 222) describes, not without understatement, as 'messy'. It is to grammarians' attempts to make sense of and bring order to this messy outcome that we turn our attention to in the next chapter.

References

Ayres-Bennett, W. (1994). Elaboration and Codification: The French Language. In W. Davies, M. Mair Perry, & R. Temple (Eds.), *The Changing Voices of Europe: Social and Political Change and Their Linguistic Repercussions, Past, Present and Future: Papers in Honour of Professor Glanville Price* (pp. 53–73). Cardiff: University of Wales Press.

Ayres-Bennett, W. (1996). *A History of the French Language Through Texts.* London: Routledge.

Ayres-Bennett, W. (2004). *Sociolinguistic Variation in Seventeenth-Century French: Methodology and Case Studies.* Cambridge: Cambridge University Press.

Baddeley, S. (1993). *L'Orthographe française au temps de la réforme.* Geneva: Droz.

de Bèze, T. (1584). *De francicæ linguæ recta pronuntiatione.* Geneva: Vignon.

Bourciez, E., & Bourciez, J. (1967). *Phonetique Française: étude historique.* Paris: Klincksieck.

Bruneau, C. (1927). *Manuel de phonétique pratique.* Paris: Berger-Levrault.

Brunot, F. (1966). *Histoire de la langue française: des origines à 1900* (13 Vols.). Paris: Colin.

Catach, N. (1997). Orthographe de la Renaissance: Perspectives d'ensemble. *L'information grammaticale, 74*, 34–38.

Darmesteter, A. (1910). *Cours de Grammaire historique de la langue française* (2 Vols.). Paris: Delagrave.

Delamothe, G. (1592). *The French Alphabet Teaching in a Very Short Time by a Most Easie Way to Pronounce French Naturally, to Read It Perfectly, to Write It Truly and to Speak It Accordingly.* London: Jillier.

Drosai, J. (1544). *Grammaticae quadrilinguis partitiones.* Paris: Perler.

Dubois, J. [J. Sylvius]. (1531). *In Linguam gallicam isagoge, una cum eiusdem grammatica Latino-Gallica*. Paris: R. Estienne.
Erasmus, D. (1528). *De recta latini græcique sermonis pronuntiatone*. Basel: Froben.
Estienne, H. (1578). *La Précellence du langage françois*. Paris: Mamert Patisson.
Ewert, A. (1966). *The French Language* (2nd ed.). London: Faber & Faber.
Ferguson, C. (1959). Diglossia. *Word, 15*, 324–340.
Fouché, P. (1952). *Phonétique historique du français*. Paris: Klincksieck.
Huchon, M. (1981). *Rabelais grammairien: de l'histoire du texte aux problèmes d'authenticité*. Geneva: Droz.
Kroch, A. (1978). Toward a Theory of Social Dialect Variation. *Language in Society, 7*, 17–36.
Lartigaut, A. (1669). *Les progres de la véritable ortografe, ou l'ortografe francèze fondée sur ses principes, confirmée par démonstrations*. Paris: Laurent Ravenau.
Lodge, R. A. (1993). *French: From Dialect to Standard*. London: Routledge.
Lodge, R. A. (2004). *A Sociolinguistic History of Parisian French*. Cambridge: Cambridge University Press.
Nyrop, K. (1935). *Grammaire historique de la langue française* (Vol. 1, 4th ed.). Copenhagen: Nordisk Forlag.
Peletier Du Mans, J. (1550). *Dialogue de l'ortografe é prononciacion françoese*. Poitiers: J. & E. de Marnef.
Picoche, J., & Marchello-Nizia, C. (1989). *Histoire de la langue française*. Paris: Nathan.
Pope, M. K. (1952). *From Latin to Modern French with Especial Consideration of Anglo-Norman. Phonology and Morphology* (2nd ed.). Manchester: Manchester University Press.
Posner, R. (1997). *Linguistic Change in French*. Oxford: Clarendon Press.
Price, G. (1971). *The French Language: Present and Past*. London: Edward Arnold.
Rambaud, H. (1578). *La declaration des abus que l'on commet en escrivant et le moyen de les eviter, et representer nayvement les paroles: ce que jamais homme n'a faict*. Lyon: Jean de Tournes.
de la Ramée, P. (Ramus). (1562). *Gramère*. Paris: Wéchel.
Thurot, C. (1881). *De la prononciation française depuis le commencement du XVIe siècle, d'après les témoignages des grammairiens* (Vol. 2). Paris: Imprimerie Nationale.
Tory. (1529). *Champfleury* (facsimile ed., 1931). Paris: Bosse.
Tranel, B. (1987). *The Sounds of French*. Cambridge: Cambridge University Press.
Zink, G. (1986). *Phonétique historique du français*. Paris: Presses Universitaires de France.

4

An Evolving Norm: Liaison in Prescriptive Grammar

4.1 Introduction

In the previous chapter, we saw how resistance by elites to word-final consonant deletion, a change led by low-status speakers, made ultimately for uncertainty over their realisation in prevocalic position. In this chapter we shall attempt to trace the development of a norm for liaison since the sixteenth century, by examining the advice and comment offered throughout this period by prescriptive commentators. However, the very notion of a normative standard, particularly in pronunciation, is far from straightforward. Prescriptive commentary on final consonants in French since the sixteenth century all too often proves vague or incomplete, and sources not infrequently contradict each other. As Poplack et al. (2015: 15) point out more generally with respect to prescriptive grammars, where consistency might be expected, we find its opposite:

> Instead of the consensus generally assumed for standard language, we find pervasive indeterminacy and contradiction, to an extent hitherto unreported. Both prescriptions and proscriptions turn out to be arbitrary and labile.[1]

[1] In similar vein, Ayres-Bennett (1994: 70, fn.16) notes that 'Inconsistency is a constant feature of the application of control'.

D. Hornsby, *Norm and Ideology in Spoken French*,
https://doi.org/10.1007/978-3-030-49300-4_4

The same authors conclude, with Milroy and Milroy (2012), that standardisation should be viewed as an ideology rather than a process with a finite end: 'there is not now, nor has there been, a coherent enduring entity that can objectively be qualified as Standard French' (p. 15). This is, as we shall see, particularly true in the case of liaison. Commentators all too readily rely on ill-defined (or undefined) notions of *euphonie* or *cacophonie* in defending their strictures, and/or advise moderation in the use of variable liaison, without specifying clearly where the boundaries between this and over- or under-use might lie.

With these caveats, we begin by examining the ideological bases for a French prescriptive norm in the sixteenth and seventeenth centuries (Sect. 4.2), before turning our attention to specific comment on liaison from prescriptive sources in the sixteenth and seventeenth centuries (Sect. 4.3). We focus in Sect. 4.4 on the period in which liaison use appears to peak, namely the eighteenth and nineteenth centuries, before looking specifically at the complex and at times bewildering prescriptions for liaison of two well-known twentieth-century grammarians, Martinon and Fouché (Sect. 4.5), and a key area of disagreement among prescriptivists, namely the treatment of nasal vowels in liaison (Sect. 4.6). We close the chapter with some general conclusions from Part II in Sect. 4.7.

4.2 The Origins of *Bon Usage*: 1529–1647

As was noted in the previous chapter, the sixteenth century first gave voice to calls for French to be given the fixity of its Latin forebear, and launched intense debate over the basis for a prescriptive norm. In exploring the ideological underpinnings of this debate, we follow Trudeau (1992) in focusing primarily on the period 1529–1647, which is bounded by the publication of two important metalinguistic works—Tory's *Champfleury* and Vaugelas' *Remarques sur la langue françoise*—and punctuated by three further notable landmarks in the codification of French: the publication of Palsgrave's *L'Esclaircissement de la Langue Françoise* in 1530, the promulgation by François I of the *Ordonnance de Villers-Cotterêts* in 1539, which made French the official language for legal and administrative purposes throughout his kingdom, and finally the founding of the *Académie Française* in 1635. This was the period in which Latin found its dominant position as a written norm challenged, and yielded increasingly to French: in Pope's (1952: 26) words 'the changed conditions of the sixteenth century turned its slow retreat into a rout'. These 'changed conditions' included relative peace and prosperity after the end of the Hundred Years War (1337–1453), which enabled the monarch to strengthen and extend his dominion at home. The growing sense of nationhood which followed was accompanied by a desire to assert the status of French as the equal both of the Latin which it was replacing in its H functions, and of its contemporary rival Italian, the aping of which in elite circles is pilloried in Henri Estienne's (1578a) *Deux Dialogues du Nouveau Langage italianisé, et autrement desguisé principalement entre les courtisans de ce temps* (see Hornsby 1998).

The introduction of the printing press towards the end of the previous century had promoted wider literacy, and favoured use of a vernacular written norm at the expense of a classical language which was no-one's mother tongue. Meanwhile, Protestantism further challenged the Latin monopoly of scripture and its interpretation, and what Pope (1952: 28) calls the 'strict purification of the Latinity', seen in a new Renaissance insistence upon Classical norms, further restricted Latin to a highly educated elite. For a number of reasons, then, circumstances favoured French, which had become by the sixteenth century a language deemed worthy of metalinguistic comment, as the works of Tory (1529), Du Bellay (1549) or Henri Estienne (1565, 1578a, 1578b), for example, testify.

The question of which variety of French should be deemed 'correct', however, remained far from settled. Complaints about the absence of a codified norm start to be heard early in the century, without there being a clear consensus on where the 'best' French is to be found. Palsgrave's complaint (1530: Vol 1: VIII) that French 'for the most generall is corrupted for want of rules and preceptes grammaticall', echoes an oft-quoted plea from Tory in *Champfleury*, published a year earlier:

> O Deuotz amateurs de bonnes Lettres, Pleust a Dieu que quelque Noble cueur semployast a mettre et ordonner par reigle nostre Langage Francois ; Ce seroit moyen que maints Milliers d'hommes se esuerturoient a souuent user de belles et bonnes paroles. Sil ny est mys et ordonné, on trouuera que

> de Cinquante Ans en Cinquante Ans La Langue Francoise, pour la plus grande part, sera changee et peruertie.....Le Langage dauiourdhui est change en mille facons du Langage qui estoit il y a Cinquante Ans ou enuiron...(quoted by Pope 1952: §79)

A *de facto* norm, that of Paris, had long been established. A number of sources (Brunot 1966: I, 330; Rickard 1989: 41–42; Lodge 1993: 98–100) cite examples of poets from the Twelfth Century onwards either boasting of their 'superior' Parisian speech or apologising for their 'rough' provinicialisms. But as the population of Paris had grown exponentially in the intervening period (see Lodge 1993: 142–44), the language of a socially stratified capital had become highly heterogeneous.[2] Vaugelas' selection, in his *Remarques sur la Langue Françoise* (1970 [1647]), not of the Royal Court but only of '*la plus saine partie* de la cour' (my emphasis) as a model for good usage is indicative of variation even at the highest social level. Further divisions were evident among higher-class Parisians between *la Cour* (the Royal Court), *le Palais* (Palais de Justice, i.e. the legal profession) and *la Ville* (the upper echelons of the bourgeoisie: see Brunot 1907), with no consensus among commentators as to which offered the best model.

Motivations for codification mix, as Lodge (1993: 169) points out, the 'disinterested' (fixing the language for use as an efficient means of written communication over space and time) and the more self-serving (a desire among members of the ruling elite to distinguish themselves linguistically from their social inferiors). What Trudeau calls a 'quête de distinction' among humanist intellectuals would have an important bearing on the conception of *bon usage* which would emerge in the seventeenth century. Unsurprisingly, these intellectuals were less than open about their motives in fashioning a norm for French, preferring to couch their

---

[2] Cf. Trudeau (1992: 16):

> Les "affaires" qui se débattent dans l'entourage royal, au Parlement et au Palais de justice créent en quelques années, au coeur de ce gros bourg qu'est encore Paris au début du XVIe siècle, une sorte de cité babélienne dans laquelle évoluent des personnages en quête de distinction.

reflections in moral or even quasi-biblical terms. Good usage (*bon usage*) was associated with the values of the *honnête homme*, and even—in Lopez's (2009: 83) words—'[le] perfectionnement moral de l'individu…qui justifie l'entreprise de re-normalisation'. In an echo of the Babelian myth,[3] French was seen by some grammarians to have lost its purety, or fallen from Grace: a return to the prelapsarian state could only be achieved via reconstruction from France's dialects. While this does not, for most writers, entail a return to Classical Latin, it does imply a preference for French forms which are seen to be closer to Latin roots. There are strong echoes in sixteenth-century metalinguistic commentary, as Trudeau (1992: 21) observes, of Dante Aligheri's (1305) *De Vulgari Eloquentia,* a text which had been translated into Italian in 1529 and was well known in France. For Dante, Classical Latin had lost, through dialectal fragmentation, all its native speakers, and now had to be replaced in its elevated functions by a 'pure' Italian vernacular (*volgare illustre*) which needed to have the fixity of its predecessor rather than the diversity of contemporary spoken Italian dialects. Rejecting the supposed 'superiority' of the Tuscan dialect, Dante saw defining linguistic elegance as the preserve of poets like himself. The ideal Italian language would thus retain those noble elements from each of the dialects which had survived from an earlier, supposedly untainted period. In similar vein, the first French grammar published in France, by Jacques Dubois ('Silvius'; 1531) offers to a classically educated readership a 'Latin-French grammar', rejecting the Parisian norm as had been promoted by Tory, in favour of a reconstructed vernacular presumed to have preceded dialectal fragmentation. For Silvius and others, French must be restored 'dans sa pureté antique, comme on fait rentrer quelqu'un dans son droit' (quoted by Trudeau 1992: 31). 'Purety' is generally measured in terms of a form's proximity to its Latin root, leading him often to prefer Norman or Picard variants over Parisian ones. Bovelles (1973 [1533]) takes such reasoning a stage further, rejecting Sylvius' notion of an *archétype vulgaire* and taking Latin itself as the ultimate reference point for good French.

For sixteenth-century commentators generally, good French is a matter for intellectuals, and too important to be determined purely on the

[3] On this point see Wagner (1951: X: 101–24) and Dubois (1970)

basis of speakers' social prestige. Etienne Pasquier (1560) rejects the Court as a model of good speech and calls for 'ceux qui auront quelque assurance de leur esprit', that is an elite of cultivated intellectuals and writers, to rule on linguistic 'purity',[4] a wish which would be granted in the next century with the founding of the *Académie Française*. The intellectual is defined by knowledge of Latin, the prism through which French must be described and codified. As Trudeau (1992: 18) observes, intellectuals' predilection for Latin as a 'pure' model for French echoes their hankering for the 'purer and morally superior' Classical norms to which they felt Latin itself had to be restored:

> C'est par la pureté de son latin, depuis la prononciation jusqu'au vocabulaire, qu'un type nouveau d'intellectuel, l'humaniste, se distingue du clerc traditionnel dont l'image ne cesse de se dégrader au cours du siècle. Le discours de la *restauratio linguae latinae* se trouve fortement imprégné de moralisme : du côté du latin classique se groupent alors les valeurs d'authenticité, de rigueur et d'intégrité scientifique et morale, en opposition au latin d'école qu'on associe à l'erreur, à l'ignorance, à la malhonnêteté et au vice. On retrouvera ces mêmes dispositions moralisantes chez les premiers grammairiens du français. Ainsi s'explique la modestie des auteurs qui s'excusent de ne pas écrire parfaitement en français. La première phase de la « culture de la langue » se déroule dans une atmosphère de censure linguistique qui dut décourager plus d'un clerc de passer du latin au français.

Reverence for Latin is seen most obviously in respect of orthography. Palsgrave for example (1530: XV), lauds the 'parfection of the Latin tong', and makes repeated reference to a 'trewe orthographie', which cleaves to ancestral Latin, notably with regard to etymological consonants:

---

[4] Quoted by Feugère (1849: 231):

> aussi veux-je que ceux qui auront quelque assurance de leur esprit se donnent loi de fureter par toutes les autres langues de notre France, et rapportent à notre vulgaire tout ce qu'ils trouveront digne d'y être approprié

> To be brefe and sodayne, and to avoyde all maner harshnesse, which myght happyen when many consonantes come betwene the vowelles, if they all shulde have theyr distincte sounde, most commonly they never use to sound past one onely consonant between two vowelles, though for keeping of trewe orthography, they use to write as many consonants as the Latin wordes have.

Accordingly for Palsgrave, the model of spoken French to be adopted is that which he identifies as being closest to the Latin ideal, i.e. the variety heard between the Seine and the Loire where the 'tonge is at this day most parfyte and hath of auncyente so continued'. As we saw in the previous chapter, the sixteenth century saw a lively debate on the subject in which progressive, revolutionary and conservative voices were heard (see Brunot 1966: II: 114), but it was the latter group, whose motives of social distinction were never far from the surface, which dominated and prevailed (p.98):[5]

> Simplifier la graphie, c'est en outre lui ôter beaucoup de sa grâce (...) C'est aussi se ravaler au niveau du vulgaire, et supprimer la différence qui doit exister entre l'écriture des doctes, et celle des gens mécaniques.[6]

This period saw a widening gap between writing and popular speech, and debate about whether to pronounce, for example, the *d* in *admonester* or *administration*, or the *m* in *calomnier*, as spelling pronunciations which restored etymological consonants became fashionable among the

[5] On this point see also Catach (1998: 46): 'L'orthographe a certes été l'objet d'un choix, à différentes époques, choix qui ne pouvait être fait que par ceux qui possédaient la culture et le pouvoir.'

[6] Brunot is paraphrasing Peletier du Mans here ('Il faut qu'il ę̀t quelque diferance antre la maniere d'écrire des g'ans doctes, e des g'ans mecaniques'; 1550: 52) and remarks, in a footnote, on the persistence of such elitist thinking:

> Ce singulier argument n'a rien perdu de sa valeur, malgré les progrès de l'esprit d'égalité. L'orthographe est toujours considérée comme la marque d'une supériorité sociale, et le désir de ne pas écrire comme sa cuisinière a encore été allégué récemment par des hommes qu'on aurait cru moins aristocrates.

educated (see Catach 1998: 25). French, in short, was left with what Cohen (1947: 197) has called 'une orthographe de caste'.

4.3 A Norm for Liaison: The Sixteenth and Seventeenth Centuries

As Posner (1997: 119) observes, final consonant deletion eventually applied more or less across the board, but encountered resistance from literate speakers influenced by a highly etymological spelling system, which led in some cases to restoration of final consonants long after the rule had ceased to operate:

> the fall of word-final consonants in the French early modern period was frequently followed by their restoration, in spelling pronunciation, a little later (cf. 6.14). The phonological rule which deleted all word-final consonants (**truncation**) seems to have operated across the board, so that there was no input left for the rule by the end of the seventeenth century. The rule therefore ceased to operate. But traces of the predeletion situation survived in the graphy, encouraging literate speakers to pronounce some words as they were written. The obsolete word-final deletion rule could not now apply to these new word-final consonants, so that the new pronunciation was sometimes accepted as the normal lexical form.

As French increasingly took over the H functions previously reserved for Latin, the question for grammarians was where the balance between popular and learned usage in this regard was to be struck. Their response would change over time and was notable for a lack of consistency, the legacy of which would be seen in the complex and idiosyncratic rules governing variable liaison, as set out in the pronunciation manuals of the twentieth century (see Sect. 4.4). By the sixteenth century, however, a measure of consensus among grammarians is evident. Authors agree that final consonants are to be deleted neither prepausally nor prevocalically (see Thurot 1881, II: 6 & 10), so liaison per se attracts little prescriptive comment. Deletion in preconsonantal environments, however, is broadly accepted, though there are disagreements in the sixteenth and early seventeenth centuries with respect to exceptions. Palsgrave recommends pronunciation of orthographic *m, n,* and *r* in all positions, while Peletier du Mans accepts non-deletion only in the case of *rr*. Exceptions for other commentators mostly concern orthographic *c, f, l,* and *r*: for De La Faye (1613), Maupas (1625) and others (see Thurot 1881, II: 4–5) all four consonants are to be realised in all environments: Peletier du Mans (1550) accepts deletion of final *r*, while Delamothe (1592), Du Val (1604) and Bèze (1584) accept final *r*, *c* and *l* deletion but make no mention of *f*. The sixteenth century sees the first overt commentary on social differences in speech: Estienne (1549: 99) for example condemns preconsonantal [f] and [r] deletion in *sauf vostre honneur* and *pour l'amour* as a lower-class Parisian usage.

In spite of grammarians' general preference for retention of final consonants in other environments, there is already evidence of instability. Final consonant deletion in prepausal position was already common among lower class speakers (see Thurot 1881, II: 14). Dubois (1531: 85) treats *sain* and *cinq* as homophones, while Palsgrave[7] and others recommend that final consonants should be pronounced only weakly. Thurot concludes for prevocalic environments (1881, II: 6) that 'la liaison se faisait plus complètement que depuis', but notes that the conjunction *et* is already an exception (see e.g. Barclay 1521: 812), and suggests that deletion in liaison environments was probably more common even in educated usage than contemporary grammarians were prepared to admit. The generally conservative Théodore de Bèze (1584) for example accepts final [t] deletion in *un so(t) et une sotte* and *un sain(t) et une sainte*. Opposition to deletion, however, is most evident in the case of loanwords, where grammarians' advice is to resist the nativising phonological tendency by realising final consonants. As Thurot (1888: 15) points out, this held not just for borrowings, but for learned or rare words of all kinds, emphasising the difference between high- and low-status usage:

[7] Palsgrave (1530: 24): 'Whan so ever a frenche worde hath but one consonant onely after his last vowel, the consonant shall be but remissely sounded'.

> Les règles précédentes ne s'appliquaient pas aux noms étrangers ni aux mots qui, venus directement du latin et du grec, en conservaient la forme. Chifflet pose en principe (6, 3), qu'« on prononce toujours les consones finales des noms étrangers ». C'est un cas particulier de la tendance générale qui porte à prononcer tout mot peu usité comme il est écrit.

The seventeenth century, by contrast, is characterised by much greater uncertainty with respect to final consonants, in spite of a plethora of codificatory activity (Thurot alone lists 91 works published over the century). The debate over orthography continued, with reformers such as L'Esclache (1668) and Richelet (1680), who sought to align orthography more closely with pronunciation, encountering fierce opposition from, *inter alia,* the anonymous (1669) author of *Les progres de la veritable orthographe française opposée à l'orthographe imaginaire du sieur de Lesclache*. The vehemence of the arguments on both sides is reflected in the title of Alemand's (1968 [1688]) work *Nouvelles observations ou guerre civile des Français sur la langue*. What is clear is that, in prepausal environments, final consonants have now largely disappeared among low-status speakers and, even among the more socially elevated, plural final /s/, infinitival /r/ and /t/ generally go unrealised in informal usage by the end of the century. That usage is variable is already evident from Garnier's (1607) advice that pronunciation of final consonants should be left optional; only fifteen years later Van der Aa (1622) encourages speakers to pronounce word-final prepausal consonants only rarely except for emphasis (see Thurot 1881: 14–15); even the more conservative Maupas (1625), who favours retention prepausally, concedes that 'Quelques consonnes a la fin des mots ne se prononcent que peu ou point, assavoir b, d, g, m, n, s, t; x, z'. By the middle of the century Chifflet (1659) advises that final consonants should not be pronounced except in the case of loan words (see Thurot 1881: 15), and finally a late seventeenth-century work (Anonymous 1696) chides Walloon speakers who do pronounce the final consonants of masculine nouns for treating them as if they were feminines ending in mute 'e', the latter having largely been lost in Parisian usage.

With respect to liaison environments, the near categorical realisation of word-final consonants which obtained in the sixteenth century had also broken down, leaving commentators uncertain of what to recommend outside of closely bonded obligatory liaison contexts. Duez (1973 [1639]) recommends liaison in a number of individual words and set phrases, while Anonymous (1624) insists on pronouncing final consonants only at the end of sense groups (Thurot 1881: 8). Chifflet (1659) favours non-realisation with certain restrictions, condemning *s*-dropping and recommending pronunciation primarily of orthographic final *n, t,* and *d* (pronounced [t]) in closely bonded syntactic contexts (e.g. Adj + N; V + N). That Vaugelas (1970 [1647]: 162) and others can condemn *velours* pronunciations with *on* (e.g. *on-z-estime*) would appear to indicate that the liaised pronunciation was already subject to hypercorrection by the seventeenth century. Thurot also notes a tendency, condemned by Tabourot, Lartigaut and others, to introduce /z/ without etymological justification, in an apparent effort to sound more educated: [8]

> *S* par vulgaire ne se prononce pas au bout de chasque mot: dont toutes fois quelques autres sont si curieux, que, pour sembler bon François et montrer qu'ils parlent proprement, ils prononcent à tort et à travers au bout de chasque mot une *s*. (Tabourot 1603: 67)

Hindret's *Art de Bien Prononcer* (1659: 201), condemns realisation of *n*, *l* and *s* in this context as 'provincial':

> Ce seroit parler comme un homme de Province, de faire sonner l'*n* du mot *on*, l'*l* du mot *il*, & l'*s* de celui d'*ils*, quoi que ces mots soient suivis d'autres mots commencés par des voyelles, en disant, *aton naverti ces Messieû, atilaité, sontizarivés* ; au lieu de dire, *a ton averti ces Messieû, ati aité, sontî arivés*, &c.

Hindret argues that formal and informal speech should be subject to different norms, establishing a pattern in which increased use of liaison is seen to be favoured notably in scripted contexts. Vaugelas' (1970 [1647])

[8] Thurot (1881: 37–58) devotes a full section to what he calls 's paragogique', i.e. the insertion of [z] in liaison environments where it is not etymologically justified, or *velours* in modern terms. That a number of commentators condemn this phenomenon in, for example, 'mile-z-amitiés' (see Thurot 1881: 38) would appear to indicate that liaison with /z/ had already established itself as a prestige form in other contexts.

Remarques have little to say regarding liaison per se, generally recommending deletion of final consonants in non-prevocalic environments, but an approach which focuses on letters rather than sounds leads him to overgeneralise and miss exceptions (see Ayres-Bennett 2004: 76–77), which are discussed by Chifflet (1659). Chifflet's critique went further than Vaugelas in offering full sections on final consonants in preconsonantal and prevocalic positions (1659: 236–55), but overall the century is notable for an absence of a settled norm in spelling or in pronunciation, with commentators often appearing uncertain as to what to prescribe. D'Aisy (1674; quoted by Thurot 1881: 9), for example, can only fall back on vague notions of 'euphonie' in his advice with respect to adjectives in non-prenominal position:

> Plusieurs, pour faire une regle certaine de cette prononciation de *d, t, l,* disent qu'on ne les doit prononcer que dans les adjectifs et les participes suivis de leur substantif et de leur regime… et qu'ailleurs ces lettres sont muettes à l'ordinaire, ex. Le grand et le petit. (…) Mais l'usage permet aussi de prononcer les finales dans ces derniers exemples, suivant l'euphonie des mots.

Hindret (1659: 711–13) likewise declares himself unable to adjudicate between what he takes to be majority informal usage in post-nominal environments, which favoured deletion, and a more conservative pronunciation which retained the final consonant:

> Je dis autant que faire se pourra, parce qu'il est bien difficile d'ètablir des Regles certaines sur une prononciation aussi douteuse et aussi partagée dans le discours familier que l'est celle de nos consonnes finales (…) Quelques-uns prononcent (…) *dē janz inconû, dē maniaîrezonaîte, dēzaîrzindolân : un discoûrzan_nuyeû, un nobjaitinsuportable, un sujaitanimé, dē bonaizadantel, un bonait a la mode, son mouchoir-à la main,* pour dire, des gens inconnus, des manières honnêtes, des airs indolens, un discours ennuyeux, un objet insuportable, un sujet animé :.. Et cependant cet union de consones finales avec les voyelles des mots qui les suivent est contre la Regle de nos mots regissans, puisque les mots de ces exemples ne sont pas regis de ceux qui les precedent : car selon cette Regle, il faut dire, *dē jan inconu, dē maniaironaite, dē zaîrzindolân : un discoûran_nuyeû, un*

nobjai insuportable, un sujai animé, dē bonai à dantel, un bonai a la mode, son mouchoi-à la main. C'est là notre ancienne & idiotique prononciation, & elle est si naturelle, que de cent personnes qui parleront dans une conversation quelles qu'elles soient, il y en aura bien quatre-vingt qui ne prononceront pas ces consonnes finales. De vous dire laquelle de ces deux prononciations est la meilleure, c'est ce que je n'entendreprendrai pas de faire jusqu'à ce que nous ayons veu l'effet des reflexions que cette remarque aura donné lieu de faire à quelqu'un de plus hardi que moi.

4.4 Peak Liaison? The Eighteenth Century and After

There is broad agreement among commentators that the tide turned against final consonant deletion, and that liaison became more common, from the eighteenth century onwards. While there are no reliable empirical data to support this claim, it is certainly plausible for a number of reasons. Firstly and most obviously, adoption by the Academy of a conservative orthography in 1694 favoured spelling pronunciations. This trend, according to Cohen (1947: 221), was particularly evident in the case of final consonants: 'Le fait général le plus notable de cette période est la restitution de consonnes finales qui s'étaient amuïes, mais qui avaient été conservées dans l'orthographe'. Thus for example non-rhotic pronunciations such as *tiroi* for *tiroir* which had found approval among grammarians in the sixteenth and seventeenth centuries were now condemned as 'vulgaires' by their eighteenth-century successors (Cohen 1947: 188); the pronunciation *fils* [fis] for [fi] also dates from the eighteenth century. The loss of final [ə] in non-meridional varieties in the previous century had also left French with considerably more word-final consonants than before, licensing the retention of other final consonants in prevocalic environments (see e.g. Clédat 1917: 139; Littré 1863–69: 54). Another factor was increased literacy: for Bruneau (1927: 135) and others, final consonant deletion was a natural phonetic development, hampered only by artificial word-boundaries on the page. The prescriptive norm for liaison therefore represented a compromise—and a complex and idiosyncratic one at that—between speech and writing (1927: 53):

> Notre orthographe présente le grave défaut de séparer les mots, non suivant la prononciation, mais suivant la logique, ou plutôt en vertu de règles d'apparence logique, mais en réalité artificielles et fausses.

For Brunot (1966, XII, 533–34), the development of the prescriptive norm in the nineteenth century needs to be set against the backcloth of France's political divisions in the wake of the Bourbon Restoration. He describes a France torn, by around 1820, between three types of linguistic norm: the traditional 'plus saine partie de la cour' of Vaugelas, the *Comédie Française* which 'fixait la prononciation déclamée', and finally what he terms *les pédants*: social climbers over-zealous in their respect for prescriptive rules, wherever they were to be found. While commentators such as Girault-Duvivier (1811), Génin (1845) and Wey (1845) yearned for the certainties of the *ancien régime*, the aristocrats who had returned to France found their own pronunciation to be in many respects out of date, and in the absence of any clear authority in respect of language, established markers of education and literacy, notably liaison, took on particular significance: 'le problème des liaisons semble avoir passionné l'opinion : les liaisons, en phonétique, ont pour un certain public la même importance que l'accord des participes de grammaire' (Brunot 1966: XII, 533). Variable liaison divided opinion between *l'école aristocratique* which favoured measured use and the *pédants* who used them liberally.[9]

The steady spread of universal free education throughout the nineteenth century,[10] which culminated with the Jules Ferry laws of the 1880s, was widely seen to favour a pedagogic norm based on the written

[9] Brunot does not disguise his disdain for the *pédants*: in a disparaging aside he quotes Génin's comment that 'Aujourd'hui il n'est pas un petit commis de magasin qui ne se pique de faire sonner les liaisons' (p. 534). He claims moreover to have resisted requests, in anonymous letters from his students, to use more liaisons in his lectures and bemoans over-use of liaison—'non sans quelques cuirs'—in school and on radio.

[10] For an overview of nineteenth-century education reform in France see Anderson (1982), Palmer (1985).

language.[11] Increased use of liaison was not universally welcomed, however, and in respect of the prescriptive norm the nineteenth century marks a clear break with the past. In a mostly pre-literate age, the signalling of literacy had high distinctive value, and accordingly sixteenth- and seventeenth-century grammarians were happy, for the most part, to recommend pronunciation of orthographic final consonants even where these had long been lost in everyday usage. The democratisation of education had now devalued the currency of literacy per se, however, and overuse of liaison—or worse, false liaison—was now associated with the social climber, desperate to vaunt his/her literate credentials in polite company, and incurring social sanction for so doing: in Martinon's words (1927: V) 'la formule *vous parlez comme un livre* n'est un compliment que dans la bouche des ignorants'. Nostalgia is expressed for the 'simplicity' of eighteenth-century usage, with its supposedly more sparing use of liaison. Wey (1845), in particular, quotes approvingly from D'Olivet's (1736) *Traité de Prosodie*, noting that 'l'homme du monde' of the eighteenth century, as a man of impeccable taste and manners, used few liaisons ('Le siècle de Louis XIV était bien plus avare de liaisons que nous'; 1845: 137). In a short section (pp. 137–40) of his *Remarques* entitled 'Des liaisons affectées', he condemns a tendency to overuse of liaison among the less educated (p. 138):

> On compte en notre langue une foule de liaisons dangereuses qui trahissent leur homme de bas lieu, et peu familier aux bons usages.

Citing such perceived affectations as *onze heures-z-un quart* for which teachers are held responsible ('le propre de la pédanterie...un défaut de maître d'écriture'; p. 137) he adds: 'vous en concluez à l'instant que vous avez affaire à quelqu'un de petite éducation, et ce qui est pire, à un sot.' Nearly seven decades later, Martinon (1913: 391–92) makes a similar contrast between the measured use of liaison among *gens du monde* and its pretentious overuse, which marks one out socially as a pedant or—worse?—a provincial:

[11] Cf. Martinon (1913: 391): 'la diffusion de l'enseignement a rétabli dans l'usage courant de la conversation beaucoup de liaisons que le XVII et le XVIII siècles n'y faisaient déjà plus'.

> Au XVIIe siècle, les personnes les plus instruites disaient couramment sans liaison, d'après les meilleurs grammairiens cités par Thurot : vene(z) ici, je sui(s) assez bien, voyon(s) un peu (…) ; et encore commen(t) avez-vous dit, ils doiven(t) arriver, nous somme(s) allés ; toutes façons qui subsistent plus ou moins dans le langage de la bonne compagnie, celle qui, par tradition, garde dans la conversation comme dans les manières cette simplicité qui est une de ces élégances. Il nous faut répéter ce que nous avons dit maintes fois dans cet ouvrage : le parler des gens du monde n'est pas celui des professeurs, des acteurs et, en général, des gens qui font profession de la parole, avocats, hommes politiques etc. (…) Depuis le temps de Molière les façons de parler prétentieuses qu'il raillait si bien ont gagné du terrain, et elles ont atteint des classes sociales qui jusqu'à présent en étaient exemptes. Mais aujourd'hui comme autrefois le dire de l'abbé d'Olivet reste vrai : 'la conversation des honnêtes gens et pleine d'hiatus volontaires qui sont tellement autorisés par l'usage que, si on parlait autrement, cela serait d'un pédant ou d'un provincial.'

It is perhaps unsurprising that the champions and arguable beneficiaries of social mobility through education, teachers (and particularly the less qualified *instituteurs*, that is primary school teachers), are singled out for criticism, and compared unfavourably with the socially secure *gens du monde*. Thus Passy asserts (1906: 130): 'ce sont surtout les instituteurs, les professeurs de diction, et encore plus les personnes peu instruites essayant de 'parler bien', qui introduisent des liaisons en masse' while for Martinon (1913: 357): 'D'une façon générale, les professeurs en font plus que les gens du monde, à cause de l'habitude qu'ils ont : les instituteurs en font trop, non pas tant en parlant mais en enseignant à lire, car ils ne savent pas que, même en lisant, il y en a qu'on ne fait pas'. Half a century later Marouzeau (1963: 23), in similar vein, would link a perceived post-war revival in use of liaison to the effects of schooling, and notably now associate conservatism with deletion rather than retention of final consonants in some liaison environments:

> L'usage de la liaison se répand dans le français d'aujourd'hui sous l'influence de l'école, de la conférence, de la radio surtout, chez les demi-cultivés (*deux heures-z-et demie, trop-p-étroit, aimer-r-à dire, le gouvernement-t-anglais, des corps expéditionnaires !*), au point où c'est devenu une marque de culture

que de résister à ce pédantisme ; on entend dire, par affectation de purisme, dans certains milieux de tendance conservatrice (fauboug Saint-Germain) : *Nou(s) aussi. Commen(t) allez-vous ?*

Advice from prescriptive grammarians on variable liaison can now be summed up by the Goldilocks principle: not too little, not too much, just the right amount. The 'right amount', however, is of course never clearly defined, and can only be gauged by those who already have had extensive exposure to the elite groups who control the norm. But with the emphasis now firmly on avoiding overuse of liaison, teachers are not infrequently berated for instilling a fear of hiatus in their pupils. Commentators are at pains to point out that French in fact has no revulsion for hiatus at word boundaries: Clédat (1917) notes that while French usage requires *les*-[z]-*ans*, it accepts [leã] without demur in, for example, *Orléans*; Tappolet (1932) likewise points out that fear of hiatus (*Hiatusfurcht*) is a myth created by poets and grammarians in the sixteenth century and, while it may be responsible for the maintenance of liaison in some cases, it is not its cause (see also Genévrier 1927: 278–79; Pleasants 1933: 127–28; Gaatone 1979).

The absence of a clear norm in the early nineteenth century prompted publication of a number of pronunciation manuals,[12] offering specific guidance on liaison use. The problem of liaison takes up most of Dubroca's (1824) work (pp. 27–62, 76–171), but there are also detailed sections in Dupuis (1836); Malvin-Cazal (1846) and Lesaint (1850). As Morrison observes (1968: 22), the typical chapter on liaison in a pronunciation manual consists of three elements: (i) a list of grammatical categories where liaison must or must not be made (ii) a paragraph explaining that liaison occurs more frequently in elevated than in conversational style and (iii) a note on 'sound changes' occurring in liaison, meaning a mismatch between sound and orthography (e.g. [t] for *d* in *grand* [t] *homme*). In nineteenth-century works, liaison is generally presented in terms of an inventory of final orthographic consonants (though some works after

[12] And ultimately, argues Brunot, led to the establishment of a Paris-based pronunciation norm which would remain largely unchallenged: 'C'est alors que s'établit, pour la France entière, une prononciation type, fondée sur l'usage de la bourgeoisie parisienne… cette prononciation ne changera guère' (Brunot 1966: XII, 532).

1880 include phonetic transcriptions: see for example Beyer and Passy 1893; Koschwitz 1893), and it is not always clear at this stage whether authors are referring to orthographic letters or sounds. Furthermore, at this stage the terms liaison[13] and enchaînement are used inconsistently and sometimes interchangeably. Guidance is generally offered on false liaison, epenthetic liaison (e.g. *a-t-il*; see Vossler 1913: 162 for earliest textual attestation of *va-t-en guerre*) and analogical liaison (e.g. *entre quatre-z-yeux*). Some twentieth-century sources additionally discuss *liaison à distance* (e.g. *chemins de fer zalgériens*; *pour vous presenter mes idées-r-ici*; see Martinon 1913: 379 fn.1; Pichon 1938), but this is unlikely ever to have been more than a marginal phenomenon. Authors variously address factors influencing liaison (e.g. grammatical relationships, prosodic factors, morphology: see Chap. 2); Dupuis (1836) offers the first detailed analysis of 'optional' liaison even if the term *facultative* is not used until Rousselot and Laclotte (1902). While they differ in their approaches and emphases (Malvin-Cazal 1846 pays less attention to grammatical relations than Lesaint 1850 for example), nineteenth- and early-twentieth-century works all suffer in at least two ways from a lack of reliable recording equipment and empirical data. Firstly, there is the basic difficulty of observing usage, given the complexity of the constraints involved and the rarity of some liaison categories; secondly, it is all but impossible to control for the interaction of factors of different kinds (e.g. prosodic, syntactic, stylistic), as we saw in Chap. 2. Detailed and robust analysis would only prove possible with the advent of annotated speech corpora in the second half of the twentieth century, and most notably in the early twenty-first century with the PFC project, which allowed access to large amounts of readily searchable recorded data. In the absence of

[13] Some twentieth-century works have argued that liaison occurs in all cases, treating hiatus as 'vocalic liaison'. For the most part, the term appears to have been employed by German-speaking sources (e.g. Quiehl 1906; Scherm 1909) who refer to *Vokalbindung*, and it is likely that such commentators are highlighting the fact that French does not follow German in using glottal stops as hiatus breakers. The term *liaison vocalique* is however used by Grammont (1914) and Goémans (1919).

such resources, authors could only report on their own, often unreliable,[14] assumptions about usage, or comment on readings of prepared texts, which are equally problematic given the gap between scripted and unscripted styles in most models of liaison usage (for critique of reading experiments, see Damourette and Pichon 1936).[15] Assessing the vitality of liaison across different time periods is therefore difficult, and complicated further by the fact that authors present data in a variety of ways, either according to final consonant, or by grammatical category, or frequency of occurrence, with some blurring of the lines in some cases between prescription and description of contemporary usage. Nonetheless there is broad agreement that use of optional liaison increased in the eighteenth century but was in decline by the early decades of the twentieth, leading Morrison to suggest (1968: 17) that the phenomenon might have reached its peak in the late nineteenth century.[16] Certainly few twentieth-century commentators contest Bruneau's view that 'nous avons l'impression que nombre de liaisons recommandées dans les traités de prononciation de la fin du XIXe siècle sont devenues insupportables' (1927: 55), nor that of Bally (1932: 319) that 'il est vrai qu'on lie toujours moins'; similar observations are made by Müller (1904: 197); Wartburg (1934: 277) and Fouché (1934: 52). What Armstrong calls the 'ebb and flow' of liaison historically had posed a particular challenge for seventeenth-century commentators, as Morrison (1968: 19) points out:

> The first source of confusion, from a historical standpoint, is the fact that between the sixteenth and nineteenth centuries the problem of liaison, in a sense, reversed. In the early period when final consonants were mostly all pronounced grammarians wrote only of troublesome exceptional cases where they were silent. But as final consonants became generally silent in

---

[14] Cf. Martinet (1947: 23; quoted by Morrison 1968: 32fn):

> On sait combien les Français, et, parmi eux, les linguistes professionnels eux-mêmes, sont tentés d'identifier leurs habitudes phonologiques avec la norme.

[15] There have also been studies of actors reading aloud or performing: see for example Block 1892; Le Roy 1911.

[16] This is certainly in line with Dauzat's (1930: 143) observation that 'elle [la liaison] a regagné du terrain du XVIIIe au XIXe, époque où elle atteint son maximum. Depuis un demi-siècle, le nombre des liaisons va en diminuant.'. If taken strictly at face value, this would put the peak at around 1880.

> French, grammarians wrote only of the troublesome exceptional cases where they were pronounced (liaison). In the transition period (the seventeenth century), there was particular confusion because grammarians could not determine which was the rule and which was the exception.

Until the late nineteenth century, most authors present an inventory of (generally orthographic) final consonants and offer advice on each, but thereafter some commentators start to present liaison data in terms of frequency, initially in terms of grammatical categories for which liaison is obligatory or forbidden, and later including examples of optional liaison.[17] This format becomes the norm in the twentieth century, though the terminology employed is inconsistent: 'most commonly occurs' only for Bayer and Passy (1893), for example; 'always/never/sometimes' for Armstrong (1932). The number of grammatical categories identified within each grouping is helpfully provided by Morrison (1968) and summarised in the table below (Table 4.1).

The gradual expansion in the numbers of grammatical categories discussed under each heading would appear to indicate a norm of increasing complexity. In fact, in many respects, the advice offered changes little from the early nineteenth century. Certainly the liaisons identified as being obligatory by Dubroca (1824), Armstrong (1932), and Fouché (1959) are essentially the same (and are not substantially different from those identified in Bauche's 1920 description of *français populaire*). Within the *interdite* grouping, for example, all three authors insist on non-liaison before the *h-aspiré* lexical set (though only Fouché attempts to offer an exhaustive list of its members: 1959: 252–58), and after *et*.

[17] The term *liaison facultative* in its current understanding is first used by Rousselot and Laclotte (1902), but Dupuis (1836) is the first to identify and discuss a category of liaisons which may or may not be realized. The first in-depth analysis of the category is provided by Müller (1904).

4.5 Two Twentieth-century Prescriptivists: Martinon and Fouché

The complexity of the norm for liaison which emerges in the twentieth century is matched only by a social significance elevated, according to Carton (2000: 39), to quasi-moral status: 'C'est une question qu'on juge très importante, au point de la présenter de la manière des préceptes moraux'. This explains the increasing attention it is afforded in twentieth-century pronunciation manuals, two of the best known of which we examine here. Both Martinon (1913) and Fouché (1959) devote full chapters to liaison. While the approaches adopted are rather different, the prescriptions offered are detailed, complex, idiosyncratic and for all practical purposes unusable.

Martinon in his introduction (1913: X) makes a point of highlighting the inclusion of a chapter offering extensive guidance on liaison:

Table 4.1 Grammatical categories within liaison frequency groupings in prescriptive sources (data from Morrison 1968)

Author	Date	'Obligatory'	'Forbidden'	'Optional'
Ploetz	1873	5	2	-
Beyer	1888	8	6	-
Beyer & Passy	1893	10	-	-
Ackernecht	1895	5	5	-
Matzke	1897	6	-	-
Dumville	1904	11	2	3
Scherm	1909	8	-	-
Nicholson	1909	10	-	15
Schmidt	1909	8	8	13
Bascan	1912	6	8	-
Bonnard	1927	9	-	-
Armstrong	1932	11	5	7
Pleasants	1933	23	14	16
Grevisse	1936	12	7	-
Peyrollaz and Bara de Tovar	1954	20	13	9
Kammans	1956	7	9	4
Fouché	1959	30	41	-

> Pour celle [la question] de la liaison, on s'en tient d'ordinaire à des conseils généraux : j'ai pris la peine d'entrer dans les détails et de classer méthodiquement les faits.

Martinon's position here and in a later work (Martinon 1927) is essentially conservative. Change is generally seen in a negative light ('Il est probable que jamais en France on n'a aussi mal parlé qu'aujourd'hui'; 1927: 7), which should be reversed where practically possible. His model for good speech is still unashamedly that of 'la bonne société parisienne', while his admiration for the fixity of the written language echoes that of sixteenth and seventeenth-century writers (1913: V):

> Un livre pratique, un livre de vulgarisation, destiné aux Français aussi bien qu'aux étrangers, doit donc partir de l'orthographe exclusivement ; il doit partir de ce qui se voit, qui est absurde peut-être, mais qui est fixe et certain, pour passer à ce qui s'entend, qui est souvent douteux ou discutable.

Martinon begins with 'Quelques observations préliminaires' (1913: 255–60), outlining the history of liaison, making the familiar link between liaison and syntactic cohesion between linked elements, and proscribing liaison before specific items such as the *h-aspiré* set and the numerals *un* and *onze*. He then moves to specific prescriptions applicable to different consonant groups (e.g. *muettes, spirantes, dentales*). Liaison with [p] is recommended with *beaucoup* and *trop*, but in verse liaison with *coup* followed by an adjective (e.g. *un coup*-[p]-*imprévu*) is also accepted, albeit with the qualification 'cela prend un air assez archaïque'. Liaison with [k] is restricted to a few items (e.g. *long, rang*) in poetry or what he terms 'style oratoire': non-liaison in prose, even in set expressions such as *long et large* is acceptable. The much more common liaison with [t] (orthographic *d* or *t*) is dealt with in greater length (pp. 363–70), and in a manner which becomes familiar in twentieth-century pronunciation manuals: a rule is offered for a particular grammatical category or lexical set, to be quickly followed by a number of qualifications and/or exceptions. Thus liaison with [t] after verbs is prescribed in all cases except for third person plural forms, where it is only recommended. Liaison is prohibited after nouns, except in verse, but accepted in *en quel endroit* [t] *avez-vous vu?* to avoid the clash of two [a] vowels in hiatus, yet Martinon rejects liaison in *le chaud aux pieds* where a similar clash applies, while accepting it in *le froid* [t] *aux pieds,* where it does not. There then follows a list of set expressions where liaison is obligatory, which includes *guet-*[t]*-apens* and *pot-*[t]*-au-feu* but not *chat Ø échaudé.* Liaison is proscribed after [r]—the actors of the *Comédie Française* who insist on *Mort* [t] *à l'impie !* are ridiculed but Martinot nonetheless recommends *mort* [t] *aux rats* 'pour éviter la cacophonie' of two successive syllables beginning with [ʁ]. Elsewhere general advice is subjective and not infrequently vague: he suggests that liaison should be made 'dans une intention d'harmonie' (p. 359) and should not be maintained 'dans le cas où elles produisent…. un son plus désagréable', without offering a clear definition of what constitutes *harmonie* or indeed of what *désagréable* might mean.

Fouché (1959), writing nearly half a century later, pays homage to Martinon for providing a manual directed as much at his compatriots as at foreign learners, but his own lengthy final chapter on liaison (pp. 434–79) approaches the question rather differently. He devotes 35 pages (41 categories) to 'cas où on ne fait pas la liaison', a further 9 to 'cas où on fait la liaison' (30 categories) and three pages of general observations in a final appendix. That there are now a greater number of proscribed categories than recommended or obligatory ones would seem to be in line with a perceived decline in liaison, coupled with a desire among prescriptive commentators to discourage overuse. The prohibitions (before *h-aspiré* words, numerals, singular nouns) and the prescribed liaisons (after determiners, prenominal adjectives, pronouns) are familiar enough, and broadly similar to those of Martinon. But the absence of an 'optional' liaison grouping proves hugely problematic, as items assigned to the 'prohibited' or 'obligatory' category become littered with exceptions and often bafflingly complex *remarques,* resulting in what Stubelius (1943: 22) has called, with reference to earlier works, 'un chaos de règles', without any reference for example to the broad phonetic principles outlined by Grammont (1914). A particularly egregious example is category 25 within the 'prohibited' section, concerning liaison after verb forms (pp. 457–62), which offers two and a half pages of examples of non-liaison, which are then qualified by 25 separate exceptions for which liaison is either required or possible ('On fait ou non la liaison'). Not even five full pages can do this single category justice, it appears—for *style soutenu* Fouché warns: 'Il est impossible d'entrer ici dans les détails' (p. 462). As Morrison observes, this is a recipe for confusion and the manual is all but impossible to use without prior knowledge of precisely the norms of liaison on which one is seeking guidance (1968: 194):

> In other words, liaisons classified as "prohibited" at the beginning are reclassified as "optional" or "obligatory" at the end. Even if there were no reclassifications, i.e., no exceptions to the "rule", a student would still have no way of finding an example of liaison unless he knew already whether it was "obligatory" or "prohibited".

Both writers, then, are happy to offer the reader general rules for liaison and then qualify (or in some cases contradict) them to the point where they provide no real guidance at all, leaving the user to rely on his/her own judgment given the circumstances and the information at his/her disposal. This reflects very real uncertainty on the part of prescriptive commentators, particularly in cases where was simply no consensus over what to recommend. This was true notably for the treatment of nasal vowels in liaison, which we review in the next section.

4.6 Prescriptive Uncertainty: Nasal Vowels in Liaison

In the OFr period, vowels were subject to nasalisation before nasal consonants, including before nasal consonant plus vowel sequences. In the latter case this was reflected orthographically from the thirteenth century via a doubling of the consonant (e.g. *abandoner* > *abandonner*). A lower-class Paris-led change, dating from the sixteenth century (see Bèze 1584: 34) saw denasalisation of the vowel in this environment, with no corresponding change to the orthography. By analogy, a similar denasalisation occurred in liaison contexts, creating a tension between those on the one hand who favoured a regularising analogical process, which treated items such *son, mon, bon* and *un* as part of the words which followed them and therefore favoured denasalisation, and those conservative commentators on the other who saw the linked words as orthographically separate and therefore maintained the nasal vowel. According to Thurot (1881, II: 555), little is known about liaison with /n/ in the sixteenth century, but available evidence for *en, bon* and *on* leads him to conclude that 'Il est probable que la voyelle nasale se dédoublait : la voyelle restait nasale et la syllabe suivante commençait par une *n*.' By the seventeenth century, the denasalised pronunciation, for example *bon ami* [bɔnami], is reported by several commentators including Anonymous (1624) and Roux (1694), and apparently accepted by Dangeau (1694), but it is not until the latter half of the eighteenth century that we see a clear division among commentators either supporting or opposing denasalisation in this context. By the nineteenth century, Littré (1863–69), Le Mare (1819) and Landais (1835) all accept Domergue's (1805) doctrine of denasalisation by analogy and Rousselot concludes (1911: 179) 'En somme, la lutte continue encore aujourd'hui entre la phonétique et l'analogie et il semble bien que c'est cette dernière qui aura raison', a view endorsed by Carton (1995: 40) who claims that the denasalised form was winning out by 1914. Denasalisation in liaison contexts favoured use of the marked feminine form with prenominal adjectives, for example *plein air* [plɛnɛʁ] , *divin enfant* [divinɑ̃fɑ̃] , while in the case of *un* three forms are attested [œ̃] , [œ] and [y], thus *un homme* [ynɔm]. While identity of masculine and feminine articles in the last of these cases is problematic for some commentators it is recommended by Dubroca (1824: 57) and Littré, but appears to have been falling out of favour in educated usage by the turn of the twentieth century (see also Langlard 1928: 32; Rousselot and Laclotte 1902: 179; Martinon 1913: 389), and is not explicitly mentioned by Passy (1906) or Fouché (1959). More generally, Grammont (1914: 134) allows denasalisation only in certain circumstances with /ɛ̃/ and /ɔ̃/ , but not at all with /œ̃/ and /ɑ̃/ , while for Langlard (1928: 132) 'la dénasalisation a presque complètement disparu de nos jours' except in isolated cases such as *bon enfant*. Martinon (1913: 388) condemns denasalisation in *plein air* as 'fétichisme de l'orthographe' which he associates (citing Rousselot) with 'certains milieux traditionnalistes et réactionnaires'. Fouché (1959: 435–36), typically, sets out a complex set of rules over two pages: generally monosyllabic forms (*bien, un, en* etc.) are seen to preserve nasality ('la prononciation avec voyelle nasale est considérée pour le moment comme la meilleure', p.436), while for masculine adjectives in *-ain* or *-ein* the denasalised feminine form is recommended, for example *ancien état* [ɑ̃sjɛneta], with the notable exceptions of *divin* and *malin*; the latter retaining the nasal vowel in *malin esprit* [malɛ̃nespri] while the former loses it in certain fixed expressions (the use of the nasal vowel in which is described as 'suranné') such as *le divin* [divin] *enfant*.[18]

For Buben (1935), denasalisation represents what he considers the 'natural' phonetic evolution of the *langue populaire* in contrast to the more complex and 'disjointed' development of *la langue des lettrés*, whose use of liaison 's'appuie en première ligne sur l'image visuelle des mots et sur l'autorité de l'orthographe' (p. 208).[19] In a clear echo of Kroch (see Chap. 1), Buben argues that the natural state of affairs, to which he sees French finally returning in the twentieth century, is for liaison to occur only between items 'étroitement liés par le sens et par l'accent' (1935: 206); in other cases liaison is attributable to the spread of literacy in the eighteenth and nineteenth centuries. For now, the conflict between the countervailing 'natural' and 'orthographic' tendencies remains unresolved (p. 214).

Similarly affected by enchaînement is the quality of the front mid-vowel in liaison, notably before [ʁ], for example after *-er* infinitives or the adjective *léger*. In accordance with the so-called *loi de position* most varieties of French apply complementary distribution for mid-vowels, with half-open [ɛ] occurring in closed syllables and [e] in open ones; conservative normative pronunciation however licences both [ɛ] and [e] in open syllables and contrasts, for example *donné* [dɔne] and *donnait* [dɔnɛ].

---

[18] Fouché broadly follows Martinon here, using the same examples, but Martinon notes that only in the case of *divin* [divin] and in compounds of the noun *vin* (e.g. *vinaigre*) is the non-nasalized pronunciation acceptable for masculine adjectives in *-in*, and recommends *esprit fin* for *fin esprit* to avoid the issue altogether.

[19] What he terms *orthographisme*, i.e. the influence of the written word on pronunciation, has been labelled 'L'effet Buben' (for discussion see Chevrot and Malderez 1999).

Dupuis (1836: 195) condemns [e] and prescribes [ɛ] before [ʁ] ,[20] while Domergue (1805) favours retention of the close [e] form. Martinon (1913: 359) by contrast recommends an intermediate vowel, while conceding that liaison in this context 'se fait de moins en moins' (p.389); Langlard (1928) similarly views liaison with *-er* infinitives as 'affectée' and 'artificielle'. Much of the heat from this latter debate was removed by a recognition that liaison with *–er* infinitives, already condemned by Dupuis (1836), had long been outmoded except in verse or scripted discourse. But it is nonetheless surprising that while commentators have been willing to present divergent opinions on mid-vowels before liaison [ʁ] , they have generally not felt the need to offer specific guidance with respect to [e] or [ɛ] before other liaison consonants (e.g. *avait* [e/ɛt] *entendu*).

4.7 Conclusions to Part II

The last two chapters have been punctuated with recurrent echoes of Kroch's ideological model of language variation. As we saw in Chap. 3, final consonant deletion from the Old French period onwards was led by lower-status speakers. As stress moved from word to rhythm-group level, final consonants in preconsonantal position were subject to the same processes of cluster simplification which had applied word-internally, leading to greater ease of articulation but at the cost of increased allomorphy. Gradually, in a simplifying change also led by lower-class speakers, use of the open syllable-final allomorph was extended to prepausal and finally pre-vocalic position, except in cases of close syntactic cohesion such as Determiner + Noun sequences which behaved essentially as single words, the final consonant of the first element forming the coda to the next syllable in what would become the familiar invariable or obligatory liaisons which are still uniformly observed today. In other cases, usage varied,

[20] Dupuis (1836: 105): 'Cette prononciation a pour garant l'usage universel et l'autorité des meilleurs grammairiens'. Later (p. 195) she claims that pronouncing a close [ɛ] in this context is 'physiquement impossible', but elsewhere her advice is less consistent: she recommends for example (p. 197) *de lègè -z-efforts* but *nos premié* [e] *z-amis*.

with higher-status speakers preferring the conservative pronunciation, in which the final consonant, retained in the orthography, was realised while lower-class speakers continued to delete. Moreover, recalling Kroch's comments regarding non-assimilation of loan words, it comes as no surprise that learned borrowings, used by high-status speakers, tended to resist the nativising tendency to erode the final consonant.

A number of commentators have alluded to the conflict between what they see as a 'natural' phonetic process led by the people but resisted by intellectual elites. Dauzat (1930: 143) for example presents this dichotomy in stark terms:

> La liaison s'est heurtée à l'hostilité du peuple, qui y répugne, tandis que les grammairiens se sont efforcés d'en étendre l'usage. Dans la bonne société, elle avait perdu du terrain du XVIIIe au XIXe, époque où elle a atteint son maximum. Depuis un demi-siècle, le nombre de liaisons va en diminuant.

In similar vein, the 'décroissance de la liaison… qu'on ne saurait nier' is interpreted by Langlard (1928: 67) in terms of overcoming an artificial resistance to natural phonetic processes by conservative purists:

> la tendance phonétique, qui avait réussi à la fin du XVIe siècle à amuïr complètement presque toutes les consonnes finales, semble avoir brisé les barrières artificielles élevées par les puristes, l'obsession de la graphie orthographique

But if the norm which emerges over the course of the nineteenth and twentieth centuries is, as Langlard (1928: 24) suggests 'un compromis entre ancien usage et tendances populaires', then it is an unstable and fiendishly complex one, which is opaque to outsiders.

For grammarians and purists between the sixteenth and eighteenth centuries, retention of final consonants carried a socially distinctive value as a marker of literacy, by virtue of its close association with a highly etymological written norm. Their defence of a conservative norm represented something of a rearguard action as final consonants were lost across the board for most speakers, and we witness grammarians struggling to strike the right balance between retention and deletion, notably in prevocalic position. A spike in liaison use in the nineteenth century, however, accompanies a general extension of educational opportunity in the post-Revolutionary period, and coincides as we saw above with a notable ideological change, in which the ostentatious signalling of literacy is no longer viewed as a mark of distinction. Those deemed to overuse liaison (notably teachers) are thus dismissed as pedants, and grammarians began openly to yearn for the 'simple' usage of the eighteenth century gentleman, or *homme du monde*. The true mark of culture in polite society is now the ability, Goldilocks like, to use just the right amount of liaison in cultivated company, as the 8th edition of the Academy Dictionary (1935: II: 118) underlines:

> Le manque de culture se trahit également par les liaisons vicieuses et par l'absence de liaisons.

Defining 'just the right amount', however, is problematic, and the Academy's own Grammar (1932: 8) is notably coy about setting the boundaries:

> Aucune règle ne détermine à la rigueur les cas où l'on doit faire et ceux où l'on doit éviter la liaison….L'usage seul en décide et il varie souvent.

Other sources had been similarly circumspect.[21] Le Roy (1911: 23), for example, offers:

> Ne pas faire assez de liaisons est blâmable et quelquefois vulgaire ; en trop faire est prétentieux et quelquefois dangereux. L'important est de se souvenir que la règle principale en cette matière est l'harmonie. (Author's emphasis).

A precise definition of *harmonie* however proves as elusive as that of its opposite, *cacophonie*, for Martinon (1913), who leaves the reader to deduce what this means from examples such as *tu le(s) za(s) zôtés*, rejected as 'inadmissible' in favour of *tu le(s) za(s) ôtés* (p. 386). As Morrison

[21] Even Nyrop (1935: 136) is frustratingly unspecific: 's'il est bon, quand on parle, d'être sobre de liaisons, il ne faut pas non plus en être trop avare'.

(1968: 120) observes, a reader seeking general guidance on variable liaison in the pages of Martinon's (or indeed Fouché's) volume is likely to be disappointed:

> even though there is some attention to style and the author's advice is intelligent, it fails to give the reader a general idea when liaison is made and when it is not. In other words, Martinon is essentially taking inventory of final consonants, rather than analyzing the problem of liaison.

For Nicholson (1909: 111) 'La liaison est une sorte d'art, un long apprentissage doit former le jugement et le goût; au début les erreurs sont inévitables, et nombreux sont les tâtonnements jusqu'à ce qu'on obtienne une sorte d'instinct', and indeed it is difficult not to conclude from the prescriptivists' own comments that the only sure route to mastering elite usage in respect of variable liaison is to be a member of the elite in the first place. The position of the outsider, meanwhile, is analogous to that of the petit-bourgeois autodidact as described by Bourdieu (1979: 378–81), aspiring to ape the manners of a higher social caste from which he/she is excluded:

> Parce qu'il n'a pas acquis sa culture selon l'ordre légitime qu'instaure l'institution scolaire, l'autodidacte est voué à trahir sans cesse, dans son anxiété même du bon classement, l'arbitraire de ses classements et, par là, de ses savoirs, sortes de perles sans fils, accumulées au cours d'un apprentissage singulier (…) Hommes de l'acquis, ils ne peuvent entretenir avec la culture la relation de familiarité autorisant les libertés et les audaces de ceux qui lui sont liés par la naissance, c'est-à-dire par nature et par essence.

That language is an intrinsic part of this culture is underlined in the same work by Bourdieu himself, who alludes specifically to the cultural capital bestowed by an ability to use optional liaison with ease. Liberty to break or flout the rules, cultural or linguistic, requires membership of the elevated social class which dictates them (p. 285):

> c'est ainsi que l'aisance en matière de langage peut s'affirmer soit dans les tours de force consistant à aller au delà de ce qui est exigé par les contraintes proprement grammaticales ou pragmatiques, à faire par exemple

les liaisons facultatives ou à substituer aux tours ou aux mots communs des mots et des tropes rares, soit dans la liberté à l'égard des exigences de la langue ou de la situation qui s'affirme dans des libertés ou des licences statutaires. Ces stratégies opposées qui permettent de se situer au-delà des règles et des convenances imposées aux locuteurs ordinaires ne sont nullement exclusives

It is against this backcloth that the scorn we saw expressed for teachers, as would-be promoters of social mobility, becomes comprehensible: the complex rules of behaviour required in elevated society are the carefully protected preserve of an elite, who neither wish them to be taught in the classroom, nor believe they can be. Those attempting to acquire them from outside the charmed circle of *initiés* betray themselves precisely by 'la tendance à l'hypercorrection, sorte de rigorisme qui porte à en faire trop de peur de ne pas en faire assez et à pourchasser, chez soi et chez les autres, les incorrections de langage' (Bourdieu 1979: 382), which incurs censure as *pédantisme* in nineteenth- and twentieth-century pronunciation manuals. The conflict between these two sources of legitimacy, social and educational, and the ideological biases of traditionalists such as Martinon are underlined by Encrevé (1988: 260–61):

Martinon (1913) opposait le « parler des gens du monde » et « celui des professeurs et, en général, des gens qui font profession de la parole » comme si l'on pouvait distinguer entre un usage gratuit de la langue relevant d'un art de vivre, pratique pure ayant en elle-même sa propre fin, et un usage intéressé de la langue au service d'un métier pour lequel elle n'est qu'un moyen, usage impur par définition, partant vicié, impropre. A cette idéologie cachée, la sociologie rappelle que le parler des « gens du monde » était une de leurs meilleurs sources de profits symboliques ; et que c'est dans la mesure où, pour les moins scolarisés, il se confondait avec celui des « gens du monde », d'où il tirait sa légitimité, que le parler des « gens qui font profession de la parole » pouvait avoir quelque efficacité et leur valoir quelques profits symboliques et matériels. En 1913, ces deux types de parlers étaient en concurrence objective pour la légitimité linguistique, et notamment pour le contrôle du pouvoir en matière de langue comme la bataille pour la réforme de l'orthographe venait de manifester.[22]

The importance of variable liaison as a marker of social distinction, therefore, can hardly be overstated, and as Kroch's model predicts, mastery of the phenomenon is jealously guarded by a narrow social elite and difficult, if not impossible, for those outside to access. The stakes are high and the attendant dangers accordingly great. As education and literacy have become more widespread, so has awareness of the potential pitfalls of *pataquès* in particular. Carton (2000: 44), writing on the post-war period, observes 'les hyperliaisons se multiplient, indice d'une incertitude croissante et du rôle de différenciateur social que joue ce phénomène.'[23] It would be unsurprising, therefore if, as Encrevé (1983: 47) argues, many speakers chose to avoid variable liaison altogether in what amounts to a 'play safe' strategy,[24] in which only obligatory liaisons are realised:

> La liaison non-obligatoire est ce territoire de la langue que ne fréquentent guère aujourd'hui que les locuteurs fortement scolarisés (ou « cultivés »), où ils éprouvent plus clairement qu'ailleurs et l'inévitable variation de leur propre usage, et le risque de commettre des fautes (par excès ou par défaut), et l'insécurité linguistique attachée à la conscience de ce risque.

Findings from over forty years of empirical research, however, suggest a rather more nuanced picture, in which variable liaison, speech style and a range of extralinguistic factors interact in sometimes surprising ways. These are explored in Part III.

[22] Cf. Kammans (1956: 245):

> dire que la liaison est facultative ne veut pas dire qu'il est indifférent de le faire ou de ne pas le faire dans tel cas déterminé. A chacun de manifester son goût et son éducation.

[23] On this point, see Sect. 7.2.3 below.

[24] On 'strategies of neutrality' see in particular Myers-Scotton (1976).

References

Ackernecht, J. (1895). Die binding in franzöischen unterricht. *Die Neueren Sprachen, III*, 393–408.

Alemand, L. (1968 [1688]). *Nouvelles observations ou guerre civile des Français sur la langue*. Geneva: Slatkine Reprints.

Anderson, R. (1982). New Light on French Secondary Education in the Nineteenth Century. *Social History, 7*(2), 147–165.

Anonymous. (1624). *Eclogue præcipuarum legum gallicæ pronunciationis*. Mons.

Anonymous. (1669). *La veritable orthographe françoise opposée à l'orthographe imaginaire du sieur Lesclache*. Paris: Jacques Bottin.

Anonymous. (1696). *Dissertation sur la prononciation de la langue française*. The Hague: Van Dole.

Armstrong, L. (1932). *The Phonetics of French: A Practical Handbook*. London: Bell.

Ayres-Bennett, W. (1994). Elaboration and Codification: The French Language. In W. Davies, M. Mair Perry, & R. Temple (Eds.), *The Changing Voices of Europe: Social and Political Change and Their Linguistic Repercussions, Past, Present and Future: Papers in Honour of Professor Glanville Price* (pp. 53–73). Cardiff: University of Wales Press.

Ayres-Bennett, W. (2004). *Sociolinguistic Variation in Seventeenth-Century French: Methodology and Case Studies*. Cambridge: Cambridge University Press.

Bally, C. (1932). *Linguistique générale et linguistique française* (4th ed.). Bern: Francke.

Barclay, A. (1521). *Here Begynneth the Introductory to Write and to Pronounce Frenche*. London: Coplande.

Bascan, L. (1912). *Manuel pratique de prononciation et de lecture française*. Rambouillet: Institut de Phonétique Française.

Bauche, H. (1920). *Le langage populaire: Grammaire, syntaxe et dictionnaire du français tel qu'on le parle dans le peuple de Paris*. Paris: Payot.

Beyer, F. (1888). *Französische Phonetik für Lehrer und Studierende. 3. Auflage in Auftrage des Verfassers neu bearbeitet von H. Klinghardt*. Cöthen: Schulze.

Beyer, F., & Passy, P. (1893). *Elementarbuch des gesprochenen Französisch*. Cöthen: Schulze.

de Bèze, T. (1584). *De francicæ linguæ recta pronuntiatione*. Geneva: Vignon.

Block, J. (1892). Zur Aussprache des Französischen. *Zeitschrift für französische Sprache und Litteratur, XIV*, 236–265.

Bonnard, G. (1927). *Manuel de phonétique française*. Lausanne: Payot.

Bourdieu, P. (1979). *La Distinction*. Paris: Minuit.

Bovelles, C. de (1973 [1533]). *Liber de differentia vulgarium linguarum et Gallici sermonis varietate* (C. Demaizière, Trans.). Paris: Klincsieck.
Bruneau, C. (1927). *Manuel de phonétique pratique*. Paris: Berger-Levrault.
Brunot, F. (1907). La Langue du Palais et la formation du « bel usage ». In *Mélanges Chabaneau, 1973* (pp. 677–685). Erlangen: Slatkine Reprints.
Brunot, F. (1966). *Histoire de la langue française: des origines à 1900* (13 Vols.). Paris: Colin.
Buben, V. (1935). *Influence de l'orthographe sur la prononciation du français moderne*. Bratislava: Faculty of Humanities, University of Bratislava.
Carton, F. (1995). La Prononciation du Français. In G. Antoine & R. Martin (Eds.), *Histoire de la Langue Française 1914–1945* (pp. 27–59). Paris: CNRS-Éditions.
Carton, F. (2000). La prononciation. In G. Antoine & B. Cerquiglini (Eds.), *Histoire de la langue française 1945–2000* (pp. 25–60). Paris: CNRS Editions.
Catach, N. (1998). *L'Orthographe (Que sais-je?)*. Paris: Presses Universitaires de France.
Chevrot, J.-P., & Malderez, I. (1999). L'effet Buben de la linguistique diachronique à l'approche cognitive (et retour). *Langue Française, 124*, 104–125.
Chifflet, L. (1659). *Essai d'une parfaite grammaire de la langue française*. Brussels: Lambert Marchand.
Clédat, L. (1917). *Manuel de phonétique et de morphologie historique du français*. Paris: Hachette.
Cohen, M. (1947). *Histoire d'une langue: le français*. Paris: Editions Hier et Aujourd'hui.
D'Aisy, F. (1674). *Nouvelle méthode de la langue française*. Paris.
D'Olivet, P.-J. (1736). *Traité de la prosodie françoise*. Paris: Gandouin.
Damourette, J., & Pichon, E. (1936). Questions de liaisons. *Le Français Moderne, IV*, 347–353.
Dangeau. (1694). *Premiere lettre d'un academicien à un autre sur le sujet des voyelles*. Paris: Coignard.
Dauzat, A. (1930). *Histoire de la langue française*. Paris: Payot.
De la Faye, A. (1613). *Institutiones linguæ gallicaæ oder Gründliche Unterweising der frantzösischen Sprachen*. Jehna: Beithmann.
Delamothe, G. (1592). *The French Alphabet Teaching in a Very Short Time by a Most Easie Way to Pronounce French Naturally, to Read It Perfectly, to Write It Truly and to Speak It Accordingly*. London: Jillier.
Domergue, U. (1805). *Manuel des étrangers amateurs de la langue française*. Paris: Pillet Ainé.

Du Bellay, J. (1549). *Defense et illustration de la langue françoise*. Paris: Arnoul l'Angelier.
Dubois, J. [J. Sylvius]. (1531). *In Linguam gallicam isagoge, una cum eiusdem grammatica Latino-Gallica*. Paris: R. Estienne.
Dubois, C. G. (1970). *Mythe et langage qu XVIesiècle*. Paris: Ducros.
Dubroca, L. (1824). *Traité de la prononciation des consonnes et des voyelles finales des mots français dans leur rapport avec les consonnes et les voyelles initiales des mots suivants*. Paris: Author.
Duez, N. (1973 [1639]). *Le vray guidon de la langue françoise*. Leiden: Elsevier. (Geneva: Slatkine Reprints).
Dumville, B. (1904). *Elements of French Pronunciation and Diction*. London: Dent.
Dupuis, S. (1836). *Traité de prononciation, ou nouvelle prosodie française*. Paris: Hachette.
Encrevé, P. (1983). La Liaison sans enchaînement. *Actes de la Recherche en Sciences Sociales, 46*, 39–66.
Estienne, R. (1549). *Dictionnaire François-latin, contenant les motz et manieres de parler Français, tournez en Latin*. Paris: R. Etienne.
Estienne, H. (1565). *Traité de conformité du langage françois avec le grec*. Paris: Delalain.
Estienne, H. (1578a). *Deux Dialogues du nouveau langage françois*. Paris: Mamert Patisson.
Estienne, H. (1578b). *La Précellence du langage françois*. Paris: Mamert Patisson.
Feugère, L. (1849). *Œuvres choisies d'Etienne Pasquier accompagnées de notes et d'une étude sur sa vie et sur ses ouvrages*. Paris: Firmin Didot.
Fouché, P. (1934). L'Évolution phonétique du français du XVIe siècle à nos jours. *Le Français Moderne, II*, 217–236.
Fouché, P. (1959). *Traité de prononciation française* (2nd ed.). Paris: Klincksieck.
Gaatone, D. (1979). Liaison et structure syllabique en français. *Français Moderne, 47*(4), 312–334.
Garnier, P. (1607). *Præcepta gallici sermonis ad pleniorem perfectioremque eius linguæ cognitionem necessaria tum breussima, tum facillima*. Bacot.
Genévrier, P. (1927). *Précis de phonétique comparée française et anglaise et manuel de prononciation française à l'usage des étudiants anglo-saxons*. Paris: Didier.
Génin, F. (1845). *Des variations du langage français depuis le XIIe siècle, ou recherche des principes qui devraient régler l'orthographe et la prononciation*. Paris: Didot.
Girault-Duvivier, C. P. (1811). *Grammaire des Grammaires, ou Analyse raisonnée des meilleurs traités sur la langue française*. Brussels: Tircher.

Goémans, L., & Antoine, G. (1919). *Traité de prononciation française*. Liège: Bénard.
Grammont, M. (1914). *Traité pratique de prononciation française*. Paris: Delagrave.
Grevisse, M. (1936). *Le Bon Usage. Grammaire française avec des remarques sur la langue française d'aujourd'hui* (7th ed.). Gembloux: Duculot.
Hindret, J. (1659). *L'Art de bien prononcer et de bien parler la langue françoise*. Paris: Laurent D'Houry.
Hornsby, D. (1998). Patriotism and Linguistic Purism in France: *Deux dialogues dans le nouveau langage françois* and *Parlez-vous Franglais? Journal of European Studies, 28/4*(112), 331–354.
Kammans, L.-P. (1956). *La Prononciation française d'aujourd'hui. Manuel à l'usage des étudiants, des comédiens, des speakers*. Brussels: Bauds.
Koschwitz, E. (1893). *Les Parlers parisiens, d'après les témoignages de MM. de Bornier, Coppé, A. Daudet, P. Desjardins, Got, Mgr d'Hulst, le P. Hyacinthe, Leconte de Lisle, G. Paris, Renan, Rod, Sully-Prudhomme, Zola, et autres. Anthologie phonétique*. Marburg: Elvert.
de L'Esclaches, L. (1668). *Les véritables règles de l'ortografe franceze*. Paris: Laurent Rondet.
Landais, N. (1835). *Dictionnaire Général et Grammatical des Dictionnaires Français*. Paris: Didier.
Langlard, H. (1928). *La Liaison dans le français*. Paris: Champion.
Le Mare, P. (1819). *Cours de langue française*. Paris.
Le Roy, G. (1911). *La Diction française par les textes*. Paris: Mellottée.
Lesaint. (1850). *Traité complet de la prononciation française dans la seconde moitié du XIXe siècle*. Halle: Gesenius.
Littré, E. (1863–1869). *Dictionnaire de la langue française* (4 Vols.). Paris: Hachette.
Lodge, R. A. (1993). *French: From Dialect to Standard*. London: Routledge.
Lopez, J. S. (2009). Langue française et éducation des élites. *Synergies Espagne, 2*, 81–97.
de Malvin-Cazal, J. (1846). *Prononciation de la langue française au XIXe siècle, tant dans le langage soutenu que dans la conversation*. Paris: Imprimerie Royale.
Marouzeau, J. (1963). *Précis de stylistique française* (5th ed.). Paris: Masson.
Martinet, A. (1947). Notes sur la phonologie du français vers 1700. *Bulletin de la Société de linguistique de Paris, XLIII*(1), 13–23.
Martinon, P. (1913). *Comment on prononce le français. Traité complet de prononciation pratique avec les noms propres et les mots étrangers*. Paris: Larousse.
Martinon, P. (1927). *Comment on parle en français. La langue parlée correcte comparée avec la langue littéraire et la langue familière*. Paris: Larousse.

Matzke, J. (1897). *A Primer of Prench Pronunciation* (Revised 3rd ed.). New York: Holt.
Maupas, C. (1625). *Grammaire et syntaxe françoise*. Paris. Jacques Cailloué.
Milroy, J., & Milroy, L. (2012). *Authority in Language: Investigating Standard English* (4th ed.). London: Routledge.
Morrison, A. S. (1968). *A Critical Bibliography of Studies of Liaison in French Speech Since 1800*. Unpublished PhD thesis, Columbia University.
Müller, K. (1904). Die Bindung sonst stummer Endkonsonanten in französischen Sprachunterricht. In *Festschrift zum elften deutschen Neuphlologentage* (pp. 149–199). Coin: Neubner.
Myers-Scotton, C. (1976). Strategies of Neutrality: Language Choice in Uncertain Situations. *Language, 52*(4), 919–941.
Nicholson, G. (1909). *A Practical Introduction to French Phonetics for the Use of English-Speaking Students and Teachers*. London: Macmillan.
Nyrop, K. (1935). *Grammaire historique de la langue française* (Vol. 1, 4th ed.). Copenhagen: Nordisk Forlag.
Palmer, R. (1985). *The Improvement of Humanity: Education and the French Revolution*. Princeton: Princeton University Press.
Pasquier, E. (1560). *Les Recherches de la France*. Paris: Mettayer & L'Huillier.
Passy, P. (1906). *Les Sons du Français: leur formation, leur combinaison, leur représentation*. Paris: Firmin-Didot.
Peletier Du Mans, J. (1550). *Dialogue de l'ortografe é prononciacion françoese*. Poitiers: J. & E. de Marnef.
Peyrollaz, M., & Bara de Tovar, M.-L. (1954). *Manuel de phonétique et de diction françaises à l'usage des étrangers*. Paris: Larousse.
Pichon, E. (1938). Genre et questions connexes (sur les pas de Mlle Durand). *Le Français Moderne, 6*, 107–126.
Pleasants, J. (1933). *Pronunciation of French: Articulation and Intonation*. Ann Arbor: Edwards.
Ploetz, K. (1873). *Systematische Darstellung der französischen Aussprache*. Berlin: Herbig.
Pope, M. K. (1952). *From Latin to Modern French with Especial Consideration of Anglo-Norman. Phonology and Morphology* (2nd ed.). Manchester: Manchester University Press.
Poplack, S., Jarmasz, L.-G., Dion, N., & Rosen, N. (2015). Searching for Standard French: The Construction and Mining of the *Recueil historique des grammaires du français*. *Journal of Historical Sociolinguistics, 1*(1), 13–55.
Posner, R. (1997). *Linguistic Change in French*. Oxford: Clarendon Press.
Quiehl, K. (1906). *Französischen Aussprache und Sprachfertigkeit. Ein Hilfsbuch zur Einführung in die Phonetik und Methodik des Französischen*. Marburg: Elvert.

Richelet, P. (1680). *Nouveau Dictionnaire François*. Geneva: J.-H. Widerhold.
Rickard, P. (1989). *A History of the French Language* (2nd ed.). London: Routledge.
Rousselot, J.-P. (1911). Dictionnaire de la prononciation française. *Revue de phonétique, I*, 169–180.
Rousselot, J.-P., & Laclotte, F. (1902). *Précis de prononciation française*. Paris: Velter.
Roux, S. (1694). *Méthode nouvelle pour apprendre aux enfants à lire parfaitement bien le latin et le françois*. Paris: Warin.
Scherm, C. (1909). *Französische Lautschule*. Nürnberg: Koch.
Schmidt, H. (1909). *Französische Schulphonetik. Praktische Anleitung für den Unterricht in der französischen Anssprache*. Cöthen: Schulse.
Stubelius, S. (1943). *Le Manuel phonétique de Nyrop à la lumière de recherches plus récentes sur le phonétisme français* (pp. 6–22). Gothenburg: Wettergren & Kerber.
Tabourot, E. (1603). *Les Bigarrures et touches du seigneur des Accords avec les apophthegmes du sieur Goulard et les escraignes dijonnoises*. Paris: Jean Richer.
Tappolet, E. (1932). Hiatusfurcht und Wohllauttheorie in Französischen. *Die Neueren Sprachen, XL*, 385–398.
Thurot, C. (1881). *De la prononciation française depuis le commencement du XVIe siècle, d'après les témoignages des grammairiens* (Vol. 2). Paris: Imprimerie Nationale.
Tory. (1529). *Champfleury* (facsimile ed., 1931). Paris: Bosse.
Trudeau, D. (1992). *Les inventeurs du bon usage (1529–1647)*. Paris: Minuit.
Van der Aa, J. (1622). *Grammatica Gallica*. Louvain.
Vaugelas, C. F. de (1970 [1647]). *Remarques sur la langue françoise* (J. Streicher, Ed.). Geneva: Slatkine Reprints.
Vossler, K. (1913). *Frankreichs Kultur und Sprache. Geschichte der französischen Schriftsprache von den Anfängen bis zur Gegenwart*. Heidelberg: Vinter.
Wagner, R. L. (1951). Contribution à la préhistoire du romanisme. *Conférences de l'Institut de Paris, X*, 101–124.
von Wartburg, W. (1934). *Évolution et structure de la langue française*. Bern: Francke.
Wey, F. (1845). *Remarques sur la langue française au dix-neuvième siècle, sur le style et la composition littéraire* (2 Vols.). Paris: Didot.

Part III

Variation and Change

5

Liaison and Geography

5.1 Invariable Liaison: The *noyau dur*

Analyses of liaison until very recently have paid little or no attention to geographical, or diatopic, considerations: generally, most commentators have assumed, with Laks (2014: 335), that any regional differences are far outweighed by socio-stylistic factors. Nonetheless, a number of commentators (see e.g. Durand and Lyche 2008; Durand et al. 2011; Côté 2017) have alluded to anecdotal comments in the literature which suggest regional variation in respect of liaison use. For francophone Europe at least, the assumption behind such comments appears to be that differences are quantitative rather than qualitative, i.e. that norms with respect to liaison are shared even if speakers vary, according to region, in the amount of liaison which they realise. Passy, for example, in the 1892 edition of *Les Sons du Français* (quoted by Côté 2017: 14) suggests that 'on fait infiniment plus de liaisons dans la Suisse romande (…) que dans la région parisienne'; *Le Bon Usage* (12th edition, Goosse 1986: 43) observes that 'Les Parisiens ont tendance à abandonner des liaisons qui se maintiennent mieux en province et en Belgique'. Such comments are generally unsupported by evidence, and sometimes boil down to little more than class prejudice with a regional guise, as can be seen in Brun's (1931: 45) observations on Marseille French:

D. Hornsby, *Norm and Ideology in Spoken French*,
https://doi.org/10.1007/978-3-030-49300-4_5

> Les liaisons sont donc beaucoup moins fréquentes qu'en français commun. (…) Cette négligence, ainsi que la paresse à articuler les groupes de consonnes donne au parler du provençal ce caractère de vulgarité qui choque le nouveau venu.

This position is directly contradicted for the south of France more generally by Fouché (1936: 202–3), who asserts that 'le nombre de liaisons est infiniment plus grand que dans le français normal (…) Les liaisons d'un groupe rhythmique à un autre appartiennent au débit de la conférence ou du sermon. Dans le Midi, on entend les unes et les autres à peu près toujours.' Neither these claims, nor a later one by Eychenne and Walker (2010: 257) for Canadian French that 'la liaison est globalement nettement moins réalisée que dans le FR', have been borne out by recent findings, but more generally the availability of a major international database has made it possible to determine empirically (a) to what extent norms are shared across the francophone area and (b) whether diatopic differences which might emerge are primarily quantitative or qualitative. These questions are explored using PFC data by Durand and Lyche 2008, Durand et al. (2011) and especially Côté (2017), the only work to consider diatopic factors in isolation.

Diatopic evidence from corpora is also essential in determining the domain in which variability applies. As will be seen particularly in Chap. 6, comparability between studies proves problematic, for two reasons: firstly, data for variable and non-variable liaison are often conflated, and secondly there is no agreement on where the boundaries between these two broad groupings lie. As Armstrong (2001: 199) observes, we lack the baseline evidence needed to determine whether items may have changed category since Delattre (1966 [1947]), or whether indeed his intuitions may in some cases have been flawed from the outset. What is certainly clear, however, is that a number of items considered *obligatoire* by Delattre have been found in recent studies (see Durand and Lyche 2008; Hornsby 2019) to be nothing of the kind. This raises the broader question of whether the claims of Delattre and others in this regard hold true for

France only, or for the francophone world as a whole, and more specifically whether a core set of non-variable liaisons can be established for all French speakers, outside which liaison contexts can be assumed to be potentially variable. This possibility is investigated by Côté (2017), who concludes that there is indeed what she terms a *noyau dur* of environments, representing a subset of Delattre's *liaison obligatoire* category, for which liaison is consistently realised by all francophones. The *noyau dur* or 'hard core' consists of four broad contexts, all exhibiting strong syntactic cohesion between elements (see Côté 2017: 15–16):

a. Determiner + Adjective/Noun
   ces [z] *amis, un* [n] *ancien voisin*
b. Proclitic + Proclitic/Verb
   on [n] *en* [n] *arrive, vous* [z] *allez*
c. verb + enclitic
   dit-[t]*on, va-t-*[t]*-on, parles-*[z]*-en*
d. en + X
   en [n] *anglais, en* [n] *allant*

Apart from performance errors, these liaisons are categorically realised by French speakers throughout the francophone world, though as we shall see below there are isolated departures from the *noyau dur* in North America. Evidence of non-liaison after *en* suggests the last of these contexts (d) is problematic, but after lengthy discussion of the counterexamples Côté (2017: 16) concludes the latter for the most part represent 'cas motivés de disjonction', for example before *un/e* used as a stressed numeral, and do not therefore invalidate the general claim of invariability in this environment. The restricted range of the *noyau dur* of non-variable liaison would appear to offer greater potential for variability than Delattre's original model envisaged. To what extent might this variability be determined by regional, national or global factors? The PFC data in particular provide an empirical basis for addressing this question both within francophone Europe (Sect. 5.2 below) and across the French-speaking world (Sect. 5.3).

5.2 Regional Variation in Francophone Europe

Setting aside anecdotal remarks of the kind quoted above, the first serious examination of regional variation in liaison is Durand and Lyche's (2008) comparison of two carefully selected rural villages, where PFC *enquêtes* had been undertaken at an early stage. Brécey in Normandy (pop. 2113) falls squarely within the *langue d'oïl* zone, while Douzens in Aude (pop. 600) lies in the *langue d'oc* area. Ancestral dialects have been preserved in both, though dialect obsolescence is reported to be further advanced in Brécey.

Focusing on *être* and *avoir* forms in the two villages to ensure a significant quantity of comparable data, Durand and Lyche found a higher incidence of liaison across the board in Douzens, where liaison (after *est*) reached 83.33%; for Brécey the highest rate recorded (after *c'est*) was only 28.84%. This finding seemed consistent with general southern conservatism with respect to the traditional orthoepic norm (as manifested e.g. in retention of word-final schwa and vowel + nasal consonant sequences), and was echoed by four later meridional and six non-meridional PFC *enquêtes*, which appeared to confirm a greater incidence of liaison in the south for three high-frequency contexts: after *est/c'est, était/c'était* and *avait*. Durand and Lyche, however, cautioned against drawing premature conclusions regarding a north-south or *oïl/oc* divide, noting that data from the three then available Belgian surveys offered a mixed picture, aligning more closely with the south for *C'est* but with the north for the other two environments, as can be seen in Table 5.1 below.

In fact, later analyses completed when more PFC data were available by Coquillon et al. (2010), who compared 67 surveys from the north and the south, and by Durand et al. (2011) found a much greater degree of homogeneity between *Oc* and *Oïl* regions. Negligible differences were observed in the reading exercise for Plural N +Adj sequences; the same was largely true for the prepositions *dans* (which showed a slightly higher realisation rate in the north), for *chez*, and for third person singular indicative + complement/adjunct sequences. Similar results were obtained for *être+allé(e)(s)* sequences, though a potentially significant difference was

Table 5.1 Liaison by region in three environments (after Durand and Lyche 2008: 48, Fig. 6)

	North		South		Belgium	
	Liaison	No liaison	Liaison	No liaison	Liaison	No liaison
(C')est	155 **33.91%**	302	146 **42.69%**	196	142 **47.33%**	158
(C')était	10 **5.34%**	177	26 **15.75%**	139	6 **4.61%**	130
avait	0 **0%**	126	11 **11.34%**	86	0 **0%**	54

observed in the cases of *suis allé(e)(s)* and *est allé(e)(s)*, for which liaison occurred more frequently in the south. Coquillon et al. conclude that the north and south of France form a relatively homogeneous space with respect to liaison, but Durand et al. (2011: 130 fn) again caution against across-the-board interpretations which fail to take into account of individual norms within the Hexagon, for example, the realisation *ils* [l] *ont* in western France, underlining once more the need for fine-grained analysis which allows for differences even at the level of the individual construction (see Chap. 6 below). Lyche et al. (2012: 379) concur, noting additionally that PFC data offer no support to the claim that wider use of word-final schwa in the south favours liaison as a hiatus-avoidance mechanism.

5.3 Liaison in the Francophone World

The PFC findings which enabled diatopic investigation of liaison to be conducted for the first time did not support claims for significant regional differentiation within metropolitan France. But what of variation in the wider francophone world? Here Côté (2017) provides an insightful synthesis of research from four global regions: Europe, Africa, Canada and Louisiana.[1] While there is general agreement with respect to the *noyau*

[1] A different division (Europe, Canada, Africa) is proposed by Durand et al. (2011) while Laks and Calderone (2014) distinguish France, first-language French areas (Belgium, Switzerland, Canada) and a second-language francophone zone (Africa).

dur of non-variable liaisons, she reports, there are different norms regarding variable liaison which are attributable to local factors, which we explore below.

PFC findings suggest that the 'espace relativement homogène' reported for France by Coquillon et al. extends broadly to francophone Europe. Liaison in the *noyau dur* environments is categorically realised both in Belgium (see Hambye and Simon 2012) and in Switzerland (Racine and Andreasson 2012). Variable liaison displays some individual differences from RF, however: liaison in the sequence *bien aimé* for example is reported to be rare in Belgium; in Neuchâtel variable liaison is largely restricted to present and imperfect forms of *être*. In both countries, as in France, the use of variable liaison declines with descending age, a finding which Hansen (2012), reporting on Paris, sees as evidence of change in progress rather than age-grading.

Turning to North America, both Barreca (2015) and Côté (2017: 18) find overall rates of variable liaison (19.6% and 19% respectively),[2] which are comparable with those observed in PFC *enquêtes* undertaken in Europe. Both Laurentian (Quebec and Ontario) and Acadian varieties (spoken primarily in New Brunswick and Nova Scotia), however, show a narrower range of variable environments than metropolitan French, and indeed a smaller number of liaison consonants. PFC data indicate that liaison is largely restricted to /z, n, t/ with only minimal incidence of /r/ and /p/. Laurentian varieties do however have /l/ as a liaison consonant, e.g. in *ça* [l] *arrive* (see Côté 2012).

Canadian PFC surveys consistently report variability outside the *noyau dur* but within the so-called 'obligatory' liaison category for RF as defined by Delattre. This is notably the case for pre-nominal adjectives: Walker (2012) notes widespread absence of liaison /t/ after *grand* in Hearst, Ontario, while Côté (2012) reports non-liaison after *premiers* in conversation style in Quebec. Non-liaison after *dans* is common in New Brunswick and Quebec, while Cichocki (2012) reports that liaison between monosyllabic prepositions and indefinite articles (e.g. *chez un*) is 'pratiquement inexistante' except after *en*, where liaison /n/ is

[2] Barreca's figure includes *en* as a variable liaison site; Côté treats *en* as non-variable but includes it for comparison with Barreca's data.

non-variable. Within the *noyau dur* itself, liaison after *on* is variable in New Brunswick and in Quebec, though in the latter case non-liaison appears to be recessive (see Côté 2017: 16), and now largely restricted to the environment involving forms of *aller* commencing with [i] (e.g. *on Ø y va, on Ø ira*). Non-liaison after *ils*, which for many Canadian speakers appears to have been lexicalised as [i], is widely reported (see Ameringen 1977; Cichocki 2012; Côté 2012). Walker (2012) reports that *ils ont* is rendered [jɔ̃] in over 90% of cases in Alberta, the RF form [izɔ̃] being restricted in Quebec to high-status speakers sensitive to mainstream normative pressure according to Côté (2012: 262). Ameringen and Cedergren's (1981) survey of 27 speakers from the Sankoff-Cedergren corpus found liaison after the pronouns *on* and *ils* to increase in line with linguistic market index (LMI),[3] and to be all but absent among working-class Montrealers.

Canadian liaison consonants do not always correspond to those of RF. Walker (2012) reports systematic use of liaison [n] after monosyllables in Alberta, irrespective of their final orthographic consonant, while in another Acadian variety, that of New Brunswick, *grand* frequently liaises with [n] rather than [t] as in RF (Cichocki 2012). Working-class Montrealers are reported by Ameringen and Cedergren (1981) and (Côté 2012: 266) to have extended use of the liaison /t/ of *est* to other present tense forms of *être*, for example *je suis* [t], *tu es* [t], and indeed to the pre-*être* context for example *ça va* [t] *être* (see Côté 2012: 267). A number of commentators remark on the behaviour of numerals. Cichocki (2012) reports that *deux* liaises only with feminine nouns in New Brunswick, e.g. *deux/hommes* but *deux* [z] *enfants* where the referents are female, while in Quebec liaison /z/ rather than canonical RF /t/ frequently occurs after *vingt* and *cent*.

[3] Defined by Sankoff and Laberge (1978: 239) as:

> an index which measures specifically how speakers 'economic activity, taken in its widest sense, requires or is necessarily associated with, competence in the legitimized language (or standard, elite, educated, etc. language)'

There is broad agreement that francophone Canadian varieties present a reduction in the range of environments in which liaison occurs, and a general paucity of liaisons in the variable category when compared with RF. In Quebec and New Brunswick liaison within the variable category is largely restricted to *est* [t], which appears for some speakers to be moving into the invariable set: a realisation figure of 87% for Trois-Rivières as reported by Côté (2012) contrasts with an average for the francophone world of about 31%.

Scripted styles in Canada show greater incidence of liaison in Delattre's *obligatoire* contexts, but reduced incidence of variable liaison overall as non-standard liaisons are eliminated in favour of zero (Côté 2012: 268), rather than the prescriptively RF correct consonant.

Although spoken in North America and bearing similarities to the Acadian varieties to which they are historically related, Louisiana merits separate treatment from the French of Canada for a number of reasons. Here French is obsolescent and an L2 variety for most speakers, and perhaps more importantly, it is not the language of formal education and its speakers are for the most part literate only in English. There is, as in Acadian varieties, some evidence of variability even within the *noyau dur*: liaison is reported to be variable rather than categorical after the object clitic *les*; after prenominal adjectives, a context classified as *obligatoire* by Delattre, liaison is almost entirely unattested (Boutin and Lyche 2014), except for a minority of speakers who have /t/ here as the default consonant in this environment (e.g. *gros* [t] *arbre*). Otherwise, variable liaison is all but negligible. Blainey (2013) cites levels below 0.5% for variable liaison in the Golden Meadow survey (5 occurrences of /n/ realised after a nasal vowel, 3 of which followed *dans*, for example *dans* [n] *un*); some variable liaison is reported after *est* in Ville Plate (Klingler and Lyche 2012: 305), in the sequence *est* [t] *arrivé(e),* and in the lexicalised expression *est* [t] *après*, where it is categorical. Otherwise liaison is reserved for plural contexts, not all of which correspond to those of RF, for example in *des petites* [z] *affaires; cinq* [z] *écoles; trop des* [z] *années, elle les* [z] *appelle asteur*. Numerals liaise with plurals but not otherwise, e.g. *il est cinq Ø heures* but *cinq* [z] *heures de temps, quatre* [z] *enfants, cents* [z] *acres* (see Blainey 2013). Lyche reports, again as in Acadian varieties, a high incidence of liaison with /t/ rather than /z/ with all present tense forms of *être* (e.g. *je suis* [t] *un peu perdu; tu es* [t] *arrivé*) and some use of liaison /t/ before *être*, for example *ta mama va* [t] *être fâchée*.

In francophone Africa, PFC data suggest norms which broadly correspond to those of RF in respect of non-variable liaison but, as in North America, a narrower range of environments for variable liaison. Frequencies in the latter category, however, may differ strikingly from those typically observed in Europe, and are subject to localised norms, determined largely by such factors as the status of French as a vehicular or vernacular language in the country in question, and the nature and influence of the relevant L1 where French is not a first language. Parallels can, in some cases, be drawn with Louisiana, where French is not a medium of instruction and competes as L2 with a language with word-level stress.

In Senegal, where French has been established since the seventeenth century, and remains the language for formal education, liaison is associated, as in RF, with the written language and follows patterns with respect to style-shifting which are similar to those observed in Europe. Boutin et al. (2012) report 50% liaison use after *est* in scripted styles but only 10.6% in conversation, and conclude (Boutin 2014: 167): 'les comportements des locuteurs africains en lecture et en conversation laissent supposer des représentations de la liaison comme très liée à l'écrit et à la norme de lecture'. Otherwise liaison is restricted almost exclusively to sequences of function and content words rather than between content words (liaison even after *très* is found to be negligible). Rather different circumstances prevail in the Central African Republic (see Bordal and Lyche 2008 and Bordal 2012 for Bangui) and in Mali (see Lyche and Skattum 2012), where French has a rather more restricted H language role. Here liaison is for the most part limited to the non-variable contexts of RF, outside of which it is found infrequently and in a narrow range of variable environments. In contrast to Senegal, there is little evidence of stylistic differentiation, and in both countries low incidence of liaison appears to be linked to L1 prosody. As Côté (2017: 20) points out, contact with other languages with greater word-level autonomy (Sango in Central African Republic; Bamako in Mali) may lead both to maintenance of word-level stress in L2 French, and the presence of glottal stops between words (see Boutin and Turcsan 2009, Boutin et al. 2012), weakening the syntactic cohesion between elements on which liaison depends. It is not yet, however, entirely clear how the countervailing factors of formality, which favours liaison, and language contact, which appears to inhibit it, affect different liaison sequences.

Since literacy in French cannot universally be assumed in francophone Africa, where French is often not a first language, it is dangerous to draw hasty conclusions from surveys which may disproportionately favour literate speakers. This is well illustrated by Côte d'Ivoire (see Boutin and Lyche 2014), where a marked difference in overall liaison use is observed between informants with and without formal education in French. The figure for the former, at 25%, is broadly comparable with that observed in continental Europe while the liaison rate for the latter group, at just 8%, is rather closer to that of Louisiana (see above). When specific variable liaison contexts are considered, a mixed picture emerges with no single global region proving dominant (see Côté 2017: 19; see Table 5.2 below). When liaison after forms of *être* is considered, for example, the only really striking differences evident are for the present tense forms *est* and *sont*, where the tendency appears to favour liaison in Canada and non-liaison elsewhere; liaison with *étais* seems variable in Africa but negligible elsewhere. Liaison after *très* is variable in Africa but mostly non-variable elsewhere. As Côté observes (ibid.), the high scores for *suis* and *étais* in Africa appear to be lexically conditioned: in twenty-five of the thirty cases where a liaison consonant was realised, the items in question were followed by the participle *allé(e)* (see also Boutin 2014); she also suggests a similar effect for *dans*, for which liaison only occurs in the sequence *dans un(e)*. The specificity of such observations, which can often relate to individual lexical sequences, point to a constant dilemma in liaison analysis, to which will return below, namely the trade-off involved between obtaining significant amounts of data (which may require conflation of contexts which behave differently), and maintenance of strict comparability (which may result in low and unrepresentative token numbers). That *être* cannot be treated as a single variable for liaison purposes is evident from the contrast in Canada between the figure for *est* (75.5%) and for *étais* (0.0%; see Table 5.2 below). But when data for *être* are

Table 5.2 Realisation of variable liaison in selected lexical contexts, by global zone (after Côté 2017: Tableau 1)

	Île-de-France	Switzerland	Canada	Africa
est	39.3%	30.6%	**75.5%**	12.8%
sont	*19.2%*	*0%*	***66.7%***	*13.7%*
suis	*15.3%*	*22%*	***28.1%***	16.0%
était	**9.3%**	4.6%	*0.0%*	*2.3%*
étais	*0.0%*	*0.0%*	*0.0%*	***19.1%***
pas	0.0%	2.0%	0.7%	**3.7%**
quand	*81.7%*	***97.0%***	*83.3%*	48.2%
très	***100%***	***100%***	*89.5%*	*68.8%*
dans	*93.9%*	***98.1%***	*78.5%*	*98.1%*

Notes: High score for each environment indicated in **bold**. Italicised figures based on fewer than 100 tokens

Table 5.3 Patterns of liaison by global region (after Côté 2017: 23, Tableau 2)

	-non-standard liaison	+non-standard liaison
+ variable liaison	Europe	Canada
- variable liaison	Africa	Louisiana

broken down by parts of the verb, only six of the twenty figures quoted are based on 100 or more tokens.

For Côté the most pertinent mode of classification for the four global zones is based on two parameters, namely (a) use of liaison in variable contexts and (b) use of liaison forms which are non-standard in RF: see Table 5.3 above.

North America, which has maintained a high degree of normative autonomy from metropolitan French since the seventeenth century, stands out for use of non-standard liaison forms, contrasting notably in this regard with Africa, and particularly sub-Saharan Africa, where French is associated with a colonial schooling system established in the nineteenth century, and has retained a largely European norm.

Both from the diachronic perspective explored in Part II and the synchronic approach adopted here, literacy emerges as a key determinant of variable liaison usage. In Canada, where speakers are generally educated through the medium of French, variable liaison is maintained, albeit in a narrower range of environments than in RF. By contrast in Louisiana, where the language of instruction and of writing is English, its use is negligible. In Africa, where the status of French and its role within formal education varies considerably, variable liaison is again associated with a very narrow range of environments but there is a sharp contrast between the behaviour of literate and non-literate speakers.

References

van Ameringen, A. (1977). *La liaison en français de Montréal.* Unpublished Masters dissertation, Université du Québec à Montréal, Montreal.

van Ameringen, A., & Cedergren, H. (1981). Observations sur la liaison en français de Montréal. In D. Sankoff & H. Cedergren (Eds.), *Variation Omnibus* (pp. 141–149). Edmonton, Alberta: Linguistic Research.

Armstrong, N. (2001). *Social and Stylistic Variation in Spoken French: A Comparative Approach.* Amsterdam, Netherlands: John Benjamins.

Barreca, G. (2015). *L'acquisition de la liaison chez des apprenants italophones. Des atouts d'un corpus de natifs pour l'étude de la liaison en français langue étrangère (FLE).* Unpublished doctoral dissertation, Université Paris Ouest Nanterre La Défense/Università Cattolica del Sacro Cuore di Milano.

Blainey, D. (2013). *First to Come, Last to Go: Phonological Change and Resilience in Louisiana Regional French.* Unpublished doctoral thesis, Tulane University.

Bordal, G. (2012). A Phonological Study of French Spoken by Multilingual Speakers from Bangui, the Capital of the Central African Republic. In R. Gess, C. Lyche, & T. Meisenburg (Eds.), *Phonological Variation in French: Illustrations from Three Continents* (pp. 23–44). Amsterdam; Philadelphia: John Benjamins.

Bordal, G., & Lyche, C. (2008). La liaison en terre africaine. In *Colloque international 'Phonologie du français contemporain: variation, interfaces, cognition' (11–13 décembre 2008).* Paris: MSH.

Boutin, B. A. (2014). Liaisons en français et terrains africains. In J. Durand, G. Kristoffersen, & B. Laks, avec la collaboration de J. Peuvergne (Eds.), *La phonologie du français: normes, périphéries, modélisation* (pp. 153–172). Nanterre: Presses Universitaires de Paris Ouest.

Boutin, B. A., & Lyche, C. (2014). Ce que nous apprenent des locuteurs francophones non-lecteurs sur la liaison. In C. Soum-Favaro, A. Coquillon, & J.-P. Chevrot (Eds.), *La liaison: approches contemporaines* (pp. 283–310). Bern: Peter Lang.

Boutin, B. A., & Turcsan, G. (2009). La prononciation du français en Afrique: la Côte d'Ivoire. In J. Durand, B. Laks, & C. Lyche (Eds.), *Phonologie, variation et accents du français* (pp. 131–152). Paris, France: Hermès.

Boutin, B. A., Gess, R., & Guèye, G. M. (2012). French in Senegal After Three Centuries: A Phonological Study of Wolof Speakers' French. In R. Gess, C. Lyche, & T. Meisenburg (Eds.), *Phonological Variation in French: Illustrations from Three Continents* (pp. 45–71). Amsterdam; Philadelphia: John Benjamins.

Brun, A. (1931). *Le français de Marseille: Étude de parler régional.* Marseille: Institut historique de Provence.

Cichocki, W. (2012). An Overview of the Phonetics and Phonology of Acadian French Spoken in Northeastern New Brunswick (Canada). In R. Gess, C. Lyche, & T. Meisenburg (Eds.), *Phonological Variation in French: Illustrations from Three Continents* (pp. 211–234). Amsterdam; Philadelphia: John Benjamins.

Coquillon, A., Durand, J., Lyche, C., & Eychenne, J. (2010). French Liaison: From Global Results to Local Varieties. In *Colloque International PHONLEX.* Université de Toulouse II–Le Mirail (8–10 septembre 2010).

Côté, M.-H. (2012). Laurentian French (Québec): Extra Vowels, Missing Schwas and Surprising Liaison Consonants. In R. Gess, C. Lyche, & T. Meisenburg (Eds.), *Phonological Variation in French: Illustrations from Three Continents* (pp. 235–274). Amsterdam: John Benjamins.

Côté, M.-H. (2017). La liaison en diatopie: esquisse d'une typologie. *Journal of French Language Studies, 27*, 13–25.

Delattre, P. (1966 [1947]). La liaison en français, tendances et classifications. In P. Delattre (Ed.), *Studies in French and Comparative Phonetics: Selected Papers in French and Englishs* (pp. 39–48). The Hague: Mouton. First Published in *French Review, 21*(2), 148–157.

Durand, J., & Lyche, C. (2008). French Liaison in the Light of Corpus Data. *Journal of French Language Studies, 18*, 33–66.

Durand, J., Laks, B., Calderone, B., & Tchobanov, A. (2011). Que savons-nous de la liaison aujourd'hui? *Langue française, 169*, 103–135.

Eychenne, J., & Walker, D. (2010). Le français en Amérique du Nord: éléments de synthèse. In S. Detey, J. Durand, B. Laks, & C. Lyche (Eds.), *Les variétés du français parlé dans l'espace francophone: Ressources pour l'enseignement* (pp. 249–264). Paris: Ophrys.

Fouché, P. (1936). Les diverses sortes de français au point de vue phonétique. *Le Français Moderne, IV*, 199–216.

Goosse, A. (Ed.). (1986). *Le Bon Usage*. Paris: Duculot.

Hambye, P., & Simon, A.-C. (2012). The Variation of Pronunciation in Belgian French: From Segmental Phonology to Prosody. In R. Gess, C. Lyche, & T. Meisenburg (Eds.), *Phonological Variation in French: Illustrations from Three Continents* (pp. 129–150). Amsterdam; Philadelphia: John Benjamins.

Hansen, A.-B. (2012). A Study of Young Parisian Speech: Some Trends in Pronunciation. In R. Gess, C. Lyche, & T. Meisenburg (Eds.), *Phonological Variation in French: Illustrations from Three Continents* (pp. 151–172). Amsterdam; Philadelphia: John Benjamins.

Hornsby, D. (2019). Variable Liaison, Diglossia, and the Style Dimension in Spoken French. *French Studies, 73*(4), 578–597.

Klingler, T., & Lyche, C. (2012). "Cajun" French in a Non-Acadian Community: A Phonological Study of the French of Ville Platte, Louisiana. In R. Gess, C. Lyche, & T. Meisenburg (Eds.), *Phonological Variation in French: Illustrations from Three Continents* (pp. 275–312). Amsterdam; Philadelphia: John Benjamins.

Laks, B. (2014). Diachronie de la liaison en français contemporain: le cas de la parole publique (1999–2011). In J. Durand, G. Kristofersen, & B. Laks (Eds.), *La phonologie du français: normes, périphéries, modélisation* (pp. 333–375). Paris: Presses Universitaires de Paris Ouest.

Laks, B., & Calderone, B. (2014). La liaison en français contemporain: approches lexicales et exemplaristes. In C. Soum-Favaro, A. Coquillon, & J.-P. Chevrot (Eds.), *La liaison: approches contemporaines* (pp. 61–89). Bern: Peter Lang.

Lyche, C., & Skattum, I. (2012). The Phonological Characteristics of French in Bamako, Mali: A Sociolinguistic Approach. In R. Gess, C. Lyche, & T. Meisenburg (Eds.), *Phonological Variation in French: Illustrations from Three Continents* (pp. 73–101). Amsterdam, Philadelphia: John Benjamins.

Lyche, C., Meisenberg, T., & Gess, R. (2012). Phonological Variation in French: Unity and Diversity Across Continents. In R. Gess, C. Lyche, & T. Meisenburg (Eds.), *Phonological Variation in French: Illustrations from Three Continents* (pp. 369–388). Amsterdam; Philadelphia: John Benjamins.

Racine, I., & Andreasson, H. (2012). A Phonological Study of a Swiss French Variety: Data from the Canton of Neuchâtel. In R. Gess, C. Lyche, & T. Meisenburg (Eds.), *Phonological Variation in French: Illustrations from Three Continents* (pp. 173–206). Amsterdam; Philadelphia: John Benjamins.

Sankoff, D., & Laberge, S. (1978). The Linguistic Market and the Statistical Explanation of Variability. In D. Sankoff (Ed.), *Linguistic Variation: Models and Methods* (pp. 239–250). New York: Academic Press.

Walker, D. (2012). Albertan French Phonology: French in an Anglophone Context. In R. Gess, C. Lyche, & T. Meisenburg (Eds.), *Phonological Variation in French: Illustrations from Three Continents* (pp. 341–368). Amsterdam; Philadelphia: John Benjamins.

6

Liaison and Social Factors

6.1 Sociolinguistics and Orderly Heterogeneity

As we saw in Chap. 2, existing models of liaison have drawn largely on the perceptive, but largely untested, intuitions of prescriptive and descriptive commentators. The emergence of sociolinguistics as a serious discipline in the 1960s provided a methodology for their claims to be tested against empirical data, taking account of variation on both the inter-speaker (social) and intraspeaker (stylistic) dimensions. Prior to this, variation had been seen as a matter of little theoretical interest and therefore largely ignored. This prevailing view was first challenged by William Labov,[1] whose pioneering work broke a long-held taboo by correlating linguistic data with extralinguistic variables (e.g. social class and sex/gender). In doing so, he laid bare the 'orderly heterogeneity', or regular social patterning in linguistic variation, paving the way for a richer understanding of the mechanics of language change, and of social meanings encoded in different ways of saying 'the same thing' which language offers at every level. It is appropriate therefore at this point to recall the methodology and key findings of what became known as the Labovian or

[1] Labov does however acknowledge a debt to Gauchat (1905), whose study of variation in the Swiss village of Charmey he describes (2006: 12) as a 'nonpareil investigation of change in progress.... full of astonishing insights', even if its author would not have known or understood the term 'socio-linguistic' in its current guise.

D. Hornsby, *Norm and Ideology in Spoken French*,
https://doi.org/10.1007/978-3-030-49300-4_6

quantitative paradigm, which will provide a baseline for understanding variability in liaison in the next three chapters.

6.2 Urban Sociolinguistic Surveys

Labov is probably best known for his celebrated New York City department stores study (see Labov 1972: 43–54), which served as a pilot for the urban survey he was later to conduct in the same city. Having selected three department stores (Saks, Macy's and Klein's) graded on a number of criteria for status, he conducted a random anonymous survey focusing on use of non-prevocalic /r/ in two contexts. New York (r) is an example of a sociolinguistic variable (conventionally indicated by brackets), that is a linguistic feature known to be used variably within a speech community. As a binary variable, it has two variants, [r] and [Ø] (zero), that is, it is either realised or not realised in non-prevocalic contexts. To ensure comparability of data, variants must be, as in this case, equivalent in that they do not encode different meanings.[2]

Labov approached shop assistants in each store and enquired about the location of items known to be on sale on the fourth floor and, once the expected response 'fourth floor' had been given, he would pretend to have misheard, eliciting a repetition. Informants had no idea that they were participating in sociolinguistic research, thereby eliminating the effects of the so-called Observer's Paradox,[3] that is the problem of obtaining natural speech in the unnatural conditions of a sociolinguistic experiment. From each speaker, four tokens of (r) were obtained: one in preconsonantal position (*fou<u>r</u>th*) and another word-finally (*floo<u>r</u>*), in two different styles, since one can assume that the repetition would generally

---

[2] Extensions of the variable concept beyond phonological level to syntax or the lexicon can be problematic for precisely this reason: see for example Lavandera (1978).

[3] Cf. Labov (1972: 209):

> the aim of linguistic research in the community must be to find out how people talk when they are not being systematically observed; yet we can only obtain this data by systematic observation.

have elicited more careful pronunciation in order to make the response clearer to the enquirer.

Use of the prestige /r/ variant was found to correlate closely with the status of the store, with the high-status Saks store employees using it most and staff in the low-status store Klein's the least. On the style dimension, an equally clear pattern was observed, with consistently greater use of the prestige variant, in all three stores, in the context of the repetition.

While the department store survey had revealed consistent patterns in variable speech data, a rapid anonymous survey of this kind could provide only limited and impressionistic information about the social background of the speakers themselves. The New York City sociolinguistic survey which followed was more ambitious in scope, applying sampling techniques drawn from sociology to obtain a cross-section of the settled city population, balanced for age, gender and socio-economic status (as determined by an index score based on the criteria of education, occupation and income). Informants were interviewed and asked to speak as naturally as possible, but Labov readily concedes that, as they were well aware of being the subjects of a linguistic investigation, the effects of the Observer's Paradox could not entirely be mitigated. He therefore sought to investigate stylistic variation by varying informants' capacity to monitor their own speech at different stages of the interview. By asking informants to read a word list, or minimal pairs (e.g. *God-guard*, two words which are homophonous for some New York speakers), he focused their attention very directly on the variables under investigation. By contrast, the general unscripted part of the interview, which covered general topics relating to family, interests and life in New York, afforded less opportunity for audio-monitoring, and Labov employed various expedients where possible to reduce this still further. The most famous of these was the 'danger of death' question, in which informants were asked to recount an experience in which they had genuinely feared for their lives.[4] The gentle pressure thereby placed on informants to convey a real sense of

[4] In stark contrast with New York, Peter Trudgill (1974a: 51–52) in Norwich found almost no-one who had had a brush with death, ands soon abandoned this question, asking informants instead to recount a situation in which they had 'had a good laugh' recently. The rationale here was similar in that the informant, who stands in a poor light if the story fails to be humorous, is gently pressured to concentrate on presenting a good narrative rather than monitor his/her own speech.

danger, Labov surmised, focused their minds on telling their story and away from their own speech, taking them closer to what he saw as the 'natural' vernacular which was all but impossible to elicit in experimental conditions.

Labov's survey, and a subsequent study conducted on similar lines by Peter Trudgill in Norwich (Trudgill 1974a), confirmed the close relationship between language use and social status. In both cities, a pattern of class stratification was evident for most variables, as can be seen in the case of the Norwich (ng) variable in gerund and present forms such as *walking, shooting, fishing*. Like New York (r), (ng) is a binary variable for which in word-final position a standard pronunciation [iŋ] and a local non-standard [ən] or [n̩] are available in Norwich:

(ng)
(ng)-1: [ŋ]
(ng)-2: [n̩]

As can be seen in Fig. 6.1 below, use of the standard (ng)-1 variant increases in line with social status. Patterns of intraspeaker variation are similarly consistent: for all social classes, use of standard or prestige forms increases with formality of style, and it is this agreement among speakers of differing social profiles regarding the forms to target in careful speech which, for Labov, is the defining characteristic of the speech community.[5]

These patterns were repeatedly observed across a wide range of variables in these and subsequent studies, and occasional departures from perfect class stratification were seen as potential indicators of change in progress. For New York (r), for example, the 'hypercorrection' of lower-middle-class speakers (Classes 6–8), who used the prestige /r/ variant more than their social superiors (Class 9) in scripted styles (see Fig. 6.2

[5] Labov (1972: 120):

> The speech community is not defined by any marked agreement in the use of language elements, so much as by participation in a set of shared norms; these norms may be observed in overt types of evaluative behavior, and by the uniformity of abstract patterns of variation which are invariant in respect to particular levels of language.

below), was initially attributed to the supposed social insecurity of a group occupying a border position between working and middle class, and acutely sensitive to linguistic change in progress for this reason.

Another important finding was consistently greater use of standard or prestige forms by women, irrespective of speech style and within all social classes. This observation, first articulated by Peter Trudgill (1974b: 85), became known as the Sociolinguistic Gender Pattern (SGP):

> In all the cases so far examined, it has been shown that, allowing for other factors such as social class, ethnic group and age, women consistently use forms which more closely approach those of the standard variety or the prestige accent than those used by men.

As sociolinguistics has matured and established itself as a discipline, many of its early assumptions have been refined or questioned. The concept of 'natural speech', something of a holy grail in early sociolinguistic research, has notably been challenged by evidence that speakers regularly accommodate, that is modify their speech behaviour, in the direction of others with whom they interact and to whom they are well disposed. This phenomenon was first investigated by the social psychologist Howard Giles, who had argued for a psychological motivation to accent convergence in a 1973 paper (quoted in Trudgill 1986: 2), stating that: 'if the

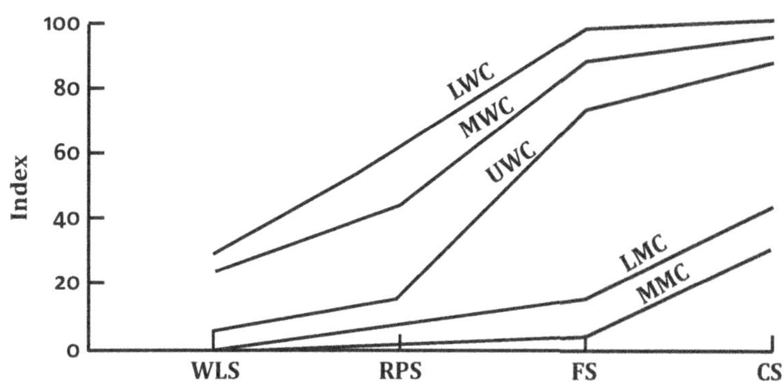

Fig. 6.1 Norwich (ng) by class and style (Trudgill 1974a: 92, Fig. 14)

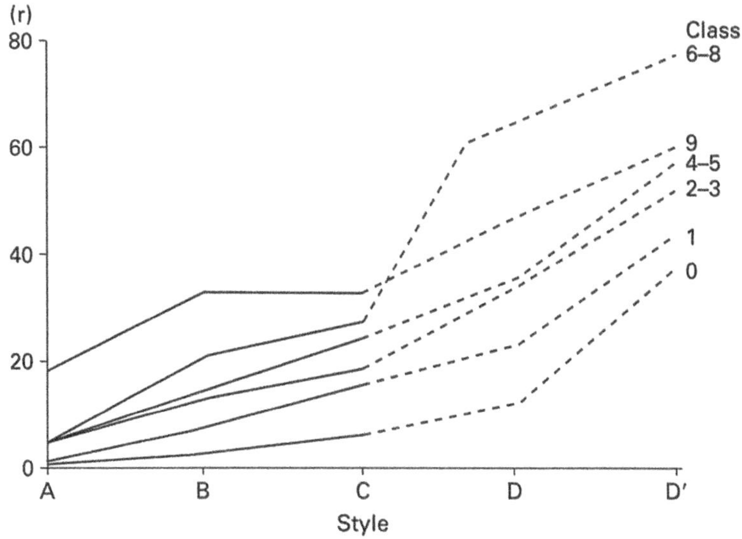

Fig. 6.2 Class stratification of non-prevocalic (r) in New York (Labov 2006: 152, Fig 7.11)

sender in a dyadic situation wishes to gain the receiver's approval, then he may adapt his accent patterns towards that of this person, i.e. reduce pronunciation dissimilarities'. This observation complicates interpretation of early survey data. As there was little evidence, for example, to suggest that the social status of staff in Labov's department store study actually corresponded to that of the store, the clear stratification observed for the (r) variable suggested that they had in fact accommodated to a target clintèle in each case and 'borrowed' the status of their customers. Of perhaps greater concern was the danger of 'self-fulfilling prophecy' in urban surveys if informants accommodate to their interviewer. Trudgill freely admits to using his home accent when interviewing working-class informants in his Norwich study, and his more standard accent when interviewing informants he perceived to be middle-class, but argues plausibly that he accommodated to his informants, and not the other way round (1986: 7–10). However, given that he also dressed 'down' for working-class and 'up' for middle-class speakers, there has at least to be the possibility that his informants were accommodating, like the New

York department store sales staff, to their perception or stereotype of their interlocutor's social profile from the very outset, and producing the results the researcher expected as a direct consequence. In the case of variable liaison, as we shall see, the question of the target audience to which a speaker might be accommodating, and whether the aim is to converge with that audience or distance him/herself from it, is a complex one with important consequences. Sociolinguists' concern to elicit 'natural speech' in early urban surveys was motivated in part by a belief, borne out by the data obtained, that the greatest variability in language is to be found in the unmonitored vernacular of working-class speakers.

With respect to the style dimension, which is of particular interest here, what became known as the 'audio-monitoring hypothesis' has also been questioned by, among others, Coupland (1980), Cheshire (1982), Bell (1984, 2001), Le Page and Tabouret-Keller (1985) and Rickford and McNair-Knox (1994). Both Labov and Trudgill assumed a continuum of formality based on attention to speech[6] and placed scripted elements, such as passages or word lists which speakers were asked to read aloud, at the most formal end of that continuum. Within the rather atypical, and for most informants unfamiliar, context of a sociolinguistic interview, these assumptions certainly seem to have been borne out by the expected patterns of correlation between use of prestige variants and formality of style: simply put, the more opportunity informants had to monitor their own speech, the more high-status forms they produced. Bell (1984: 147) however has argued that, since all speech is continually designed with an audience in mind, the very notion of attention to speech as a determiner of speech style is, in his words, a 'non-starter'. Far from being a successful ruse to reduce audio-monitoring, he suggests, the 'danger of death' question should be seen as inviting informants to select the style appropriate for the telling of an exciting tale, which for most speakers in this case meant New York vernacular.[7] He proposes an alternative 'audience design' model in which, in descending order of importance, interlocutors

[6] Cf. Labov (1972: 208): 'Styles may be ordered along a single dimension, measured by the amount of attention paid to speech'.

[7] Similarly one might argue that Trudgill's request that his Norwich informants recall a situation in which they 'had had a good laugh' appeals to an established British tradition, in which a working-class accent is an important part of the persona of professional comedians.

(seen, ratified and addressed), auditors (seen and ratified but not addressed), overhearers (seen, but neither ratified nor addressed) and finally eavesdroppers (not seen, ratified or addressed) all influence the way in which a speaker presents himself/herself in speech. In similar vein, Le Page and Tabouret-Keller (1985) argue that speech is designed through identification with notional 'model groups' which are perceived by the speaker but may not necessarily exist in any objective sense: witness for example Trudgill's (1983) analysis of UK pop music performers' identification with a general 'American' model which bore little relation to the behaviour of real US English speakers, to whom they had had only limited exposure. Labov subsequently qualified the audio-monitoring hypothesis and attention to speech effects as 'heuristic devices to obtain a range of behaviors within the individual interview, not as a general theory of style shifting' (Labov 2006: 59; also 1972: 97).

Bell's paper also raises the question of how speakers style shift, and the relationship between interspeaker and intraspeaker variation. Bell argues that variation on the style dimension mirrors that observed on the social dimension. However, since few if any individuals can have regular and full access to the full range of variation within the speech community, the stylistic range of any speaker can only be an imperfect reflection of variation observable in society. It would therefore follow that what he calls 'hyper-style' variables, in which the range of variation observed on the style dimension exceeds that of the social dimension, should be a theoretical impossibility.

The development of social network based approaches to variation (see especially Milroy 1980; Milroy and Milroy 1985) shifted the emphasis away from membership of abstract groupings such as social class and focused instead on the relationships contracted by individuals within a community. Vernaculars in Belfast, for example, were found by Milroy (1980) to be focused (showing consistent use of local variants) where social networks were dense and multiplex (i.e. where individuals mostly knew one another well, and often in more than one context), and diffuse (i.e. a local norm was less consistently observed) where networks were loose and uniplex. This was because the network ties of close-knit communities acted as a vernacular enforcement mechanism, promoting accommodation to local group norms. This insight refined our understanding of variation and change in a number of important ways. 'Hypercorrection' of the kind witnessed in New York, for example, was now viewed not in terms of a putative lower-middle class social insecurity but instead as the product of looser network ties. The greater range of contacts outside the immediate community which is typical of middle-status groups favours the adoption of new variants, while the social or geographical isolation more commonly associated with lower status groups in particular inhibits it.

Differences in social network structure also offered an explanation for what became known as the 'gender paradox', expressed by Labov (2001: 293) thus: 'Women conform more closely than men to sociolinguistic norms that are overtly prescribed, but conform less than men when they are not.' While the sociolinguistic gender pattern as expressed by Trudgill above still appears to hold true—in spite of significant changes in the social and employment position of women in the last half-century—in cases of stable variation, women have been found to lead change both towards and away from established prestige norms. In Newcastle, for example, Milroy et al. (1994) found younger middle-class women to be leading changes away from highly localised non-standard forms. The variants they favoured, however, were not standard or prestige forms as the sociolinguistic gender pattern might lead us to expect, but rather non-standard forms of wider regional currency. The recessive localised forms were associated notably with traditional working-class males, whose lives typically centred on a single workplace and set of locally-based workmates, and whose social networks were accordingly dense and multiplex. By contrast women, and particularly here more mobile middle-class women, had a wider range of contacts and looser social network ties, which required a broader linguistic repertoire and made them more receptive to levelled variants which were not necessarily standard ones. Indeed, when the traditional gender roles are reversed, as for example in Clonard (see Milroy 1980: 144), an area of high female and low male employment in the 1970s, the familiar sociolinguistic gender pattern of men using vernacular forms more consistently than women can be quite dramatically inverted, as the norm-enforcement mechanism associated with strong network ties is now found to affect women to a greater degree than men.

Our brief overview of key findings in variationist sociolinguistic research has provided a set of working assumptions for the investigation of variable liaison. Firstly, it seems reasonable to expect a clear pattern of class stratification in all styles, with use of prestige forms increasing consistently in line with social status. Secondly, we can expect to find considerably greater overall variability at the bottom end of the socio-economic scale than at the top. Thirdly, if variation is stable, we would expect to see a clear pattern of higher scores among women for prestige or standard forms; if on the other hand there is evidence of change in progress, then women would be expected to lead, showing greater use of the innovating variant than men. Finally, we would expect to see a clear relationship between variation on the social and stylistic dimensions, such that the latter mirrors the former and no speaker's stylistic repertoire ever exceeds the range of interspeaker variation observed within a single style. As we shall see below, variable liaison confounds all of these expectations. Only in the case of those whom Encrevé (1988: 55) has labelled *professionels de la parole publique*, to whom we turn in Chap. 8, do we find patterns consistent with findings elsewhere that change is in progress, with women in the vanguard. Yet, as we shall argue below, the atypicality of this group, and of the style its members employ for professional purposes, makes this in fact a surprising rather than expected finding. The enigmatic behaviour of variable liaison, which we attempt to unravel in Part IV, can only be understood in terms of ideology and sources of the prescriptive norm explored in Parts I and II, and confirms its status as, in Encrevé's (1988: 45) words, 'un phénomène sociolinguistique inversé'.

6.3 French Language Corpora

The availability since the 1970s of French spoken-language corpora has enabled variation research to move from the realm of expert intuition (e.g. Delattre 1966a, b and c) or self-report (e.g. Martinet 1945) to a firmer basis of empirical data. Some of these corpora have focused on specific groups or locations, while others, most notably that of the Phonologie du Français Contemporain (PFC) or the 'Four Cities' project (see Chap. 7

below), have been designed wholly or partly with the study of liaison in mind. In stark contrast to the classic urban surveys described in Sect. 6.2, a number of liaison studies have specifically targeted higher-status rather than working-class speakers, or favoured those for whom speaking in public is an occupational requirement, the so-called *professionnels de la parole publique*.

Malécot's corpus, on which he reports in a series of articles published in the 1970s, consists of fifty half-hour conversations recorded in 1967–1968 with members of what the author describes variously as 'the Paris "establishment"' (1972: 346, 1975a: 51), or 'the educated middle-class of Paris' (1975b: 161). Findings reported in Malécot (1975b) suggest overall liaison rates ranging between 57.6% and 70.8% (see Table III, pp. 168–69), according to the extralinguistic parameters involved. These figures combine variable and non-variable contexts, but with respect to former, Malécot observes:

> Perhaps the most important of our false notions concerns the so-called 'optional' liaisons. That designation has led many to assume that liaison is made in such cases much more than it actually is, that is, more or less half the time. Our statistics show that, on the contrary, the figure is very low indeed, especially for certain grammatical categories.

While the absence of hard statistical analysis on use of variable liaison (or even a clear working definition of the concept) is disappointing, its relative absence from the spontaneous speech of precisely the group one would expect best to control the prestige norm, albeit in what appears to have been a relaxed speech style, is noteworthy. Green and Hintze (1990, 2001) also target upper middle-class *oïl* French speakers, controlling for age and gender. Informants fall into two age-groups 35–40 and 55–65, and again show high overall liaison rates (over 80% for all five informants: p. 69) when scores for variable and non-variable contexts are conflated.

Ashby (1981b) introduces a socioeconomic class dimension to his investigation of liaison use in Tours, a city widely perceived in France to be a bastion of 'correct' French, and accordingly associated with high levels of linguistic security (p. 47). Ashby's informants are assigned to two groups established informally on the basis of education and occupational status, and balanced also for age and gender, but a sample of only sixteen speakers allows for only two speakers per cell, with the attendant danger that data may be skewed by an anomalous individual and/or be generally unrepresentative of particular subgroups. At 34%, Ashby's overall liaison rate is rather lower than for Malécot's data, but this figure includes only variable contexts, which he is careful to separate from non-variable environments. The latter are defined broadly according to Delattre's classification and include fixed locutions (e.g. *de temps en temps*) and subject clitic + verb sequences, but also more controversially the monosyllabic prepositions *dans* and *en*.

De Jong (1988, 1994) reports an overall liaison rate of of 49.2% for both variable and non-variable contexts in data described as 'careful speech', and taken from a gender-balanced sample of 45 speakers and around 16,000 tokens from the Orléans corpus, recorded in 1969 (see Blanc and Biggs 1971). De Jong controls for age (three groups) and social class (five groups established on the basis of education and other socio-economic factors).

Liaison was one of a number of variables explored by Armstrong (2001) in data from Dieuze (Moselle), recorded in 1990 among younger (11–12 years) and adolescent speakers (16–19 years) in the town's *lycée* and *collège.* Armstrong does not control for social class but identifies two styles, 'interview' and 'conversation', based respectively on data from one-to-one interviews with the researcher and what he calls 'peer conferences' involving two or more informants of the same age and gender, recorded in conversation in the researcher's absence. What little variable liaison Armstrong found in either style occurred mostly after monosyllabic adverbs (e.g. *très*) or prepositions (*dans, chez*).

6.3.1 The *Phonologie du Français Contemporain* (PFC) Project

While all studies above provide a snapshot of variation in one place or among a particular social group, the more recent *Phonologie du Français Contemporain* (PFC) project, launched by Jacques Durand, Bernard Laks and Chantal Lyche in 1999, aims at global coverage of the francophone world, using a common research protocol. The PFC project was born of general dissatisfaction with available databases and survey material on contemporary French phonology, which had had different goals and lacked methodological consistency, making comparisons between them difficult and complicating rather than illuminating our understanding of change in progress.[8] The methodology and aims are set out in the first of a series of PFC bulletins uploaded to the project website (Durand et al. 2009), providing regular updates. Compiling a robust and comprehensive database of contemporary francophone speech would counter the *de facto* normativity of descriptive theories built on expert intuition, repeated unquestioningly over and again by successive sources:

> A y regarder de près, la quasi-totalité des études phonologiques publiées depuis les années soixante repose soit sur des intuitions des auteurs, soit sur les données héritées de la tradition normative et orthoépique dont Fouché (1959) constitue l'exposé le plus systématique. Bien loin donc de la perspective cumulative pour laquelle nous avons plaidé ailleurs Durand (1996), la phonologie du français souffre ainsi de psittacisme: les mêmes données normatives, les mêmes pseudo observations sont reprises ad nauseam, finissant par constituer par leur répétition même ce Français de Référence dont Morin a si justement souligné les limites (Morin 2000). (Durand et al. 2009: 22)

In respect of intraspeaker variation, the PFC approach mirrors that of Labov by employing a 'structured interview' technique, designed to manipulate informants' capacity to audio-monitor their own speech, and includes reading exercises, seen by the researchers as ranged at the formal end of a style continuum. Over the course of an hour, all informants are asked to read the same reading passage and word list, and at least twenty minutes are devoted to what the researchers term 'guided interview', which loosely follows a common format and topics for all informants. This is supplemented later by a second session, in which a further twenty minutes of 'free conversation' (*discours libre*) are recorded,

[8] 'L'hétérogénéité sociolinguistique des données disponibles rend périlleuse toute vision diachronique fiable' (Durand et al. 2009: 18).

involving groups of 2–3 informants, freeing them from the question-answer format of the interview and allowing them greater control of the subject-matter. Once the data have been obtained, the reading tasks and about five minutes from each of the interview styles are transcribed in conventional orthography alongside the speech signal as Tier 0 for analysis within the PRAAT programme (see Boersma and Weenink 2016). Liaison, one of the principal foci of the project, is coded in PRAAT on a separate tier using two symbols. The first refers only to the number of syllables in the linking word W_1: one for monosyllables, two for polysyllabic words. The second figure refers to the syntagm as a whole and defines the type of liaison involved:

0 no liaison
1 liaison enchaînée
2 liaison non-enchaînée
3 unclear
4 epenthetic liaison

After the codings have been entered, the liaison consonant itself (if present) is noted, or *h* for a pause or hesitation, as in the following examples (see Durand et al. 2009):

est11t en *liaison enchaînée* with [t], after monosyllabic W_1
ont12t e *liaison non-enchaînée* with [t] after monosyllabic W_1
visites20h officielles no liaison after polysyllabic W_1; pause or hesitation after W_1.

Use of standard orthography on Tier 0 avoids the potential pitfalls of idiosyncratic notation or transcription on the part of researchers and allows for easy searchability. The approach to coding has been widely adopted outside the PFC project, including in the 'Four Cities' study (see Chap. 7), for which the Dolmen tool (Eychenne and Paternostro 2016) was additionally used to search the database.

Each interview in a given city or town forms part of an *enquête* consisting ideally of 10–14 informants, providing a snapshot rather than a representative cross-section of the community under investigation. While representativity on the basis of social or demographic criteria is not an aim of the PFC (Durand et al. 2009: 8), the age and gender of each informant is recorded, together where possible with data on education level and profession, in order to facilitate comparisons between groups and apparent time observation of change in progress. Use of a reading exercise provides a style contrast for each speaker and ensures comparability of data, but inevitably skews the sample towards literate speakers, and poses a particular challenge for the PFC in places where French is not used as a medium for writing. In Louisiana, for example, where French is obsolescent and most informants, particularly younger speakers, are English-dominant, the reading passage had to be replaced by a translation task, and some items on the word list were changed in favour of others from the Louisiana lexicon.

6.4 Liaison and Class

As we saw in Sect. 6.2, evidence from a wide range of sociolinguistic surveys supports Bell's contention that variation observed on the social dimension finds its imperfect mirror image on the style dimension in the behaviour of individual speakers. We will consider the question of style in relation to liaison more closely in the next chapter, but it seems reasonable at this point to suggest that a phenomenon associated for more than a century in prescriptive manuals with elevated speech styles is likely to be the preserve of higher-status speakers. Armstrong's (2001: 177) claim that 'it [variable liaison] is mostly used by middle-class speakers in formal speech styles' would seem therefore to do little more than state the obvious. But as Durand et al. (2011: 110–11) observe, this association is generally assumed rather than demonstrated empirically, and a more complex and nuanced picture emerges from the few reliable studies which have attempted to correlate social status and use of liaison.

Perhaps the most compelling evidence in support of Armstrong's claim comes from Laks' 1975 recordings of lower working-class adolescent informants in Villejuif (see Laks 1983), re-examined by Encrevé (1988: 48–49). Encrevé found that while 525 of 1084 possible liaisons were realised (48.5%) overall, only 17 of a possible 576 variable liaisons were realised (2.9%), 13 of which were produced by two speakers and 12 of which involved *dans.* But if liaison use proved strikingly low among working-class informants, its incidence among upper middle-class Parisians recorded by Malécot in what appears to have been informal style (1975: 176) at about the same time was scarcely greater, in spite of the very significant social distance between his own speakers and those of Laks.

Malécot's conflation of findings for variable and non-variable liaisons makes them difficult to interpret, but he groups his informants under four different categories of occupation (students, teachers, professionals, administrators), and only for the last of these observes what he considers a significantly higher than average use of liaison (i.e. 10% or more above the overall average figure of 64%). He finds, moreover, no significant effects from 'situational' variables such as topic and attitude. That there is relatively little difference between findings from opposite ends of the social spectrum comes as something of a surprise, and stands in stark contrast to the variables studied in New York and Norwich, which for all variables in all styles showed high-status speakers consistently and strongly outscoring low-status speakers for use of prestige variants. In this connection it is worth noting that Ashby's (1976) examination of Malécot's data found high rates of *ne* retention, suggesting for the variably deleted negative particle a pattern of behaviour rather more in line with expectations.

Social class, determined on a rather impressionistic basis by Laks and Malécot, is notoriously difficult to define and operationalise (for discussion see Gadet 2007: 92–93), and studies which have attempted to introduce a class comparison have either applied a social class index (see e.g. De Jong 1988, 1994), or used a proxy such as education for the same purpose (e.g. Mullineaux and Blanc 1982; Meinschaeffer et al. 2015). Neither approach yields evidence of systematic correlation between linguistic and social factors.

Ashby's Tours study compares speakers from two 'informally defined' (1981b) socioeconomic classes, established on the basis of education and employment status, and finds, as expected, a lower incidence of variable liaison among working-class speakers than among their middle-class counterparts. Within the working-class population, however, younger female informants were found significantly to outscore both their female middle-class peers and working-class males of all ages. As noted above, Ashby's sample is small and with three extralinguistic parameters (age, sex and class) under investigation and only two informants per cell, there is the potential for data to be skewed significantly by unrepresentative speakers. Nonetheless this result is something of a surprise for which no satisfactory explanation is offered.

Ashby's findings contrast with those of De Jong (1994), who examines a rather larger, socially stratified sample of 45 Orléans informants recorded in careful style in 1969. Here very sharp differences were observed between the highest group (upper middle-class), with an overall liaison frequency of 61.6%, and the lowest-ranked group, labelled lower working-class, with a corresponding figure of 29.6% (findings reported by Armstrong 2001: 192). Once again, however, aggregate data prove a little misleading: while liaison after *est* correlates closely with socio-economic class, liaison after *suis* is found not to (see Eychenne et al. 2014: 37), and again lower socioeconomic groups are found in some cases to show unexpectedly high uses of variable liaison. De Jong (1994) also explored variable liaison in a sample of data from the socially stratified Sankoff-Cedergren corpus, recorded in 1971 in Montréal (see Sankoff et al. 1976), comparing these data with those obtained in the later Thibault and Vincent corpus of the same speakers (see Thibault and Vincent 1990). What is of particular interest here is the behaviour of different social groups with respect to local Canadian and supranational norms (see Chap. 5 above).

With respect to liaison after the clitic pronoun *ils*, De Jong identified three groups of speakers. The largest group (A) did not liaise in this context, while a smaller group (B) did so categorically, leaving a third group (C) whose behaviour in this context was found to be variable. Use of /z/ at all as the link consonant was found to be 'the exclusive privilege of the members of the highest social class' (p. 132), recalling the tendency identified by Kroch for high-status individuals to borrow high-prestige forms from outside their speech community. Lower-status Montrealers by contrast appeared to have internalised /i/ rather than /iz/ for *ils*, and predominated in Group A, for whom liaison was the exception rather than the rule. Three groups were similarly identified with respect to variation after *suis*, where liaison in Montreal French favours /t/ rather than /z/.

Here liaison was found to *decrease* significantly with increasing socio-economic status because higher-status individuals avoided the local liaison variant, opting for a 'play-safe' strategy of zero liaison in the face of a complex norm.

A number of researchers have started from the reasonable assumption that educational attainment is generally an indicator of social advantage, and would therefore tend to favour greater use of variable liaison. Free compulsory education established following the Jules Ferry reforms of the 1880s (see Sect. 4.4) promoted literacy and instilled what has been called 'la peur de l'hiatus', favouring restoration of some variable liaison forms which had fallen out of use and were no longer prescribed in normative works. But while Durand et al. (2011: 111) are certainly right in their observation that: 'Il semble bien… que l'école publique ait joué ici un rôle fondamental', evidence of a systematic relationship between liaison and education level proves as elusive as a linear relationship between liaison and social class does for Ashby and De Jong.

Among Mallet's (2008) speakers, for example, the highest overall liaison rate (54%) is observed among speakers who have finished middle school without obtaining a high-school diploma, while the lowest rate (38%) is reported among those with higher (Bac+2) qualifications. Meinschaeffer et al.'s (2015) findings similarly reverse expectations. In the spoken French sample from the C-Oral-Rom corpus, speakers with less formal education were again found to use more variable liaison consonants than those with university or equivalent qualifications (30% and 23% respectively; p. 388), but the difference was found to be statistically significant only for females (p. 390).[9] Their conclusion that their findings are 'compatible with the claim that French liaison is a linguistic feature with overt prestige for most speakers—with the exception of males with little education' (p. 391) offers little by way of explanation for what would seem to be a surprising result. Durand et al. (2011: 128) similarly report no significant correlation between education level and use of variable liaison in the PFC data. Dividing speakers into three groups, based on time

[9] Use of statistical methods presupposes comparability of data, which for the reasons outlined at the end of the previous chapter cannot be assumed in the case of liaison, and is therefore problematic here.

spent in formal education (fewer than 14 years; 14–20 years; 20+ years), they find only a modest difference—less than 3%—separating the highest scoring middle group (48.91%) and the least educated group, which had the lowest figure (46.46%). It must be stressed that these are aggregate figures which combine invariable and variable environments, and that Durand et al. provide no data for scripted styles: as they themselves point out these figures might well have been different had the speakers been placed in 'situations de forte tension linguistique' (p. 128), for example in public speaking. There is, moreover, the possibility that a fine-grained analysis might have yielded different results for individual liaison environments. But nonetheless the failure of an important and reliable extralinguistic parameter to manifest any consistent pattern of correlation is striking, Might that other key extralinguistic factor from sociolinguistic surveys, gender, prove a more reliable determinant of liaison usage?

6.5 Liaison and Gender

As we noted in Sect. 6.2, the relationship between gender and language variation has proved to be one of the most robust and consistent findings of the last fifty years, in spite of major changes in the social position of women during that period. The close association between variable liaison and elevated style would suggest that, if variation is stable, we should expect to find a clear and consistent pattern, as per the SGP, of women using more of the prestigious liaison forms than men in all styles. If, however, if liaison is in decline as some have suggested, then conversely we would expect to see women leading a change in the direction of non-liaison in variable contexts. In fact, survey evidence supports neither of these conclusions and, as proved to be the case with social class, liaison again defies normal sociolinguistic expectations.

It should first be noted that a number of studies do reveal patterns of variation which appear to be consistent with the SGP. Malécot (1975b), De Jong (1994), Eychenne (2009), and Meinschaeffer et al. (2015) all report a higher incidence of liaison among women than among men, but the difference in most cases is small. Malécot dismisses the gender difference (66.9% for men; 62.0% for women) in his own data as insignificant; the gap for De Jong's (1993) Montreal data is again less than 4% (50.8% women; 46.9% men), the figures in both cases conflating variable and non-variable environments. Green and Hintze's study of 'bourgeois oïl speakers', however, indicated a much stronger lead for women over men for overall liaison use (81.25% for women, 71.75% for men).

Ashby (1981b), by contrast, reports a higher overall variable liaison score for men in his sixteen-speaker Tours sample, but again the difference is slight (32% for women, 34% for men). However, as can be seen from Table 6.1 below, the female score is inflated notably by the apparently anomalous figure for working-class women, to which we referred above: at 34% the liaison frequency for this group is twice that of working-class men and higher than that of working-class informants of both sexes in the older group. In all other cases, where age and class are held constant, the gender gap favours males, most strongly younger for middle-class informants who lead their female peers by 19%.

An apparently anomalous figure for younger women would normally, of course, be consistent with a pattern frequently observed when change is in progress. But such an interpretation is difficult to square with Ashby's findings more generally. As can be seen above, the younger working-class female score is exceptionally high but the apparent-time evidence of Ashby's data strongly points towards less use of liaison among younger speakers, not more. As noted in Sect. 6.3, data based on cells containing only two informants must be treated with caution and can be skewed by unrepresentative speakers. Ashby however is certainly not alone in finding no systematic correlation between liaison and gender. Ranson's (2008) study finds no significant difference in the behaviour of the genders, as does Hornsby (2011) with respect to *pataquès*, that is use of prescriptively incorrect liaison consonants, among *lycée* students in three francophone cities (see Chap. 7). Ranson's position finds further support from the PFC data, from which Durand et al. (2011: 128), conclude: 'Toutes nos interrogations globales sur les liaisons, à ce jour, ne laissent apparaître aucune différence significative entre les taux de liaison réalisés par les hommes et les femmes.'

The striking observation in this and the previous section is the absence of any consistent pattern of correlation between liaison and the most

Table 6.1 Variable Liaison in Tours (Ashby 1981b; after Armstrong 2001: 190, Table 2)

	Age 14–21		Age 51–64	
	(N)	%	(N)	%
WC female	293	34	293	19
WC male	203	17	386	25
MC female	527	24	622	45
MC male	408	43	450	48

salient and reliable social parameters from five decades of sociolinguistic research. The analysis of his own Dieuze data leads Armstrong (2001: 193) to a very similar conclusion: 'What is most immediately striking about these results is the lack of systematic variation along the usual sociolinguistic dimensions'. Even allowing for the problems of aggregated data and conflation of variable and non-variable environments, this finding is surprising and demands explanation. Perhaps even more surprising is that few commentators have felt the need to offer one. As we shall see in Chap. 8, only in the case of a select group—the so-called *professionnels de la parole publique*—will we see compelling evidence of a gender-related pattern of variation which, we will argue, is actually surprising and unexpected. We turn next, however, to a final extralinguistic variable, age, for which something resembling a consistent pattern of correlation does begin to emerge.

6.6 Variation and Change in Apparent Time

A major driving force behind the emergence of variationist sociolinguistics as a discipline in the 1960s was the need to develop a theory of language change, which mainstream linguistics had largely ignored (see for example Labov et al. 1968). This aim underscores the importance of speaker age as an extralinguistic variable in surveys. The essential insight that differences in the behaviour of young and old speakers with respect to specific linguistic variables might be indicative of change in progress was implicit in the approach of traditional dialectologists such as Gilliéron, who targeted NORMs (non-mobile, older rural males), and was central to Gauchat's (1905) early variation study in the Swiss village of Charmey. Studies in 'apparent time', which explore age-group comparisons from a single survey, have been used either in lieu of or as a complement to studies in real time, in which a researcher returns to a community or group he/she has investigated earlier (see e.g. Trudgill 1988).

Investigating change with respect to liaison presents two problems. The first, alluded to above, is that only in the case of a very particular group, the so-called *professionnels de la parole publique*, do we have sufficient baseline data from earlier periods against which to make comparisons with contemporary usage. This leaves researchers reliant on apparent time data from a single point in time, which are reliable indicators of change in progress only in so far as speakers' linguistic behaviour can be taken to be more or less fixed, and not subject modification at different stages in their lifetime. As Blanche-Benveniste and Jeanjean (1987) have pointed out with respect to variable deletion of the negative particle *ne*, this is far from a safe assumption (for discussion see Ashby 1981a). In this particular case apparent time data which appeared to signal the imminent demise of *ne* were in fact found to be more compatible with an age-grading effect, in which young speakers' use of the negative particle increased with age as they became embedded in workplace hierarchies, where (particularly for those in white-collar occupations) both formal discourse and the written word acquired greater prominence.

In contrast to the rather inconclusive findings observed for both class and gender, a fairly clear pattern emerges for the parameter of age. Here the broad consensus among researchers is that younger speakers realise fewer variable liaisons than older speakers (see e.g. Ashby 1981b; De Jong 1994; Eychenne 2009; Léon 1992, 1993; Lyche and Østby 2009; Mallet 2008, Pustka 2009 and Ranson 2008).

Agreement even here, however, is not absolute, and two studies in particular, published forty years apart, reveal higher overall liaison use among younger rather than older or middle-aged speakers. Among the age-groups determined by Malécot (1975b) for his upper middle-class Parisian sample, the highest overall liaison frequency was observed among the youngest informants (20–29 years). Meinschaeffer et al. (2015: 389) similarly find that 'Younger speakers realize the liaison consonant significantly more often than older speakers'. These findings are, however, based on small (and in Malécot's case, socially marked) speaker samples. More recent PFC data from a larger population of 293 informants, reported by Durand et al. (2011), confirm the general pattern observed of declining liaison use with age. This is evident in both in scripted and in unscripted styles (Table 6.2).

The PFC data appear to show a consistent pattern of age stratification with a difference of 9.31% separating the oldest and the youngest informants. However, the oldest (over 60s) group appears to be an outlier in both scripted and unscripted contexts, the gap between this group and the rest (4.57%) accounting for roughly half this difference. Differences between the three younger groups in the text element of the PFC interview (where data are more strictly comparable) amount to just 1.37% and only 0.28% separates the under 20s and 20–40 groups. The low score for the under-20s group is based on a relatively small sample (21 speakers), but is consistent with Armstrong's (2001) findings for his own young and adolescent speakers in Dieuze, who were found to use variable liaison only sporadically except after monosyllabic adverbs and prepositions, and after *est* only with a full noun phrase subject. Armstrong concludes (2001: 193) that his informants may not yet have 'achieved the communicative competence necessary to enable them to style-shift using liaison', but this interpretation seems hard to reconcile with the PFC data for scripted styles, in which younger speakers liaise almost as frequently as speakers in the two age groups immediately above them. It also raises the question of whether his younger speakers in fact *need* to acquire the communicative competence required to style shift using liaison, to which we will return in Chap. 9, after consideration of a particular group who

Table 6.2 Liaison by age (after Durand et al. 2011: 127, Table 5)

	Age < 20 (21 speakers)	Age 20–40 (108 speakers)	Age 40–60 (92 speakers)	Age > 60 (72 speakers)
% liaisons realized	42.26	45.83	47.00	51.57
% liaisons Conversation	38.74	42.25	43.88	47.95
% liaisons Text	56.56	56.84	57.93	64.33

certainly do need to style-shift, namely the *professionnels de la parole publique*, in Chap. 8.

The findings also leave open the question of whether the patterns observed should be interpreted in terms of change in progress (i.e. a general ongoing decline in the use of liaison), or of age-grading. On the one hand, the differences between younger and older speakers in the PFC data are clear and consistent, with the group born before 1951, which for the most part reached adulthood before 1968, being the outliers by some margin. Léon (1992) concludes that liaison is an indicator of conservative speech, citing an experiment (Léon and Tennant 1990) on speaker perceptions, which suggested that speakers who used more liaison were perceived to be older and/or better educated. Against this, one might counter that, for the PFC data at least, differences between age-groups for speakers of working age (20–60) are minimal. These PFC data represent, of course, observations in apparent rather than real time, but in Chap. 8, we consider some real-time findings which suggest that, for one group at least, there is in fact clear evidence of change in progress. There are, moreover, good grounds for speculating, as we shall see in Chap. 9, that this may be a lasting rather than merely a passing trend.

6.7 Conclusions

From the above review of social factors, two surprising observations emerge. Firstly, as we saw, there was no consistent correlation between liaison use and either of the two most widely employed and reliable extralinguistic parameters, namely social class and gender. The lack of any systematic pattern for liaison and social class, or proxies such as education or profession, is particularly puzzling given the close association between liaison and elevated speech styles, and the evidence from the PFC and elsewhere of higher incidence of liaison in scripted styles, which within the Labovian paradigm are seen to occupy the most formal end of a style continuum. If, as Bell (1984) has suggested, variation on the style dimension mirrors that observed on the social plane, then the reverse relationship should in theory also apply and we should expect a marker of formal style to be associated with the usage of higher status speakers in all styles.

In unscripted style at least, we find no such consistent correlation, and in some cases there are unexpected and contradictory results. Where variation is stable within a speech community, we would expect to see evidence of the sociolinguistic gender pattern (SGP), in which women outscore men for use of prestige variants, but again we do not find this with any consistency in the data. Nor do we find evidence of women leading change, as we would expect in cases of unstable variation. While there was evidence in apparent time at least of a decline in variable liaison with age, there was little to suggest that women were leading this change and indeed in one notable case we saw evidence of younger women apparently leading change in the 'wrong' direction.

The second surprising observation is that few if any commentators meaningfully address the mounting evidence that liaison does not behave in the way we would expect of a conventional sociolinguistic variable. Encrevé's choice of the term '*phénomène* sociolinguistique inversé' (my emphasis) is perhaps telling in this regard (see Sect. 9.2 below), and likewise Armstrong (2001: 207) is aware of the apparent incompatibility between liaison and a general Labovian framework:

> The linguistically and socially highly constrained nature of variable liaison means that it does not comfortably fit into an analytic framework that we have sought to develop here: that which seeks to explore the sociolinguistic function, for an entire speech community, of variation on the different levels of linguistic analysis considered in relative isolation from each other.

Armstrong does not however speculate on why this might be the case, and elsewhere a succession of less than convincing *ad hoc* explanations for anomalous or unexpected patterns seems indicative of researchers' perplexity as to why liaison fails to follow the model of, say, a New York (r) or Norwich (ng) in survey data. Thus Ashby, faced with what appears to be an abnormally high use of liaison among his younger working-class female informants, questions his own class categorisation and suggests that the two informants involved might in fact have belonged to a higher social class (1981b: 52–53) than had initially appeared to be the case. This explanation fails notably to explain why younger women originally assigned to a higher social class in fact had significantly lower rates of liaison than these speakers (see Table 6.1). In similar vein, unexpectedly high incidence of liaison among Malécot's 20–29 year old informants is attributed speculatively to the notion that this group—and presumably this group alone—is possessed of a conservatism which stems from their desire to be acceptable to the 'establishment' (1975b: 169). This might seem a surprising suggestion in the immediate aftermath of *les événements* of 1968, often invoked as a pivotal moment in French history, which saw young people in the vanguard of change towards a more informal and less socially conservative society. High rates of variable liaison among less rather than more educated speakers are attributed by Meinschaeffer et al. (2015: 391, quoting Laks 2009: 243, note 9) to their presumed social insecurity: 'un fort taux de liaison facultative [...] est un signe [...] d'insécurité sociale propre à une bourgeoisie [...] dominée par la norme écrite et emportée par son insécurité scolaire', echoing Labov's initial explanation for hypercorrection in New York City (see Sect. 6.2); elsewhere higher than expected rates of liaison are explained by the same authors, with little supporting evidence, in terms of 'groups assumed to be striving for higher status' (ibid.).

Analysis thus far has been severely hampered by a lack of compatibility between research methodologies, population samples, and taxonomies of variable and invariable liaison contexts, together with the problems posed by aggregate results, which have been seen to be potentially misleading on several levels. The 'Four Cities' corpus, findings from which we consider in the next chapter, was conceived in response to these concerns, and attempts as far as possible to ensure comparability of both of data collection and of population samples in the four francophone cities in which research was undertaken.

References

Armstrong, N. (2001). *Social and Stylistic Variation in Spoken French: A Comparative Approach*. Amsterdam, Netherlands: John Benjamins.

Ashby, W. J. (1976). The Loss of the Negative Morpheme *Ne* in Parisian French. *Lingua, 39*, 119–137.

Ashby, W. J. (1981a). The Loss of the Negative Particle *Ne* in French: A Syntactic Change in Progress. *Language, 57*, 674–687.

Ashby, W. J. (1981b). French Liaison as a Sociolinguistic Phenomenon. In W. W. Cressey & D. J. Napoli (Eds.), *Linguistic Symposium on Romance Languages 9* (pp. 46–57). Washington, DC: Georgetown University Press.

Bell, A. (1984). Language Style as Audience Design. *Language in Society, 13*(2), 145–204.

Bell, A. (2001). Back in Style: Reworking Audience Design. In P. Eckert & J. R. Rickford (Eds.), *Style and Sociolinguistic Variation* (pp. 139–169). New York: Cambridge University Press.

Blanc, M., & Biggs, P. (1971). L'enquête socio-linguistique sur le français parlé à Orléans. *Le Français dans le monde, 85*, 16–25.

Blanche-Benveniste, C., & Jeanjean, C. (1987). *Le français parlé: transcription et édition*. Paris: Didier.

Boersma, P., & Weenink, D. (2016). Praat: Doing Phonetics by Computer. Retrieved from http://www.fon.hum.uva.nl/praat/ [Computer Program. Version 6.0.10].

Cheshire, J. (1982). *Variation in an English Dialect: A Sociolinguistic Study*. Cambridge: Cambridge University Press.

Coupland, N. (1980). Style Shifting in a Cardiff Work Setting. *Language in Society, 9*, 1–12.

De Jong, D. (1988). *Sociolinguistic Aspects of French Liaison*. Unpublished PhD thesis, University of Amsterdam.

De Jong, D. (1993). Sociolinguistic Aspects of Montreal French Liaison. In W. Ashby, W. Mithun, G. Perisonotto, & E. Raposo (Eds.), *Linguistic Perspectives on the Romance Languages* (pp. 127–138). Amsterdam: Benjamins.

De Jong, D. (1994). La sociophonologie de la liaison orléanaise. In C. Lyche (Ed.), *French Generative Phonology: Retrospective and Perspectives* (pp. 95–130). Salford: European Studies Research Institute.

Delattre, P. (1966a [1947]). La liaison en français, tendances et classifications. In P. Delattre (Ed.), *Studies in French and Comparative Phonetics: Selected Papers in French and English* (pp. 39–48). The Hague: Mouton. First Published in *French Review, 21*(2), 148–157.

Delattre, P. (1966b [1955]). Les facteurs de la liaison facultative en français. In P. Delattre (Ed.), *Studies in French and Comparative Phonetics: Selected Papers in French and English* (pp. 55–62). The Hague: Mouton. First Published in *French Review, 29*(1), 42–49.

Delattre, P. (1966c [1956]). La fréquence des liaisons facultatives en français. In P. Delattre (Ed.), *Studies in French and Comparative Phonetics: Selected Papers in French and English* (pp. 49–54). The Hague: Mouton. First Published in *French Review, 30*(1), 48–54.

Durand, J., Laks, B., & Lyche, C. (2009). Le projet PFC (Phonologie du Français Contemporain): une source de données primaires structurées. In J. Durand, B. Laks, & C. Lyche (Eds.), *Phonologie, variation et accents du français* (pp. 19–61). Paris: Hermès.

Durand, J., Laks, B., Calderone, B., & Tchobanov, A. (2011). Que savons-nous de la liaison aujourd'hui? *Langue française, 169*, 103–135.

Eychenne, J. (2009). Une variété de français conservatrice en Languedoc. In J. Durand, B. Laks, & C. Lyche (Eds.), *Phonologie, variation et accents du français* (pp. 265–290). Paris: Hermès.

Eychenne, J., & Paternostro, R. (2016). Analyzing Transcribed Speech with Dolmen. In S. Detey, J. Durand, B. Laks, & C. Lyche (Eds.), *Varieties of Spoken French: A Source Book* (pp. D35–D52). Oxford: Oxford University Press.

Eychenne, J., Lyche, C., Durand, J., & Coquillon, A. (2014). Quelles données pour la liaison en français: la question des corpus. In C. Soum-Favaro, A. Coquillon, & J.-P. Chevrot (Eds.), *La liaison: approches contemporaines*. Bern: Peter Lang.

Fouché, P. (1959). *Traité de prononciation française* (2nd ed.). Paris: Klincksieck.

Gadet, F. (2007). *La variation sociale en français* (2nd ed.). Paris: Ophrys.

Gauchat, L. (1905). L'unité phonétique dans le patois d'une commune. In *Aus Romanischen Sprachen und Literaturen: Festschrift H. Mort* (pp. 175–232). Halle: Max Niemeyer.

Green, J., & Hintze, M.-A. (1990). Variation and Change in French Linking Phenomena. In M.-A. Hintze & J. N. Green (Eds.), *Variation and Change in French: Essays Presented to Rebecca Posner on the Occasion of Her Sixtieth Birthday* (pp. 61–88). London: Routledge.

Green, J., & Hintze, A.-M. (2001). The Maintenance of Liaison in a Family Network. In M.-A. Hintze, T. Pooley, & A. Judge (Eds.), *French Accents: Phonological and Sociological Perspectives*. London: AFLS/CILT.

Hornsby, D. (2011). Getting It Wrong: Liaison, *Pataquès* and Repair in Contemporary French. In D. Lagorgette & T. Pooley (Eds.), *On Linguistic Change in French: Studies in Honour of R. Anthony Lodge* (pp. 69–83). Chambéry: Presses Universitaires de Savoie.

Labov, W. (1972). *Sociolinguistic Patterns*. Philadelphia: University of Pennsylvania Press.

Labov, W. (2001). *Principles of Linguistic Change, Vol. 2: Social Factors*. Malden, MA: Blackwell Publishers.

Labov, W. (2006). *The Social Stratification of English in New York City* (2nd ed.). Cambridge: Cambridge University Press.

Labov, W., Weinreich, U., & Herzog, M. (1968). Empirical Foundations for a Theory of Language Change. In W. P. Lehmann & Y. Malkeil (Eds.), *Directions for Historical Linguistics: A Symposium* (pp. 95–188). Austin: University of Texas Press.

Laks, B. (1983). Langage et pratiques sociales: étude sociolinguistique d'un groupe d'adolescents. *Actes de la recherche en sciences sociales, 46*, 73–97.

Laks, B. (2009). Les hommes politiques et la liaison (1908–1998). In L. Baronian & F. Martineau (Eds.), *Le français d'un continent à l'autre: mélanges offerts à Yves-Charles Morin* (pp. 237–269). Quebec: Presses Universitaires de Laval.

Lavandera, B. (1978). Where Does the Sociolinguistic Variable Stop? *Language in Society, 7*(2), 171–182.

Le Page, R., & Tabouret-Keller, A. (1985). *Acts of Identity: Creole-Based Approaches to Language and Ethnicity*. Cambridge: Cambridge University Press.

Léon, P. (1992). *Phonétisme et prononciations du français avec des travaux d'application et leurs corrigés*. Paris: Nathan.

Léon, P. (1993). *Précis de phonostylistique: Parole et expressivité*. Paris, France: Fernand Nathan.

Léon, P., & Tennant, J. (1990). "Bad French" and Nice Guys: A Morphophonetic Study. *French Review, 63*, 763–778.

Lyche, C., & Østby, K. (2009). Le français de la haute bourgeoisie parisienne: une variété conservatrice? In J. Durand, B. Laks, & C. Lyche (Eds.), *Phonologie, variation et accents du français* (pp. 203–230). Paris, France: Hermès.

Malécot, A. (1972). New Procedures for Descriptive Phonetics. In *Papers in Linguistics and Phonetics to the Memory of Pierre Delattre* (pp. 345–355). The Hague: Mouton.

Malécot, A. (1975a). The Glottal Stop in French. *Phonetica, 29*, 51–63.

Malécot, A. (1975b). French Liaison as a Function of Grammatical, Phonetic and Paralinguistic Variables. *Phonetica, 32*, 161–179.

Mallet, G.-M. (2008). *La liaison en français: descriptions et analyses dans le corpus PFC*. Doctoral thesis, Université Paris Ouest Nanterre la Défense, Paris, France. Retrieved from http://www.projet-pfc.net.

Martinet, A. (1945). *La Prononciation du français contemporain*. Paris: Droz.

Meinschaeffer, J., Bonifer, S., & Frisch, C. (2015). Variable and Invariable Liaison in a Corpus of Spoken French. *Journal of French Language Studies, 25*, 367–396.

Milroy, L. (1980). *Language and Social Networks*. Oxford: Blackwell.

Milroy, J., & Milroy, L. (1985). Linguistic Change: Social Networks and Speaker Innovation. *Journal of Linguistics, 21*, 339–384.

Milroy, J., Milroy, L., Hartley, S., & Walshaw, D. (1994). Glottal Stops and Tyneside Glottalization: Competing Patterns of Variation and Change in British English. *Language Variation and Change, 6*, 327–357.
Mullineaux, A., & Blanc, M. (1982). The Problems of Classifying the Population Sample in the Sociolinguistic Survey of Orléans in Terms of Socio-Economic, Social and Educational Categories. *Review of Applied Linguistics, 55*, 3–37.
Pustka, E. (2009). PFC et la phonologie du français en Vendée. In J. Durand, B. Laks, & C. Lyche (Eds.), *Phonologie, variation et accents du français* (pp. 307–335). Paris, France: Hermès.
Ranson, D. (2008). La liaison variable dans un corpus du français méridional: l'importance relative de la fonction grammaticale. In J. Durand, B. Habert, & B. Laks (Eds.), *Congrès mondial de linguistique française. Recueil des résumés et CD-ROM des actes*. Paris: Institut de Linguistique Française & EDP Sciences, 1657–1671.
Rickford, J. R., & McNair-Knox, F. (1994). Addressee- and Topic-Influenced Style Shift: A Quantitative Sociolinguistic Study. In D. Biber & E. Finegan (Eds.), *Sociolinguistic Perspectives on Register* (pp. 235–276). New York: Oxford University Press.
Sankoff, D., Sankoff, G., Laberge, S., & Topham, M. (1976). Méthodes d'échantillonage et utilisation de l'ordinateur dans l'étude de la variation grammaticale. *Cahiers de Linguistique de l'Université du Québec, 6*, 85–125. Montréal: Presses de l'Université du Québec.
Thibault, P., & Vincent, D. (1990). *Un corpus de français parlé. Montréal 84: historique, méthodes, et perspectives de recherche*. Quebec: Department of Languages and Linguistics, Laval University.
Trudgill, P. (1974a). *The Social Differentiation of English in Norwich*. Cambridge: Cambridge University Press.
Trudgill, P. (1974b). *Sociolinguistics: An Introduction to Language and Society*. Harmondsworth: Penguin.
Trudgill, P. (1983). Acts of Conflicting Identity: The Sociolinguistics of British Pop-Song Pronunciation. In P. Trudgill (Ed.), *On Dialect: Social and Geographical Perspectives* (pp. 141–160). Oxford: Blackwell.
Trudgill, P. (1986). *Dialects in Contact*. Oxford: Blackwell.
Trudgill, P. (1988). Norwich Revisited: Recent Changes in an English Urban Dialect. *English World-Wide, 9*, 33–49.

7

The Four Cities Project

7.1 Introduction

The Four Cities project, for which fieldwork was conducted by the author between 1998 and 2003, was conceived partly to counter anglophone dominance within variationist sociolinguistics by reporting on francophone Europe, where the Labovian or quantitative paradigm has generally made little headway.[1] As a complex variable subject to multiple constraints, for which the variants could be relatively easily identified, liaison seemed well suited to a quantitative approach. A diatopic dimension was introduced by selection of fieldwork sites in large socially stratified urban areas at some distance from Paris. The three cities selected within France, namely Lille (pop. 233,000; metropolitan area 1.15m); Strasbourg (pop. 281,000; metropolitan area 786,000); and Perpignan (pop. 122,000; metropolitan area 269,000) are geographically dispersed in the north, east and south of the country and incorporate both the *Oc/Oïl* division and different substrate varieties (Picard/Flemish, Alsacien and Catalan respectively), while the fourth site, Mons, with a rather smaller population (95,000), lies across a national border in Belgium, but shares a substrate language (Picard) with Lille.

To ensure comparability of the speaker sample, participants in each city were recruited from two schools: one a traditional *lycée* with a broadly

[1] On this point see Hornsby and Jones (2013).

D. Hornsby, *Norm and Ideology in Spoken French*,
https://doi.org/10.1007/978-3-030-49300-4_7

academic curriculum, geared to preparing its students for *Baccalauréat* and possible admission to a university or *grande école*, the other a more vocationally orientated *Lycée d'Enseignement Professionnel* (LEP).[2] Once permission had been obtained from the Headteacher or Director of the institution, interviews were recorded in each school with twelve students (six male, six female) aged 15–20. The ninety-six informants were interviewed individually on general topics relating to their studies, interests and opinions of life in their city and region, for around twenty minutes. Although every effort was made to put them at their ease, no attempt was made to mitigate the effects of the 'Observer's Paradox', and indeed both the research methodology and setting were designed to steer informants towards the formal end of their repertoire, in the expectation of eliciting the greatest number of variable liaison consonants. The interviews, conducted individually in the informant's school by an unfamiliar and formally dressed researcher introduced by a member of teaching staff, followed a loose question/answer format controlled by the interviewer which included, in an attempt to address the lack of empirical data from scripted styles in the literature, a short reading exercise. After about five minutes, informants were asked to read aloud twenty-one short stimulus sentences (see below), containing a total of fifty-four variable liaison sites:[3]

1. La France subit une vague de froid depuis quelques jours, tout comme d'ailleurs la plupart des pays européens.
2. Sachez encore que les sans-papiers qui occupent actuellement la cathédrale d'Orléans souffrent, eux aussi, du froid.
3. Je vais aller aussi voir des films anciens, qui ne sont pas amusants.
4. Les agents immobiliers arrivent en une demi-heure.
5. Jean a été le dernier à parler, mais le premier à parler de manière intelligente.

[2] The closest approximation to the *lycée/LEP* division in Belgium is that of *athénée/CEFA*. A school of each type was identified in Mons with the help of a local contact, and was found in each case to be broadly comparable in mission and status to its French counterparts.

[3] The Four Cities project predates the launch of the PFC by one year, but unlike the latter focuses exclusively on liaison; the reading exercise for the PFC consists of a text containing thirty-three potential liaison sites.

6. Les étudiants écoutaient encore le professeur, mais Anne regardait un petit écureuil dans la forêt.
7. Jean-Paul est modeste, mais il est beaucoup aimé.
8. Ce fut un long été.
9. Alors, pourquoi attend-on?
10. Nous sommes allés chez une copine.
11. Depuis une paire d'années, ils aimaient chanter en chœur.
12. Nous attendons un second enfant.
13. Je le trouve bien aimable et extrêmement intelligent.
14. Pour Paul, c'était un long apprentissage.
15. Aujourd'hui, il vient à Strasbourg; demain, il doit aller à Marseille.
16. Vous êtes trop aimable!
17. Cela n'a été qu'un léger incident, lors duquel la victime n'a pas été beaucoup agressée.
18. Ses anciens étudiants américains annoncèrent un grand exploit.
19. À Lille, il y a des appartements à louer à des loyers élevés, mais d'autres appartements à des loyers plus modestes sont disponibles ailleurs.
20. Ils n'ont pas trop apprécié un certain ami de Mme Lefebvre.
21. Qu'un sang impur abreuve nos sillons!

The sentences were drawn or adapted from textbooks, recent television news reports (in which liaisons had been realised), or other sources (e.g. the French national anthem for Variable 54 *sang impur*), and included three forms unambiguously associated with formal written French (two verbs in the past historic and a question by inversion), which were unlikely to occur in spontaneous speech. Care was taken to include as wide as possible a range of potential variable liaison environments, often at the expense of more commonly occurring ones (forms of *être* for example, on which data were fairly plentiful elsewhere, were excluded), but obviously it was impossible to include all types of potential liaison site in a manageable exercise. All six canonical liaison consonants, however, and all of Delattre's frequency rankings (A-F in Table 7.1 below) were represented.

At the start of the interview, informants were asked to state their age, and provide information about their parents' occupations. Recorded data were analysed using PRAAT (Boersma and Weenink 2016) and the data management software program Dolmen (Eychenne and Paternostro 2016), having been coded according to the conventions of the *Phonologie du Français Contemporain* project (see Sect. 6.3.1). The fifty-four potential liaison sites from the reading exercise (reading style: RS) were treated as individual numbered variables; in the unscripted part of the interview (interview style: IS), all liaison sites outside of Côté's *noyau dur* of invariable contexts and not identified as *interdite* by Delattre were treated as potentially variable, with the exception of set phrases such as *Jeux* [z] *Olympiques*, which were treated as invariable.

7.2 Intraspeaker Variation: Scripted and Unscripted Styles

A total of 5191[4] potential variable liaison sites were generated in Reading Style (RS) and a further 3366 occurred in unscripted interview style (IS), giving a total of 8557 liaison sites (see Table 7.2).[5]

At 32.6% the global RS score predictably exceeds that of IS (19.9%), but a breakdown of these data by Delattre's *obligatoire* (Sect. 7.2.1) and *facultative* groupings (Sect. 7.2.2) reveals some surprising results.

7.2.1 Delattre's *Liaison Obligatoire*

Given the long-established association between liaison use and scripted styles, the RS/IS style dimension here is of particular interest. As noted above, many liaison environments identified by Delattre as *obligatoire* in fact demonstrate variability. Data for three such categories are provided in Table 7.3 below.

While overall incidence of liaison again favours RS, the expected pattern is reversed for two of the three categories, which show greater use of

[4] This figure excludes variables for which no data are available (for example because of omissions or misreads) but includes repetitions (see Sect. 7.2.3 below).

[5] Much of the data for this section is taken from Hornsby (2019), where the style dimension is considered specifically in the context of the diglossia hypothesis (see Massot 2005).

Table 7.1 Frequency categories for variable liaison (after Delattre 1966c: 54)

Frequency category		Liaison type	Example variable
A	très fréquente	*Être*+ adjective Monosyllabic preposition or adverb + noun	26 *chez une copine*
B	assez fréquente	Verb + past participle or adjective After polysyllabic adverb or preposition	27 *depuis une paire*
C	mi-fréquente	Verb + complement After negative adverb	40 *pas été*
D	peu fréquente	Plural noun + adjective After monosyllabic conjuctions	43 *étudiants américains*
E	rare	Plural noun or adjective + verb or conjunction After polysyllabic conjunctions After plural past participle	44 *américains annoncèrent*
F	très rare	After singular nouns ending in *s* or *t* After infinitive in *-er*	37 *aller à Marseille*

Table 7.2 Variable liaison in two speech styles: RS and IS (from Hornsby 2019; Table 2)

	Total	Liaison	No Liaison	Liaison %
Interview style (IS)	**3366**	671	2695	**19.9**
Reading style (RS)	**5191**	1694	3497	**32.6**
Total	**8557**	2365	6192	**27.6**

liaison in unscripted IS than in RS. In the case of Adjective + Noun sequences in particular, the IS score is significantly higher, at 92%, than the corresponding RS figure of 66%. It is only when one looks more closely at the composition of the categories in the two speech styles that an explanation becomes apparent. The reading exercise, it will be recalled, was deliberately constructed to include as wide a range of liaison environments as possible, some of which proved rather rare in spontaneous speech. In RS (see Table 7.4 below), this grouping showed considerable internal variation, with scores for individual variables ranging from 96% to 42%.[6]

[6] Figures quoted here and below, unless otherwise indicated, include all liaison consonants. When only prescriptively correct consonants are counted, these figures fall to 95% and 24% respectively.

Table 7.3 *Liaison obligatoire* for three morphosyntactic categories in IS and RS (after Hornsby 2019; Table 3)

	Interview Style (IS)			Reading Style (RS)		
	Tokens	Liaison Realised	Liaison %	Tokens	Liaison Realised	Liaison %
Adj + N	65	60	**92**	885	580	**66**
Monosyllabic Prepositions +	276	268	**97**	190	160	**84**
Monosyllabic Adverbs +	415	85	**20**	496	300	**60**
Total	756	413	**55**	1571	1040	**66**

By contrast, a much narrower range of liaison sites occurred spontaneously in IS, the vast majority of which (57/61 tokens), involved liaison after plural adjectives (which accounted for only two of the nine variables in RS). The canonical liaison consonant in all but two cases (*plein, premier*) was /z/ or /t/, and there were only four cases of non-liaison, all of which involved final consonant clusters inhibiting liaison with plural /z/ (in *autres*, *grandes*, *plusieurs* and *simples*).

Two variables in RS contained monosyllabic prepositions: Variable 12 *en une*, for which the liaison rate was 67/92 tokens = 73% and Variable 26 *chez une* (90/98 = 92%). Liaison proved equally categorical in IS for *chez* (5/6 tokens = 83%), but perhaps surprisingly was even more consistent in IS for *en* (146/151 tokens = 97%).

Monosyllabic adverbs showed the more expected pattern of high liaison incidence in RS and low incidence in IS, but here the range of potential liaison sites was wider in IS than in RS, underlining once again how even single items can be subject to multiple linguistic constraints. The item *bien* for example with a score of 89% shows near categorical liaison in RS, while in IS the score is just 18% (7/38 occurrences). The RS figure however is based exclusively on *bien aimable* (Variable 31), a sequence which has been all but lexicalised, and in which the adverb is closely bound to the adjective it qualifies. In IS *bien* also occurred in sequences in which it bore a stronger syntactic relationship with the preceding element (e.g. *j'aimerais bien être institutrice*), in none of which liaison occurred (30 tokens). Incidence of liaison in sequences comparable to

Table 7.4 Liaison in Adj + N sequences in RS and IS

RS				IS				
No	Variable Sequence	Canonical liaison consonant	Liaison %	Left context	Canonical liaison consonant	Liaised tokens	Total	Liaison %
46	*grand exploit*	t	96	*grand*	t	4	4	100
19	*petit écureuil*	t	95	*petit*	t	3	3	100
30	*second enfant*¤	t	83	*gros*	z	1	1	100
42	*anciens étudiants*	z	72	*plein*	n	1	1	100
53	*certain ami*	n	62	*premier*	r	1	1	100
23	*long été*	k/g	55	Plural Adj	z	47	51	94
34	*long apprentissage*	k/g	54					
49	*autres appartements*	z	49					
39	*léger incident*	r	42					

bien aimable in fact proved similar to that observed in RS (6/7 tokens: 86%), bearing out Delattre's intuition for monosyllabic adverbs but subject to the proviso that *bien* must qualify a following element.

7.2.2 Delattre's *Liaison Facultative*

Items identified by Delattre as variable show a clear difference between IS and RS, but here liaison proves the exception rather than the rule in both styles: overall liaison scores for RS were 16% (556/3521 tokens), and 9% for IS (216/2469; see Hornsby 2019, Table 7). The broad category of post-verbal liaison, however, was again noteworthy for internal variability. A breakdown of post-verbal environments is provided in Table 7.5.

Sub-categories 1 and 2 show relatively high rates of liaison and significant differences between RS and IS scores. The only data for the latter in RS is the sequence *sommes allés* (Variable 25), which had been specifically selected as a form associated with the written rather than the spoken language (where it is frequently replaced by *(on) est allé*),[7] and offers a poor basis for comparison with the range of sites in IS. An interesting contrast did however emerge for Subcategory 1, impersonal *être*, as can be seen in Table 7.6 below.

Liaison after *c'était* occurred in 72% of cases, but sixteen informants who misread this sequence as *c'est* also liaised in all but one case (94%). These figures stand in stark contrast to the corresponding IS figures, 0% and 9% respectively, presenting the only clear evidence within the corpus for a sharp style differentiation between scripted and unscripted styles.

7.2.3 False Liaison and Repair in RS and IS

Thus far we have merely reported incidence of liaison without commenting on the nature of the consonant selected. It could not be assumed that liaison consonants realised would always correspond to those prescribed, and data were accordingly monitored for mismatches between canonical and realised liaison consonants. The phenomenon of *pataquès*, or 'false

[7] The single occurrence of *sommes* in IS was liaised—incorrectly—in *sommes* [st] *arrivés*.

Table 7.5 Post-verbal liaison in RS and IS (after Hornsby 2019: Table 8)

			Interview Style (IS)			Reading Style (RS)		
	Description	Frequency Band	Tokens	Liaison Realised	Liaison %	Tokens	Liaison Realised	Liaison %
1	Impersonal *être* +	très fréquente	531	44	8	90	73	81
2	Verb + past participle or adjective	assez fréquente	164	25	15	93	67	72
3	Verb + Adverb	assez fréquente	80	0	0	366	25	7
4	Verb + complement	mi-fréquente	715	33	5	676	98	14
5	Plural past participle +	rare	7	0	0	ND	ND	-
6	Singular past participle +	très rare	16	2	13	ND	ND	-
7	Infinitive -er +	très rare	227	1	0.4	272	12	4

ND: No data

Table 7.6 Liaison with impersonal *être* in RS and IS (after Hornsby 2019: Table 9)

Variable Sequence		Interview Style (IS) Tokens	Liaison Realised	Liaison %	Reading Style (RS) Tokens	Liaison Realised	Liaison %
33	c'était +	34	0	0	81	58	72
	c'est+	495	43	9	16	15	94

Table 7.7 *Pataquès* (false liaison) in RS

Prescribed liaison consonant	Number of variables	Actual consonant realised: z	t	Other	Total
k/g	3	1	52	0	**53**
n	3	7	14	3	**24**
p	4	23	15	1	**39**
r	6	8	11	2	**21**
t	15	4	-	34	**38**
z	23	-	5	20	**25**
Total:	**54**	**43**	**97**	**60**	**200**

liaison', to which we alluded in Chap. 2, and which might be seen as a form of hypercorrection, is almost entirely restricted in our data to RS. Only two IS liaison tokens in fact involve an incorrect liaison consonant: in one case *dans* liaised with [n] rather than [z], while in another an unexpected liaison was produced with the single IS token of *sommes* (*sommes* [st] *arrivés*). There were also two cases of sporadic liaison, one in proconsonantal position (*des* [z] *matières*) and another a plural agreement marker with a singular referent in *je suis né* [z] *en Belgique*. While these four isolated cases might reasonably be attributed to performance error, a very different picture emerges in RS. Here, fully 220 of 1694 (13.0%) liaisons realised across the four sites were prescriptively incorrect (Table 7.7).

A clear majority of the RS false liaisons are *cuirs* (where /t/ is incorrectly realised), but over a third are neither *cuirs* nor *velours* (involving inappropriately placed /z/). The figures exclude /g/ for the item *long* (20 tokens), but include /d/ for *attend* and *second* (26 tokens), and a couple of misreadings, for example *doit* [v] *aller* (presumably by analogy with *doivent*), and *pas* [st] *amusants*. The two lowest frequency liaison consonants in both IS for this corpus and in the PFC, namely /p/ and /k/, which are restricted to a small number of items (*beaucoup* and *trop* for the former and *long* and *sang* for the latter) were both especially subject to *pataquès*: *long* in particular (Variables 23 *long été* and 34 *long apprentissage*), was wrongly liaised in 51 of 189 tokens (27%). The liaison consonant in these cases was invariably /t/ (50/51 tokens), suggesting perhaps a cognitive link with sequences such as *l'ont* or *lent*. By contrast *pataquès* examples with *trop* (Variables 38 *trop aimable* and 52 *trop apprécié*) and *beaucoup* (Variables 21 *beaucoup aimé* and 41 *beaucoup aggressé*) were more likely to be *velours*, with thirty-three cases involving /z/ and only fifteen involving /t/. The most likely explanation for this is that both *trop* and *beaucoup* are associated with expressions of quantity and may therefore be cognitively associated with /z/ as a plural marker. The *pataquès* tokens were disproportionately produced by female rather than male informants (125 to 71), and slightly more by type B than A school speakers[8] (108 to 88).

The reading exercise, loaded as it was with variable liaison sites, posed problems for some of our informants, who stumbled not infrequently at points where liaison was possible, and then attempted to reread. Changes made to the liaison consonant in such cases are summarised below:

Although not in this case elicited directly by the researcher, these rereadings are analogous to the repetitions of *fourth floor* in Labov's (2006: 40-57) New York department store study, where the additional focus led invariably to greater use of the prestige /r/ variant in non-prevocalic position. Surprisingly, no such pattern is evident here. As can be seen in Table 7.8 above, the second reading was almost as likely to result in a

Table 7.8 Rereadings of RS liaison sequences (Hornsby 2019: Table 10)

		First reading		
		Correct	Zero	Incorrect
Second reading	**Correct**	24	16	15
	Zero	4	33	16
	Incorrect	1	4	7 (3)*

*3 changes; 4 repetitions

[8] LEPs in France and the Mons CEFA: see below Sect. 7.3.3.

'zero' reading (fifty-three tokens) as a correct one (fifty-five tokens), with twelve incorrect second readings. Far from moving consistently in the direction of the prestige form as expected in a more careful style, our informants were as likely to opt on rereading for the 'safe' option of no liaison at all.

7.3 Interspeaker Variation

The availability of a comparable population sample from four sites provides an opportunity to explore interspeaker variation in three of the four dimensions discussed in Chaps. 5 and 6: diatopic variation, variation by gender, and finally variation by socio-economic status, for which school type provides a proxy measure. We begin by comparing liaison rates by city.

7.3.1 Liaison and Diatopic Variation

As we saw in the previous chapter, comparing aggregate data for liaison is fraught with difficulties, given major frequency differences between variable liaison categories, and the intracategorial differences which may affect single items (as seen above, for example, with *bien*). In short, we can rarely be sure of comparing like with like, and even when we can, the likelihood is that we will be dealing with token numbers too small to be statistically significant, casting doubt on any general conclusions. The comparability of the population sample in each city here, however, and the scripted sentences read by all informants do allow a like-for-like comparison in this case, albeit for RS only. Liaison scores by city for both styles are listed in Table 7.9 below, from which it is noteworthy that Perpignan is something of an outlier, showing the lowest overall rate of liaison in both styles (Table 7.9).

The Perpignan score, while lowest in both cases, is closer to that of the other cities in IS than RS, where it falls a full 11.1 percentage points below that of the highest placed city (Strasbourg). These figures would seem to be at odds with a general finding for the PFC reported in Durand

Table 7.9 Four Cities Corpus: overall liaison rates by city

	RS			IS		
	Liaised tokens	Total tokens	Liaison %	Liaised tokens	Total tokens	Liaison %
Lille	422	1300	**32.5**	181	785	**23.1**
Mons	435	1298	**33.5**	144	675	**21.3**
Perpignan	346	1293	**26.7**	126	728	**17.3**
Strasbourg	491	1300	**37.8**	220	1178	**18.7**

(RS figures include data from rereadings)

Table 7.10 Perpignan as lowest ranked city by variable

Variable no.	Sequence	Liaison consonant	Grammatical category
5	*vais aller*	z	Aux + Inf
9	*agents immobiliers*	z	NPlu + Adj.
12	*en une demi-heure*	n	Prep + Det.
19	*petit écureuil*	t	Adj + N
25	*sommes allés*	s	Aux + P.Part
38	*trop aimable*	p	Adv + Adj.
39	*léger incident*	r	Adj + N
43	*anciens étudiants*	z	Adj + N
46	*grand exploit*	t	Adj + N
48	*loyers élevés*	z	NPlu + Adj
52	*trop apprécié*	p	Adv + P.Part

and Lyche (2008) which suggested that southern varieties liaised more, not less, than their northern counterparts, a finding about which the authors expressed scepticism, and on which Durand et al. (2011) would cast further doubt when data from later *enquêtes* became available. Might similar scepticism be in order here? While caution should be exercised in evaluating data based on one token per individual, it is instructive to note the specific RS variables in which Perpignan showed a noticeably lower incidence of liaison than the other three cities. For this purpose, we have selected only those variables for which the Perpignan informants produced three or more liaisons fewer than the third placed city, corresponding to a difference of around 3% (Table 7.10).

The data above do not offer strong evidence for a localised norm in respect of one or more the canonical liaison consonants, all six of which are represented here. Might the behaviour of liaison in certain grammatical category types, however, be locally constrained? Three categories which appear promising in this regard: four of the Perpignan low-score variables involve Adjective + Noun sequences (Variables 19, 39, 43 and 46); a further two involve Plural Noun + Adjective sequences (Variables 9 and 48), while another two involve the adverb *trop* (Variables 38 and 48). The behaviour of these categories in IS, unfortunately, offers little evidence to support or refute this hypothesis. In the case of *trop*, only three of twenty tokens from the whole corpus were liaised, in two cases by Perpignan informants; for Adjective + Noun sequences (see above) all twelve Perpignan tokens were liaised; finally only one token (from a Strasbourg informant) out of fifty-five tokens from the four cities showed liaison in Plural Noun + Adjective environments. While we cannot draw definitive conclusions from piecemeal data like these, it seems unlikely that the main categories of liaison sites are subject to is subject to localised norms, particularly given the evidence to the contrary of a much larger survey, the PFC (see Sect. 5.2).

7.3.2 Gender and Liaison in RS and IS

The availability of a gender-balanced population sample also provided an opportunity to explore a key extralinguistic variable which, as we saw in 6.5 had surprisingly failed to correlate consistently with liaison in previous studies. Here a rather clearer picture emerged. Global figures for liaison by gender (Table 7.11) show females leading males in both styles, as would be predicted by the SGP.

While the gender gap, at 3.5% for RS and 3.2% for IS, is not large in either style, the pattern of females outscoring males is repeated almost across the board in each fieldwork site. The data for gender are broken down by city in Table 7.12.

Only in one case (Strasbourg in RS) is the pattern of female speakers leading males reversed; in the other seven cases the gender gap ranges from to 0.9% (Mons RS) to 8.4% (Perpignan RS). Differences appear to be quantitative rather than qualitative, i.e. there is no evidence that particular liaison consonants or environments are gendered. But while on the one hand these findings do appear to be in line with the predictions

Table 7.11 Variable liaison rates by gender in RS and IS

	RS		IS	
	F	M	F	M
Liaised tokens	888	806	348	323
Unliaised tokens	1696	1801	1261	1434
Liaison %	**34.4**	**30.9**	**21.6**	**18.4**

Table 7.12 Percentage variable liaison rates by gender and city in two styles

	RS		IS	
	F	M	F	M
Lille	36.3	28.4	25.3	21.1
Mons	34.0	33.1	22.9	19.8
Perpignan	31.1	22.7	19.0	15.8
Strasbourg	35.9	39.6	20.1	17.4
Total	**34.4**	**30.9**	**21.6**	**18.4**

of the SGP for stable variation, we have seen evidence throughout this book that, far from being stable, liaison may well be in decline. Early twentieth-century prescriptive commentators seemed to agree that liaison use had peaked by the mid-nineteenth century (see Chap. 4); apparent and real time studies reviewed in Chap. 6 suggested more recent falls in usage, and the evidence both of Côté's *noyau dur* in Chap. 6 and our RS data for this corpus in Sect. 7.2.1 above seemed to suggest that Delattre's grouping of *liaison obligatoire* environments had in fact contracted considerably, with supposedly invariable liaison environments now clearly demonstrating variability. We will, moreover, see further evidence of falling use among *professionnels de la parole publique* in the next chapter. If liaison is in decline, as a number of pieces of evidence suggest, then we might expect female informants to be leading change towards non-realisation, but this corpus offers almost no support for that case.

The most likely explanation for the patterns observed here lies not in the SGP as typically observed for 'normal' sociolinguistic variables, but in levels of literacy, which as we saw in Part 2 has been closely associated with liaison use since at least the seventeenth century. This is a domain in which girls in most western European countries consistently lead boys. Johnson and Johnson (2016: 56) for example note:

> France, like most other Western European countries, witnesses continuing gender differences in many aspects of education and work (DEPP 2015). Attainment surveys, both national and international, have repeatedly confirmed a general tendency for girls to be ahead of boys on average in their early language development, and in reading and writing throughout compulsory schooling.

For all the researcher's assurances to informants that the interview did not represent a 'test', the context and setting of the interview, in an educational establishment and conducted by what must have appeared to be an external authority figure, are likely to have framed the speech event and notably the reading exercise in terms of educational attainment in an area in which females appear to have an advantage. In the circumstances, it is perhaps surprising both that the gender gap was not in fact greater.

7.3.3 Social Class: A Proxy Measure

As we saw above (Sect. 6.4), social class is notoriously difficult to measure, and posed a particular problem in this case in so far as the informants were still in full time education and could not be graded in terms of their involvement in the labour market, income, or similar measures, as for example in New York or Norwich. The contrast between the two types of educational establishment did, however, appear to offer a proxy measure. *Lycées* and the *athénée* in Mons were labelled type A schools; the LEPs and the CEFA in Mons were labelled as type B. French *lycées*, which are geared towards preparing students for higher education, are generally held to attract students of more elevated social status than the more vocationally oriented LEPs *(lycées d'enseignement professionel)*. To test this hypothesis, information provided by informants about their parents' occupations (a familiar social status indicator used by both Labov and Trudgill), was graded on a simple three-way occupational status measure as proposed by Marceau (1977), in which 3 points were given for professional, 2 for semi-skilled and 1 for manual occupations, giving an index score for each of informant of between 2 and 6. Results for three of the fieldwork sites (Lille, Strasbourg and Mons) were collated in Hornsby (2009), and revealed as expected noticeably higher occupational index

Table 7.13 Liaison by School type and City in RS and IS

		Lille	Mons	Perpignan	Strasbourg	Total
RS	**A**	33.4	34.9	31.7	42.5	**35.6**
	B	31.5	32.1	21.8	33.1	**29.7**
IS	**A**	19.9	23.2	17.6	20.1	**20.2**
	B	25.5	18.2	17.0	16.8	**19.6**

(OI) scores for the type A schools (Lille 5.25; Strasbourg 4.67; Mons; 4.42) than for the corresponding B schools (Lille 3.00; Strasbourg 3.75; Mons; 3.58).[9] It is worth mentioning in passing that none of the nine informants with an occupational index score of 6 attended a B school, and none of the seven informants with a score of 2 attended an A school. One might reasonably conclude that the children of white-collar and blue-collar workers are disproportionately attracted to schools which prepare them for similar careers to their parents, but to what extent would this division manifest itself in respect of liaison? Liaison rates by city and school type are shown in Table 7.13.

A clear pattern of A school informants leading their B school counterparts is evident in both styles and in all four cities, with the exception of Lille in IS. The overall gap is noticeably greater for RS (5.9%) than for IS (0.6%), though arguably both sets of figures are skewed by an outlier: the exceptionally low figure in RS for Perpignan and the exceptionally high one for Lille in IS. These findings are nonetheless in line with those of Hornsby (2009), where the OI scores for informants in three of the four sites were correlated with number of liaisons realised (out of a possible 54) in RS. These showed regular social stratification, with liaison use

[9] The number of informants reporting that they had a 'mère/père au foyer' was almost certainly rather lower than would have been the case for Labov or Trudgill some three decades earlier, but such cases nonetheless raised the same problem encountered by those researchers, namely the appropriate way to classify partners not in paid employment. The option of simply setting aside informants with only one employed parent seemed unsatisfactory; the alternative, adopted here, was to take the score for the parent in paid employment and double it. This, of course, raises the objection that some people, in all likelihood mostly women, would thereby be graded solely and inaccurately according to their partner's social profile. It moreover presupposes a degree of social immobility which makes marriage or partnership across social divides exceptional rather than normal. While this assumption is not historically unreasonable for France and Belgium, it cannot simply be taken as a given. Concerns such as these prompted the decision not to pursue the occupational index measure across all four sites here.

Table 7.14 Liaisons realised in RS, by occupational index (OI) score (after Hornsby 2009)

SEI	No. of informants	Mean RS liaisons realised
6	9	**17.22**
5	17	**15.76**
4	26	**15.50**
3	13	**14.85**
2	7	**12.14**

increasing with OI score, albeit with less than one point separating the middle groups (see Table 7.14 above).

While far from conclusive, based as they are on single tokens per informant for each variable, findings on both proxy class measures pointed to a clear pattern of differentiation in RS. As with the findings for gender, however, we suspect that that the clear correlations observed, which have not been consistently replicated in other studies (see Sect. 6.4), can be largely attributed to the setting and context of the interview, which were likely to have recalled a classroom test conducted by a teacher, favouring the more academically orientated (and often the most socially advantaged) pupils. It is, moreover, not unreasonable to surmise that students in type A schools are more likely to be targeting higher education and careers in which higher level literacy skills are required.

7.4 Conclusions

Once more our findings point to the importance of literacy in understanding liaison use, but the nature of the link between the two remains unexplained. If liaison were straightforwardly associated with reading aloud, then we would expect to find a clear and consistent style division between RS and IS, strongly favouring liaison in the former. In fact, we found this pattern only in the case of *c'est/c'était*, and in some cases (e.g. after *en*) the expected pattern was reversed.

Overall style differentiation, moreover, would be more reasonably described as gradient than sharp, with liaison in categories defined by Delattre as *facultative* in particular very much the exception rather than the rule. The Four Cities project is far from the first to report low overall incidence of liaison in interview style, but the relatively modest scores for RS are nonetheless something of a surprise, given a carefully constructed reading exercise and research protocol which, in terms of the audio-monitoring hypothesis (see Sect. 6.2), would seem to have maximised speakers' attention to speech, and informants for whom the daily school *dictée* and its reinforcement of French spelling conventions were still very familiar. We reconsider these findings in Chap. 9, after turning attention in Chap. 8 to a very different group of speakers, whose use of liaison has been consistently found to exceed that of the general population: the so-called *professionnels de la parole publique*.

References

Boersma, P., & Weenink, D. (2016). Praat: Doing Phonetics by Computer. Retrieved from http://www.fon.hum.uva.nl/praat/ [Computer Program. Version 6.0.10].

Delattre, P. (1966c [1956]). La fréquence des liaisons facultatives en français. In P. Delattre (Ed.), *Studies in French and Comparative Phonetics: Selected Papers in French and English* (pp. 49–54). The Hague: Mouton. First Published in *French Review, 30*(1), 48–54.

DEPP. (2015). *Filles et garçons sur le chemin de l'égalité de l'école à l'enseignement supérieur.* Paris: Ministry of National Education, Division for Evaluation, Forecasting and Performance.

Durand, J., & Lyche, C. (2008). French Liaison in the Light of Corpus Data. *Journal of French Language Studies, 18*, 33–66.

Durand, J., Laks, B., Calderone, B., & Tchobanov, A. (2011). Que savons-nous de la liaison aujourd'hui? *Langue française, 169*, 103–135.

Eychenne, J., & Paternostro, R. (2016). Analyzing Transcribed Speech with Dolmen. In S. Detey, J. Durand, B. Laks, & C. Lyche (Eds.), *Varieties of Spoken French: A Source Book* (pp. D35–D52). Oxford: Oxford University Press.

Hornsby, D. (2009). *Liaison and Reading Styles in French.* Paper to Cambridge University Linguistics Society, 2.4.2009.

Hornsby, D. (2019). Variable Liaison, Diglossia, and the Style Dimension in Spoken French. *French Studies, 73*(4), 578–597.

Hornsby, D., & Jones, M. (2013). *Exception française*? Levelling, Exclusion and Urban Social Structure in France. In M. Jones & D. C. Hornsby (Eds.), *Language and Social Structure in Urban France* (pp. 94–109). Oxford: Legenda.

Johnson, S., & Johnson, R. (2016). *Literacy in France: Country Report. Children and Adolescents*. European Literacy Policy Network (ELINET).

Labov, W. (2006). *The Social Stratification of English in New York City* (2nd ed.). Cambridge: Cambridge University Press.

Marceau, S. (1977). *Class and Status in France: Economic Change and Social Immobility 1945–75*. Oxford: Clarendon Press.

Massot, B. (2005). *Français et diglossie: Décrire la situation linguistique française contemporaine comme une diglossie: arguments morphosyntactiques*. Thèse de doctorat, Université de Paris 8. Retrieved from http://inferno.philosophie.uni-stuttgart.de/~benjamin/pdf/these-benjamin-massot-version-soutenance.pdf.

8

Professionnels de la Parole Publique

8.1 Introduction

Thus far we have reported on speakers from a wide range of studies, including our own, whose incidence of variable liaison has generally been low, and whose usage in a number of respects runs counter to usual sociolinguistic expectations. In this chapter, we consider a group of speakers whose behaviour with respect to liaison has consistently been found to diverge from that of the general population. For those whom Encrevé (1988: 55) has labelled 'professionnels de la parole publique', speaking in a public and/or communicating with a wide audience is a regular rather than occasional occupational requirement,[1] which appears to elicit a style in which a significantly greater number of variable liaisons, in a wider range of environments, is used than in conversational speech.

In the category of *professionnels de la parole publique* Encrevé includes politicians and union leaders, journalists, broadcasters, lawyers, ministers of religion and academics, but he excludes teachers, whose relationship with a specific, younger audience is rather different from that of the occupational groups cited and uniquely involves, inter alia, teaching of the written norm (1988: 77). He also notes the growth of 'media experts'

[1] Cf. Encrevé (1988: 76 fn):

> Par *professionnels de la parole publique* nous entendons toutes les catégories de locuteurs dont la profession implique régulièrement la prise de parole en public.

D. Hornsby, *Norm and Ideology in Spoken French*,
https://doi.org/10.1007/978-3-030-49300-4_8

drawn from a variety of professions in which public speaking is not a typical occupational activity (e.g. writers, economists, doctors, military personnel), who are regularly consulted by broadcast media as 'experts' in their field and become 'quasi-professionnels de la parole publique'. Though Encrevé does not state this explicitly, what links all members of the group is a presumption of authority which confers the right to speak to a wide audience in the expectation of being listened to, for the most part without interruption. For this reason other occupations which involve regular interaction with the public, for example shopkeepers, flight attendants, or travelling salespeople, have attracted little scholarly interest in respect of liaison.

8.2 Radio Broadcasting: Ågren's (1973) Study

John Ågren's (1973) investigation of France-Inter radio programmes recorded in 1960–1961 represents the first major study of liaison in broadcast media. His corpus of 8441 tokens of variable liaison is drawn from 134 × 20-minute editions of *Tribune de Paris*, a panel show devoted to discussion of the arts, politics and current affairs, and *Club des Jeunes*, a discussion programme aimed at young people. The speakers are described as 'le plus souvent des journalistes, des écrivains et des hommes politiques', generally well educated and possessing specific areas of expertise (1973: 2), who had been invited to discuss issues relating to current affairs and culture.

While Ågren ignores the social dimension of variation, his analysis offers a groundbreaking investigation of linguistic and stylistic constraints on liaison, which are found to interact in a variety of ways. He is careful to exclude speech he believes to have been scripted, but argues for a stylistic division within his data between *niveau soigné* and *niveau courant*, established on the basis of a number of independent criteria (pp. 17–20).

Within an overall variable liaison rate of 61.6% for his corpus, Ågren notes significant variability even in structurally similar environments. For forms of *être*, for example (pp. 32–61), liaison rates vary between 97% (after *est*) and 21% (after *étais*), the highest incidence being observed among the most frequently occurring third-person forms and the stylistically elevated item *étant* (74%: 22/29 occurrences). The syntactic category of the second element is found to be less important, with scores here ranging from 96% (*être* + indefinite article + noun) to 77% (*être* + prepositional phrase). Similarly, the hypothesis that the presence of an existing consonantal enchaînement would inhibit liaison finds little support for *être*: both *sommes* (58%) and *êtes* (71%) which have a fixed final consonant have noticeably higher scores than *suis* (47%) and *serait* (41.4%) which do not.

The overall liaison rate for *pas* is reported at 23%, but this single item too exhibits significant internal variation according to context. Liaison is realised in 43% of cases before adjectives, but considerably less frequently where the syntactic bond is weaker, for example before prepositional phrases (9%; 10/103 occurrences) or adverbial constructions (0%; 0/5 occurrences). Of particular importance here is the position of *pas* in the rhythm group: in final position ('pas terminal'), as in Ågren's example *si l'adversaire n'a pas|accepté de parler*, liaison, while not impossible, is very much the exception. The rarity in his data of *pas terminal* in pre-adjectival position offers a partial explanation for the higher incidence of liaison in this context.

Interaction between constraints complicates determination of their relative importance. For adverbs, for example, Ågren's *longueur des termes à lier* seems particularly relevant in that liaison occurs predominantly with monosyllabic forms, but this effect is difficult to disentangle from that of *fréquence d'emploi* in so far as the most commonly occurring adverbs—*bien* and *trop* for example—are mostly monosyllabic. For *niveau de langue*, or style in Labov's terms,[2] Ågren contrasts the recordings or parts of recordings which meet his criteria for the more formal *niveau soigné* with those he categorises as *niveau courant*, and finds consistently higher incidence of liaison in the former case. On one notably simple measure, Ågren explores liaison in the context of *ne* deletion, a phenomenon associated with informal spoken French, and finds 95%

[2] The terms 'style' and 'register' are used inconsistently in French linguistics, each being deployed by anglophone linguists to denote intraspeaker variation linked to sociosituational formality. As this book attempts to examine liaison through the prism of quantitative sociolinguistic methodology, it seems appropriate to use 'style' in Labov's sense, and reserve 'register' for reference to language associated with a particular profession or activity, e.g. 'the register of sports reporting'.

incidence of liaison after *pas* where *ne* is retained but only 5% incidence where the negative particle is deleted. Ågren concludes:

> à chaque niveau de langue convient un certain nombre de liaisons, de sorte que, si l'on dépasse les bornes du langage accepté, on court le risque de faire des liaisons qui détonnent. Les LF [liaisons facultatives] contiennent ainsi une quantité non négligeable d'informations extra-linguistiques relatives au milieu social, à la formation, à l'origine géographique, à l'âge, etc. du locuteur.

On the specifics of this claim, however, Ågren is circumspect: there is no attempt to explore social factors, nor any indication of where the 'bornes du langage accepté' might lie, or indeed of which precisely are the 'liaisons qui détonnent' in any given style. We find ourselves back in the realm of Goldilocks, as outlined in Chap. 5, in which mastery of an unfathomable prescriptive norm requires an ill-defined 'right amount' of liaisons of the appropriate kind at each stylistic level. The question of whether the differences between styles might be quantitative (greater incidence of some or all variable liaisons as formality increases) or qualitative (a wider range of liaisons used in formal styles), or indeed both, is also left open.

8.3 Political Discourse

Perhaps unsurprisingly, one highly prominent sub-group among the *professionnels de la parole publique* has attracted particular attention. For politicians, public speaking is not merely a professional requirement but a matter of record, leaving them open within democratic societies to charges of double standards, or failure to deliver on promises, when inconsistencies are brought to light. One would reasonably assume, therefore, than this is a group whose professional fortunes depend heavily on an ability to choose words with care. Politicians have been the subject of three important liaison studies. Encrevé (1988) examines data from twenty-one high-profile French figures recorded between 1978 and 1981, while Laks' corpus (HPOL1) of data from forty-three politicians in seventy-three interventions between 1908 and 1998 (see Laks 2009) is supplemented by a second (HPOL2), taken from a further forty-one figures (17 women, 24 men) born between 1927 and 1977 and politically active between 1999 and 2015 (see Laks and Peuvergne 2017). These high-profile individuals are observed in speech events ranging from press conferences to speeches and televised debates, all of which demand from a politician a style which Encrevé calls 'calculé, surveillé' (1988: 57), notwithstanding the occasional 'stratégie de décontraction ostentatoire' (p. 58) designed to make the candidate appear relaxed and confident.

Encrevé reports an overall liaison rate of 48.6% (5787 of 10,816 possible occurrences) which, in spite of the fact that it conflates data from variable and invariable sites, is somewhat lower than Ågren's figure of 61.6% for variable liaison only in a radio corpus recorded some twenty years earlier. A number of findings however are consistent with Ågren's: liaison after *est*, for example, is again near-categorical for this group of speakers (p. 66), and liaison after monosyllabic adverbs and prepositions, both classified by Delattre as *obligatoire*, once more proves in fact to be variable.

Encrevé reports very wide intraspeaker variation within his speaker sample, with realisation rates proving noticeably higher in speeches which Encrevé describes (p. 61) as 'interventions monologuées assurément écrites et apprises par coeur', than in debates or interviews. François Mitterrand's liaison rate ranges from 54.5% in debate with Valéry Giscard-D'Estaing in 1981 to 81% for his first Presidential New Year Address on 30th December of the same year.[3] Encrevé (1988: 61) concludes: 'le taux de liaisons facultatives réalisées croît pour chaque locuteur avec la « hauteur » du style'. Encrevé finds evidence too of variation within the same speech event, but there is a hint of circularity about his claim (1988: 258) that it is the 'tension' of the event which determines the incidence of variable liaison.

Very significant interspeaker differences are also evident from Encrevé's data. Overall liaison scores range from 18.8% for *Parti Communiste*

[3] Pierre Léon (1971: 134) reports an even wider range of variability—between 9% and 100%—for ten speeches by Charles De Gaulle recorded between 1959 and 1961.

Français leader Georges Marchais to 66.7% for former Gaullist Justice Minister Alain Peyrefitte (see Table 8.1 below).

While these are aggregate figures and must, as we have seen more than once, be treated with caution, it seems reasonable to ask whether differences on this scale might be explained in terms of inequalities of social and educational capital. As a former mechanic, and the son of a quarryman, Georges Marchais would appear to belong to a very different world from that of the Academician and *énarque* Alain Peyrefitte. But anything resembling a linear relationship for these speakers between social background and use of variable liaison proves elusive. Lionel Jospin, whose social profile resembles that of Peyrefitte, has the fourth lowest incidence of liaison (32.2%) of the twenty-one politicians investigated, with a rate almost identical to that of Charles Fiterman (32.5%), a PCF minister under Mitterrand whose background is closer to that of Georges Marchais. Perhaps political authority might be a more promising determinant here: with the exception of Peyrefitte (not insignificantly a member of the Académie Française), all the public figures with liaison rates above 59% had either served as President or been candidates for the presidency.[4]

The inter- and intra-speaker variation observed reflects a careful strategic calculation, based on a constellation of competing factors, designed to maximise a politician's appeal to his/her electorate. Firstly and most obviously, this requires identification with a target audience. Mindful no doubt of the socio-economic differences between their core supporters, left-leaning figures are found to use noticeably fewer variable liaisons than politicians on the right (Encrevé 1988: 266). At the same time, a certain distance between a politician and those he/she aspires to lead is essential. Even Georges Marchais' variable liaison rate—the lowest in Encrevé's sample—is significantly higher than the figure of 2.9% for Laks' adolescent informants, recorded in Marchais' own constituency of Villejuif (see Encrevé 1988: 266). The importance of this distance arguably increases in proportion to the credibility of the candidate's aspiration to high office, as he/she seeks to burnish his or her (in France,

[4] While this was also true of Marchais, Lecanuet and Garaud, none of these had a serious chance of election to the Elysée Palace. Jospin himself would be a more credible presidential candidate for the *Parti Socialiste* (PS) later in his career (in 1995 and 2002), losing the second-round run-off to Jacques Chirac in 1995.

Table 8.1 Liaison rates among politicians 1978–1981 (after Encrevé 1988: 56, Tableau 2)

	Variable liaisons realised (%)	Variable liaisons without enchaînement as % of total realised
Barre	62.3	13.5
Cheysson	51.7	8.5
Chirac	59	15.2
Couve de Murville	49	9.7
Debré	49	18.7
Fiterman	32.5	13.5
Garaud	33.7	3.2
Giscard d'Estaing	61.1	11.1
Jospin	32.2	16.7
Lecanuet	38.4	4.5
Maire	19.9	17.7
Marchais	18.8	18.6
Mauroy	35.2	6.7
Mendès-France	33.7	5.2
Messmer	30.2	6.9
Mitterrand	62.5	12.5
Pelletier	48.7	10.8
Peyrefitte	66.7	1.7
Poniatowski	42.2	14.7
Rocard	61.5	0
Veil	52.3	7.6

generally his) credentials as a statesperson able to stand above the fray and speak on behalf of the nation. This might explain the higher liaison rates observed for two left-wing figures—François Mitterrand (President of the Republic 1981–1995) and Michel Rocard (Presidential candidate in 1969 and Prime Minister 1988–1991), who outscore many of their counterparts on the right. Such parallels should not however be extended too far: Pierre Mauroy also served as Prime Minister (1981–1984) but has a noticeably lower liaison rate than Rocard, who also outscores Laurent Fabius, another reform-minded, centrist former Prime Minister (1984–1986) from the *Parti Socialiste.*

Laks and Peuvergne (2017) compare findings for their HPOL2 corpus (1999–2015) both with those of Encrevé (1978–1981) and with Laks' earlier HPOL1 corpus (1908–1998) and find a remarkable stability in overall liaison rates for public figures throughout the twentieth Century. At 56.7%, the global liaison rate for HPOL2 is, as they point out, broadly in line with an average rate for political figures which remained consistently above 56% throughout the twentieth century. Even the figure of 54.4% for the most recent available period (2010–2015) is only marginally down from this figure, casting doubt on impressionistic claims that overall liaison is in decline (for example Ågren 1973: 1). Encrevé's figure of 72.5% for 1978–1981 seems something of an outlier in data from over 100 years and 81,837 liaison sites (Laks and Peuvergne 2017: 61). As in Encrevé's data, higher realisation rates are reported in speeches (which they classify as 'situation formelle'; p. 67) than in interviews ('situation moins formelle'). The figures quoted generally amalgamate data from variable and from invariable liaison sites,[5] and for that reason are probably not very meaningful. But where data allow, a more fine-grained analysis of variable liaison environments only presents a rather different picture. Over the sixteen-year period 1999–2015, the average figure for liaison in variable environments is 32.3%, with fluctuations by period between 40.1% (for 1999–2001) and 26.4% (for 2006). These figures are rather lower than those observed by Encrevé, and mask differences between speakers corresponding to age-group. Apparent-time data for three age groups A1 (born 1927–1945), A2 (born 1946–1958) and A3 (born 1961–1976)—corresponding to pre-war, 4th Republic and 5th Republic respectively, appear to suggest change in progress, as can be seen in Fig. 8.1 below.

The highest incidence of variable liaison is observed in the Group A1 politicians born before the second world war, that is during the first and second post-Jules Ferry generations, which the authors describe as 'une période de forte légitimité scolaire et culturelle' (2017: 65) in which use of liaison associated with the written code was inculcated throughout the school curriculum. In Encrevé's words (1988: 261):

> L'usage de la plupart des dirigeants politiques s'exprimant en public reflète évidemment beaucoup plus le langage de leurs enseignants des facultés de

[5] Compare for example an overall liaison rate of 47.7% for the socially mixed PFC corpus and 41.4% for Laks' working-class Villejuif adolescents, who as we saw above, realized only a miniscule number of variable liaisons.

droit, de Sciences-po ou de l'ENA et celui de ces autres enseignants que sont pour eux les journalistes des médias audiovisuels que celui de Swann, des Guermantes ou de monsieur de Norpois.

Encrevé's reference to three pillars of the Proustian fictional aristocracy underlines the change observed within French society in this period, driven by the secular education system, in favour of an ideology based on educational merit rather than inherited wealth and its associated notions of 'tone' and 'manners'. This contrast he sees neatly encapsulated in the liaison scores of Alain Peyrefitte (66.7%) and Maurice Couve de Murville (49%). For the latter, a member of what Encrevé terms the 'haute société protestante' (1988: 261), a more modest usage accords with what Encrevé memorably describes as a 'sens des « convenances » (celles que seuls reconnaissent les pairs)', appropriate for a time when the vaunting of literacy, shorn of its previous distinctive value, might appear vulgar. By contrast, the greater vigilance manifested by the Academician Peyrefitte, the son of *instituteurs*, stems from 'un savoir-parler tout scolaire' which draws its legitimacy from recognition by the educational system. For this reason, Encrevé suggests, Peyrefitte's behaviour, for all his exalted status as an

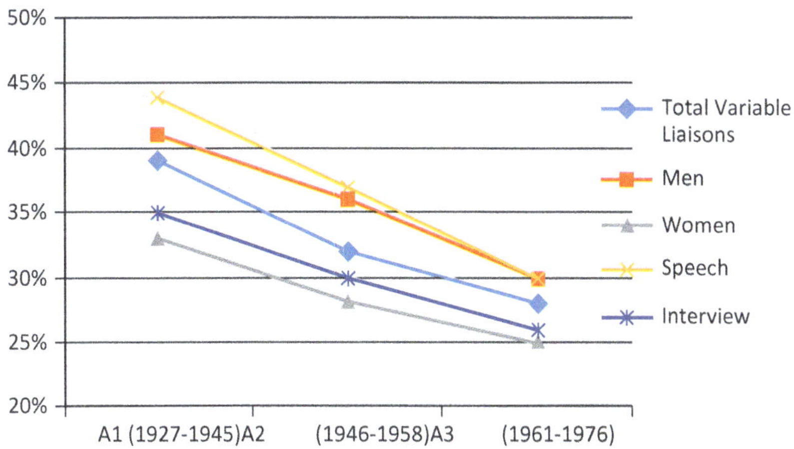

Fig. 8.1 Variable liaison among national political figures, by age group (after Laks and Peuvergne 2017: 66, Figure 2)

Establishment figure, recalls the hypercorrection of Labov's (1966) lower middle-class speakers with respect to the variable (r) in New York.

The increase observed both in the use of variable liaison and of *liaison sans enchaînement* (see Sect. 8.4) in for the period 1978–1981 is consistent with this group coming to political prominence in their forties and fifties. The second group A2 experienced the changed conditions of the Fifth Republic, and notably *les événements* of 1968, which marked an ideological shift towards a less rigidly hierarchical society,[6] into which the third group, A3, which uses the fewest variable liaisons, was born and raised. The usage of these latter speakers reflects, in Laks and Peuvergne's (2017: 65) words 'l'existence de dynamiques plus fortes et de tendances beaucoup plus abruptes' (original emphasis), with notably a 9% fall in overall variable liaison use for age groups separated by just thirty years (compared with a figure of 10% for the twentieth century as a whole). When variable liaisons alone are considered an overall fall of 5% for all generations over a fifteen-year period is observed. In a world in which authority is questioned rather than accepted uncritically, it is perhaps unsurprising that, in their words, 'la distinction stylistique et le style oratoire du grand discours politique régressent massivement' (p. 67), with a consequent decline in liaison use. Two important observations need, however, to be made in respect of this finding.

Firstly, change appears to have occurred on an item-by-item rather than a categorial or 'across the board' basis. Laks and Peuvergne observe little change in the behaviour of obligatory liaison environments, in which items subject to what they term *figement* (such as 'des amis' or 'nous allons') behave effectively as single lexical items.[7] They do, however,

---

[6] For Encrevé (1988: 262), this found expression in a breakdown of rigid social distinctions and codes: from male teachers no longer feeling obliged to wear ties at work, to the first swear words published in *Le Monde*. A marked decline in non-reciprocal use of V and T pronouns had also been reported by Brown and Gilman (1960).

[7] Cf. Laks and Peuvergne (2017: 68):

> Il s'agit bien d'un phénomène catégorique, constant, stable dans l'espace temporel comme dans l'espace social ou l'espace stylistique. Ce phénomène est si catégorique que l'on peut en effet défendre avec de très nombreux grammairiens l'existence en français, et pour tous les français, de mots uniques composés par figement de liaisons toujours réalisées.

acknowledge occasional cases of *défigement*, for example in the case of *pas important* or *trop important*, for which liaison is realised categorically by older speakers, but now only variably by younger speakers. Within the category of adverbs, liaison proves three times as likely with monosyllabic forms as with polysyllables. Even for monosyllabic adverbs, however (categorised as obligatory by Delattre), a decline in real time from 48% to 30% across the three generations is evident; the comparable figures for polysyllabic items are 17% and 4%. The adverbs *bien, mieux*, and *moins* present global liaison scores ranging between 38% and 65%. The negative adverb *pas*, however, 'présente, en temps apparent, une évolution brutale vers la non-liaison' (2017: 69), falling from 21% for A1 to 12% for A3, though as we noted above this single item is subject to variability according to context, and the degree of cohesion with a following element (see Chap. 6), making comparisons difficult. Variation is also evident among conjunctions, where *quand* shows 96% liaison overall, and unusually appears to be moving towards invariable status in apparent time (93% for A1 rising to 100% for A3), with the final consonant often realised even in pre-consonantal position. *Mais*, by contrast, shows an overall liaison rate of 11% but no apparent correlation with age (p. 70).

A second, striking observation is that women appear to be leading change. For all three age groups there is a gap of between 4% and 8% between the genders, with women in all age-groups using fewer variable liaison forms than their male counterparts, a pattern observed equally consistently in both formal speech and interview styles (see Fig. 8.1 above). Laks and Peuvergne see this pattern as consistent with findings elsewhere in which women have been found to lead linguistic change (see Sect. 6.2 above). But the evidence of Chaps. 6 and 7 should make us wary of interpreting variable liaison data in conventional variationist terms, and this finding is in fact rather more surprising than it seems. Firstly, it is clearly out of step both with the inconclusive findings for gender observed in Chap. 6 and those of the 'Four Cities' survey discussed in Chap. 7, which showed female informants using more liaison forms than males. We have, essentially, been able to find one kind of 'typical' pattern of gender-based variation only by turning to a population which is highly atypical. Secondly, it is worth recalling the terms of Labov's (2001: 261–93) 'gender paradox', and the explanations offered for it, as discussed above (Sect. 6.2). Where women lead change, they tend to outscore men in use of innovating variations generally adopted from outside the speech community. Zero liaison, however, far from being an innovative variant, is by some distance the default form for most speakers in the majority of variable liaison contexts thus far examined. Women's greater receptivity to outside forms, moreover, has been explained in terms of gender-based differences in social network structures, those of women being typically wider and more loose-knit than those of men, by virtue of having a generally more diversified set of roles.

Such explanations are rooted in the effects of accommodation in face-to-face interaction (see Giles 1973), which are very far removed from the conditions of modern broadcast media in which professional politicians, male and female, attempt to woo an audience they cannot see, who are watching them from their living rooms. Why then do we observe what in some respects seems a typical gender pattern in such highly atypical circumstances? Laks and Peuvergne (2017: 66) offer only the following: 'c'est surtout parce qu'elles [les femmes politiques] apparaissent beaucoup moins sensibles à la formalité des situations de discours' (2017: 66), which does little more than restate the problem, in the absence of evidence that sensitivity to style is linked to gender *per se*, except in so far as women's 'outsider' status in a very male-dominated arena[8] might in fact be expected to render them *more* rather than less sensitive to its norms and conventions. A more promising approach would be to reframe the question in terms of power and authority, noting that both have largely been denied to women within the French political system. At the time of writing, no woman had ever risen to the rank of *Président(e) de la République*, and only one, Édith Cresson, had served as Prime Minister (1991–1992). Only one female Presidential candidate, Ségolène Royal in 2007, had reached the second-round run off (losing to Nicolas Sarkozy). One consequence of relative inexperience at the highest level is that women are considerably less likely than men to be required to demonstrate the authority of office or the bearing of a statesperson, and we have

[8] Laks and Peuvergne admit to having had difficulties in balancing their HPOL2 sample, which includes 17 women and 24 men. Women barely figure at all in Encrevé's 21-speaker sample, which includes only two female politicians: Marie-France Garaud and Simone Veil.

seen that it is consistently in set-piece speeches, which underline the authority of the speaker, that the highest rates of liaison are observed (an example being Charles de Gaulle's 100% liaison rate for his address to Parliament during his state visit to London, April 7th 1960: see Encrevé 1988: 258).

8.4 Liaison Without Enchaînement

In Part II, we discussed the historical link between liaison and literacy, and notably the greater incidence of variable liaison in scripted speech. One phenomenon in particular, *liaison sans enchaînement* (LSE), is of particular interest here in that it appears to bring spoken French closer to the written norm from which it notoriously diverges. LSE involves liaison without resyllabification, as for example in *jugeais essentiel* [ʒy.ʒɛz.ʔe.sɑ̃.sjɛl] (example from Encrevé 1988: 35). LSE appears only to affect variable liaison contexts, and generally involves either a glottal stop (as in the example above) or a pause between the final liaison consonant and the onset of the following syllable. LSE had largely slipped under observers' radar until Encrevé (1983) identified and defined the phenomenon: Ågren (who appears to have believed that glottal stops block liaison), for example, does not mention it at all. Encrevé himself saw LSE as an important and growing and feature of public discourse, particularly among politicians. Most of the public figures in his eleven-speaker sample (p. 69, Table 7) realise around 15% of their variable liaisons without *enchaînement*, and for seven of these incidence of LSE increases between 1978 and 1981 (a decrease is observed only in one case).

Encrevé links increased use of LSE with increased time spent in a public education system which promoted a pronunciation closely aligned with the written norm, and with it a tendency to avoid hiatus and individualise words (1988: 272). LSE might be seen as advantageous to politicians in that it arguably promotes clarity in a language with a high propensity for homophony. But, as with variable liaison itself, use of LSE defies correlation with social or ideological factors, even if the phenomenon itself seems to be restricted to what Encrevé (1988: 278) calls 'locuteurs légitimes'. Several commentators (see, e.g. Armstrong 2001: 180; Gadet 2007: 83–84) have noted the potential for confusion (or worse) in a misjudged variable liaison, quoting in particular an unnamed former Prime Minister, speaking in 1978: 'Quand Monsieur Mitterrand était ministre, et Dieu sait qu'il l'a beaucoup [p] été, euh beaucoup-[p] [ʔ] été'. The unwitting and unforutunate *calembour* (cf. 'beaucoup pété') is hastily repaired, not by deleting the variable liaison, but by repeating the liaison without enchaînement, and inserting a glottal stop in the onset position of the following syllable, indicating, as Gadet suggests, that social distinction is derived from use of variable liaison rather than enchaînement, allowing the latter to be sacrificed.

By realising the link consonant in coda position, mirroring its orthographic place in the word, Encrevé (1988: 283–84) suggests, LSE would seem to be symptomatic of a wider realignment of speech with writing, this being the only strategy available for bridging the chasm between speech and writing, given the dismal failure of successive orthographic reform projects:[9]

> Il y a plus d'un siècle que les linguistes français lancés dans la lutte pour la réforme de l'orthographe soulignent l'immense écart entre forme orale et forme écrite de la langue. Il se pourrait que l'écartèlement entre l'une et l'autre devienne pour les usagers tellement coûteux qu'il ne leur soit plus supportable. Puisque l'orthographe est intouchable, divinité archaïque dont les sectateurs sont assez puissants pour imposer à toute la communauté un culte exigeant des sacrifices incalculables, il ne serait pas étonnant que les locuteurs empruntent, petit à petit, la seule voie demeurée ouverte pour un rapprochement: prononcer comme on écrit, puisqu'il paraît exclu qu'on puisse jamais écrire légitimement comme on prononce. Il est tout à fait logique que cette tendance se manifeste d'abord dans la parole des professionnels du discours public, qui sont aussi des professionnels de l'écrit.

[9] Encrevé's remarks came two years before the modest reforms set out in the 1990 *Rectification de l'Orthographe*, which would be widely condemned by France's elite (see Ball 1997: 191–92). These followed a long line of tepid and largely unsuccessful proposals including those of the Beslais commissions of 1952 and 1965 which, in spite of their 'caractère incontestable de modération' were quietly shelved (see Désirat and Hordé 1976: 220–21).

However, the suggestion that LSE should be seen primarily a response to a gap between writing and speech which for most French speakers has become 'tellement coûteux qu'il ne leur soit plus supportable', is implausible on a number of levels. The suggested alignment between speech and writing is of a piecemeal kind at best, affecting only variable liaison contexts in those cases—generally a minority—where that liaison is actually realised. It is, moreover, a phenomenon largely restricted to *professionnels de la parole publique*, and only used marginally outside this group: Durand et al. (2011: 114) report only 0.35% of liaison forms in the PFC project as being produced without enchaînement; the corresponding figure for the Four Cities project was 1.35%. Moreover, as Encrevé himself observes (1988: 281), near-universal literacy in the wake of the introduction of free compulsory education, which might have been expected to favour spelling pronunciations,[10] did not in fact lead to increased use of variable liaison generally or LSE in particular. Far from being 'la seule solution au problème de l'orthographe à laquelle les linguistes n'aient pas songé' (1988: 284), LSE is more likely a strategy of distinction, employed by privileged users to accentuate rather than reduce the gap between scripted and unscripted speech, and thereby lay claim to the authority associated with the written word.

The popularity of LSE as a rhetorical device grew significantly during the post-war period, as politicians experimented with styles appropriate for regular and frequent interaction with broadcast media. From available data for the period 1928–1958, Encrevé reports an LSE rate of less than 5% of realised variable liaisons, rising to nearly 10% over the next twenty years, and then again to 14% for political speeches between 1978 and 1981 (and most notably 35% for the Presidential debate of 1981: see Laks and Peuvergne 2017: 62–63). But after a peak in 1981 (13.3% for

[10] Encrevé (1988: 281–82) cites the famous first *dictée* scene from Pagnol's *Topaze* (2004 [1928]) in which Topaze stresses implausibly the final consonants ('Des moutonsse…étai-eunnt'), as an example of how spelling pronunciation was inculcated in schools. Concern over over-emphasis on the daily dictation had been expressed by none other than Jules Ferry, in a speech to Directors of *Ecoles Normales* in April 1880: 'A la dictée—à l'abus de la dictée—il faut substituer un enseignement plus libre […]. C'est une bonne chose assurément que d'apprendre l'orthographe (…) mais épargnons ce temps si précieux qu'on dépense trop souvent dans les vétilles de l'orthographe, dans les pièges de la dictée, qui font de cet exercice une manière de tour de force et une espèce de casse-tête chinois' (quoted by Chervel 2006).

Encrevé's corpus, 12.6% for Laks' HPOL1), a sharp fall in LSE use among political figures is observed. The corresponding figure for 1999 is only 6.5%, and for the HPOL2 corpus covering the period 1999–2015 the LSE rate falls again to 3.7% of variable liaisons realised. Laks and Peuvergne describe LSE now as 'purement erratique' with, once again, no clear patterns of correlation emerging from the data with respect to education, party allegiance, or political status. François Hollande and Nicolas Sarkozy (presidents from left and right respectively) do not use the feature at all; nor does the far-right European Parliament member Marine Le Pen; by contrast Mme Le Pen's father Jean-Marie (also an MEP) joins Socialist former Prime Minister Manuel Valls and four others in the group of speakers for whom 10% or more of variable liaisons are realised without enchaînement.

8.5 Newsreaders

While politicians' first imperative is to persuade, newsreaders' overriding professional commitment is maintain credibility: their audience must be able to trust that the news[11] that they are hearing is reliable and (for the most part at least) objective and unbiased. The basis for such trust is an assumption on the viewer's part that the news has been carefully investigated, prepared and presented, which can only be maintained if newsreaders' material is scripted in advance and read aloud or, in the case of, say, political interviews, if the interviewer is well briefed in advance to ask

[11] The dangers to credibility of an inappropriate newsreading style are well illustrated by the experience of the United Kingdom, where authority is associated with the accents of power, and in particular RP (see Hornsby 2019). Citing the example of the wartime broadcaster Wilfred Pickles, Lynda Mugglestone (2003: 270–72) recalls an experiment in which he was asked by the BBC to read the news in the accent of his native Yorkshire, apparently in an attempt to confuse the Nazis. This led to complaints from listeners—not infrequently from Yorkshire themselves—that they could no longer believe the news they were hearing. While broadcasters in recent years have striven for greater inclusivity (estimates put the number of RP speakers at only 3–4% of the UK population), objections to news presenters with marked regional accents continue to be heard. In 2014 a viewer sent the BBC Breakfast presenter Steph McGovern £20 towards 'correction therapy' for her Middlesbrough accent, which the viewer called a 'terrible affliction' (https://www.theguardian.com/media/mediamonkeyblog/2014/nov/25/viewer-offered-bbcs-steph-mcgovern-20-to-correct-her-northern-accent; accessed 24.7.2019).

relevant searching questions on behalf of the viewer. This expectation however conflicts with a countervailing (and no doubt ratings-driven) imperative that the viewer should feel at ease with the newsreader, who should strive to project the persona of relaxed and trusted guest in the living room, rather than merely a distant mouthpiece for words written by others. Just as politicians must strive simultaneously to stand together with and apart from their electorates, so successful newsreaders must signal to their audience that their material is scripted, while at the same time overtly maintaining the illusion that it is not. Resolving this dilemma has been greatly facilitated by the advent of autocue, which enables the newsreader to look directly at the viewer ('Madame, Monsieur, bonsoir. Les titres de ce journal de vingt heures…'), while reading from a prepared text. This relatively new presentation style, labelled 'style faussement parlé' by Encrevé (1988: 262), has been a focus of scholarly attention and found to favour both higher incidence of variable liaison than would typically occur in spontaneous speech, and frequent use of liaisons classified by Delattre and others as 'rares' or 'très rares' (see Pustka et al. 2017). Here again, however, there seems to be tentative evidence of change in progress.

Smith (1998, 1999) compares a sample of newscasters recorded from France-Inter in 1995–1996 with Ågren's findings from the same station, based on recordings made in the early 1960s. While his data do not offer a strictly like-for-like comparison with Ågren's, he reports a significant fall in incidence of variable liaison overall (from 61.6 to 46.8%), and notably in all six of Ågren's categories (see Table 8.2 below).

Pustka et al. (2017) examine Chalier's corpus of data from 60 news journalists drawn in equal numbers from France, Switzerland and Canada. Each informant was recorded in three contexts: guided interview (10 minutes), the PFC reading task (3 minutes), and finally three minutes of newsreading or voice-over, which, as it had generally been prepared for autocue, is described as *écrit oralisé* by the authors. The presenters' behaviour in the two scripted styles was found to differ notably from that observed in the unscripted guided interviews (see Table 8.3 below).

That figures in all three styles are generally higher, for this very particular group of informants, than those observed in the PFC or Four

Table 8.2 Variable liaison in two radio speech corpora (after Armstrong 2001: 197, Table 4)

	Ågren (1960–1961)		Smith (1995–1996)	
Category	(N)	%	(N)	%
être	3858	87.9	1301	78.8
avoir	1140	51.4	411	28.0
semi-auxiliary verbs	851	50.2	407	25.8
pas	965	23.1	379	21.4
polysyllabic adverbs	988	40.3	234	12.8
plural nouns	639	26.6	309	22.0
Totals	8441	61.6	3041	46.8

Table 8.3 News journalists and liaison by speech style (data from Pustka et al. 2017)

Environment	PFC text (%)	Newsreading (%)	Guided interview (%)
Adj + N (sing.)	100	100	90
N (plu) +.	25	9	1
N (plu) + Adj.	37	25	7
est +	100	94	50
Inf *-er*	2	0	1
Adverbs (monosyllabic)	93	72	35
Adverbs (polysyllabic)	8	4	0
Prepositions (monosyllabic)	100	99	99
Prepositions (polysyllabic)	N/A	27%	0

Cities corpora should come as no surprise. Near categorical incidence of liaison in scripted styles was observed after *est*, monosyllabic adverbs and prepositions,[12] and Adjective + Noun sequences, but there are notable differences between scripted and unscripted styles for monosyllabic adverbs and after *est*. A consistent pattern of stratification from the reading exercise, where incidence of liaison is highest, to interview style, where it is lowest,[13] via newsreading style (or *style faussement parlé* in Encrevé's terms) is broken only in the case of post *-er* infinitival

[12] In the PFC reading exercise, the only preposition in a liaison context was *dans*, which was liaised in 30/30 cases.

[13] Hornsby (2019) asks whether *professionnels de la parole publique* are ever truly 'off the record': the question remains open but the evidence of Pustka et al.'s data suggests that there is indeed a significant gap between their scripted and non-scripted performance.

environment, where liaison incidence is marginal in all three styles but slightly higher in the guided interviews than in newsreading style. Here its total absence in autocued news output comes as something of a surprise, given that this liaison, otherwise described as *extrêmement rare* by Laks and Peuvergne, had been seen as typical in this particular style (see Pustka 2016: 170). This would certainly appear to lend further support to the claim that variable liaison among *professionnels de la parole publique* is in decline.[14] But these speakers remain under-researched, and any conclusion that wholesale change is in progress would be premature, particularly as findings in another context, as we shall see in the next section, appear to point in a very different direction.

8.6 Audiobooks

As we saw in Sect. 2.3, acquisition of variable liaison is acquired rather later than non-variable liaison: generally by age 6–8, as literacy skills are developed at school. An intriguing possibility, however, is that audiobooks, disproportionately used within socially advantaged families in France (Pustka 2017a), may expose children from such backgrounds to written styles, and therefore to variable liaison, from an earlier age and before formal literacy training has commenced. Pustka examines use of variable liaison in thirty-two audiobooks aimed at children and read aloud by actors. This corpus of 17 hours and 35 minutes' data yielded 7348 liaison environments, results for which were compared with those of other corpora for four high-frequency categories. Figures for Pustka's corpus are for the most part significantly higher than those observed in the oral corpora of De Jong and Mallet, but comparable in many cases with those of Ågren (1973), based on data recorded some fifty years previously, as illustrated for example by her data for liaison after *être* in Table 8.4 below:

[14] Coutenson (forthcoming 2021) observes a similar pattern among another group of *professionnels de la parole publique*. Her survey of chart-topping French language pop songs between 1956 and 2017 shows a sharp fall in use of variable liaison by francophone artists over this period.

Table 8.4 Liaison after forms of *être* in four corpora (after Pustka 2017a: 201, Tableau 4)

		Ågren	De Jong	Mallet (PFC)	Audiobooks (Pustka 2017a)
Present indicative	*suis*	47	29	13	45
	es	88	0	0	41
	est	97	69	44	86
	c'est	–	–	28	87
	sommes	58	71	44	11
	êtes	71	0	31	75
	sont	86	46	19	69
Imperfect indicative	*étais*	21	5	–	16
	était	75	19	8	73
	c'était	–	–	–	63
	étaient	63	21	11	82

A global variable liaison rate of 73% for *être*, however, masks considerable stylistic variation both within and between texts, which Pustka interprets broadly in terms of Koch and Oesterreicher's (1985) distance-proximity model. Koch and Oesterreicher see proximity in terms of familiarity and closeness between interactants, as reflected in a number of features of informal spoken French (e.g. *ça* for *cela*, *on* for *nous*; *ne* deletion etc.), while distance is marked by features largely restricted to the written language (e.g. use of past historic, interrogative inversions, *l'on* for *on* etc). On the basis of these and similar criteria (see Pustka 2017a: 197–98, Tableau 3), what Pustka calls *contes musicaux*, *contes de fée* and *contes du monde* are essentially written in *français de distance* while *fables modernisées* and *Le Petit Nicolas* in particular are written in what she calls *oral simulé*. It is the latter works which show lowest overall liaison scores for *être*, though there are additionally stylistic differences within each text. In the case of *Le Petit Nicolas* for example liaison after *c'est* in the narrative occurs in 67% of occurrences (16/24 tokens) but in only 25% of occurrences in direct speech between children (1/4), as opposed to 83% for direct speech between adults (5/6). Non-liaison with *est*, *c'était* and *était* likewise is largely confined to *Le Petit Nicolas* or, within the other works, to direct speech. The formula *Il était une fois* was consistently liaised (9/9 occurrences), perhaps unsurprisingly as a fixed expression associated with children's stories, which behaves like a single lexical item. Aggregate data are problematical, as we have seen above, but where like-for-like comparisons are available, we see very high rates of liaison overall in audiobooks, particularly in narrative elements and/or texts which otherwise adopt a literary style rather than attempting to imitate natural speech.

Adverbs similarly showed generally higher rates of liaison than in the other corpora, notably for the most frequently occurring forms *très, bien,* and *pas.* There is some evidence, too, that differences in this genre are qualitative as well as quantitative, that is that different kinds of liaison may be acceptable in audiobooks from those used elsewhere, even by *professionnels de la parole publique.* Pustka notes three surprising occurrences in her children's corpus of liaison after singular nouns, which are treated as *interdite* for pedagogical purposes by Delattre (1966 [1947]), but accepted by the same source in classical theatre (1955: 59): *un instant* [t] *auparavant; l'expert* [t] *en la matière* and *De tout temps* [z], *en tous lieux.* In more recent work, she has focused additionally on audiobooks aimed at adults, and found not only significantly higher rates of realisation than in spontaneous speech, but also a number of liaisons which she qualifies as 'erratiques' such as the above, or after second person indicative present verb forms (*Tu es* [z] *à Paris ?*). The term *erratique* has been borrowed from Encrevé as a non-prescriptive equivalent for Delattre's *interdite,* but far from being irregular and unpatterned as this term would seem to imply, she finds such liaisons to be systematic, and goes so far as to suggest (2017b) that different norms may apply for this emerging genre: 'Ces résultats suggèrent de modifier les règles de liaison au profit d'une classification morphologique plus régulière (même traitement des substantifs au singulier et au pluriel; des verbes à la 2ième et à la 3ième personnne)'.

8.7 Conclusions

Our survey of speech professionals has found noticeably higher incidence, and a wider range of variable liaisons than was observed in studies targeting the general population, and in stark contrast to our findings in Chaps. 6 and 7, we do find some fairly consistent patterns in the data which are in line with sociolinguistic expectations. Most notably, we observed a real time decline in use of some variable liaison forms, which appeared to be confirmed by inter-generational apparent time data where these were available. There was some evidence too in Encrevé's data of something akin to class-based variation in that politicians from more humble origins seemed to use fewer variable liaisons than those from more privileged backgrounds, though this was by no means consistent and there was evidence of interaction between socioeconomic factors and others such as political ideology and age. We found women leading change away from use of variable liaison, and a stronger and more consistent pattern of style shift, favouring greater use of variable liaison in scripted styles, than was observed in either the Four Cities or the PFC data. Finally, Pustka's analysis of audiobook data suggested a correlation between use of variable liaison and what she calls *français de distance*, correlating with a high incidence of written only and/or high status forms, and a low incidence of variable liaison in works which target a more immediate style, and use a high number of *français populaire* forms.

But even these findings have probably raised as many questions as they have answered. Why, for example, do we find a clear pattern of gender-based variation among politicians, but not among the general population? And how are we to explain the higher liaison scores observed among newsreaders in the PFC reading task than those obtained when reading from an autocue? How might these findings inform a general theory of liaison and speech style? We will attempt to address these questions in Chap. 9.

References

Ågren, J. (1973). *Etude sur quelques liaisons facultatives dans le français de conversation radiophonique: Fréquences et facteurs*. Uppsala: Acta Universitatis Upsaliensis.

Armstrong, N. (2001). *Social and Stylistic Variation in Spoken French: A Comparative Approach*. Amsterdam, Netherlands: John Benjamins.

Ball, R. (1997). *The French-Speaking World: An Introduction to Sociolinguistic Issues*. London; New York: Routledge.

Brown, R., & Gilman, A. (1960). The Pronouns of Power and Solidarity. In T. A. Sebeok (Ed.), *Style in Language* (pp. 253–276). Cambridge, MA: MIT Press.

Chervel, A. (2006). *Histoire de l'enseignement du français du XVIIeau XXesiècle.* Paris: Retz.

Coutenson, G. (forthcoming 2021). La liaison dans un corpus de hits francophones (1956–2017). In E. Pustka, A. Dufter, & D. Hornsby (Eds.), L'Oralité mise en scène; *Special Issue of Journal of French Language Studies.*

Delattre, P. (1966 [1947]). La liaison en français, tendances et classifications. InP. Delattre (Ed.), *Studies in French and Comparative Phonetics: Selected Papers in French and English* (pp. 39–48). The Hague: Mouton. First Published in *French Review, 21*(2), 148–157.

Delattre, P. (1966 [1955]). Les facteurs de la liaison facultative en français. In P. Delattre (Ed.), *Studies in French and Comparative Phonetics: Selected Papers in French and English* (pp. 55–62). The Hague: Mouton. First Published in *French Review, 29*(1), 42–49.

Désirat, C., & Hordé, T. (1976). *La Langue française au 20esiècle.* Paris: Bordas.

Durand, J., Laks, B., Calderone, B., & Tchobanov, A. (2011). Que savons-nous de la liaison aujourd'hui? *Langue française, 169*, 103–135.

Encrevé, P. (1983). La Liaison sans enchaînement. *Actes de la Recherche en Sciences Sociales, 46*, 39–66.

Encrevé, P. (1988). *La Liaison avec et sans enchaînement: phonologie tridimensionnelle et usages du français.* Paris: Seuil.

Gadet, F. (2007). *La variation sociale en français* (2nd ed.). Paris: Ophrys.

Giles, H. (1973). Accent Mobility: A Model and Some Data. *Anthropological Linguistics, 15*, 87–105.

Hornsby, D. (2019). Variable Liaison, Diglossia, and the Style Dimension in Spoken French. *French Studies, 73*(4), 578–597.

Koch, P., & Oesterreicher, W. (1985). Sprache der Nähe – Sprache der Distanz. Mündlichkeit und Schriftlichkeit im Spannungsfeld von Sprachtheorie und Sprachgeschichte. *Romanistisches Jahrbuch, 36*, 15–43.

Labov, W. (1966). *The Social Stratification of English in New York City.* Washington, DC: Center for Applied Linguistics.

Labov, W. (2001). *Principles of Linguistic Change, Vol. 2: Social Factors.* Malden, MA: Blackwell Publishers.

Laks, B. (2009). Les hommes politiques et la liaison (1908–1998). In L. Baronian & F. Martineau (Eds.), *Le français d'un continent à l'autre: mélanges offerts à Yves-Charles Morin* (pp. 237–269). Quebec: Presses Universitaires de Laval.

Laks, B., & Peuvergne, C. (2017). La liaison en français contemporain dans la parole publique (1999–2015). *Journal of French Language Studies, 27*(1), 55–72.

Léon, P. (1971). *Essai de phonostylistique*. Paris: Didier.

Mugglestone, L. (2003). *Talking Proper: The Rise of Accent as Social Symbol* (2nd ed.). Oxford: Oxford University Press.

Pagnol, M. (2004 [1928]). *Topaze: pièce en quatre actes*. Paris: De Fallois.

Pustka, E. (2016). *Einführung in die Phonetik und Phonologie des Französischen* (2nd ed.). Berlin: Erich Schmidt Verlag.

Pustka, E. (2017a). L'écrit avant l'écriture: la liaison dans les livres audio pour enfants. *Journal of French Language Studies, 27*, 187–214.

Pustka, E. (2017b). *Liaisons 'interdites': infractions à la norme dans un style de parole hautement contrôlé*. Paper Presented at AFLS Annual Conference, Glendon College of York University, Toronto, August 8–10. Published Abstract.

Pustka, E., Chalier, M., & Jansen, L. (2017). A la recherche d'une norme de prononciation: le modèle des présentateurs de télévision. *Journal of French Language Studies, 27*, 101–115.

Smith, A. (1998). French Variable Liaison: A Proposed Simplification. *Francophonie, 17*, 11–14.

Smith, A. (1999). *Linguistic Change on British and French Public Service Radio*. Unpublished PhD thesis, University of Newcastle-Upon-Tyne.

Part IV

Conclusions and Implications

9

An Inverted Sociolinguistic Phenomenon?

9.1 Interpreting the Findings

We began this book by outlining a model developed by Anthony Kroch, which linked language variation closely to ideology, or the pursuit of social distinction in Bourdieu's sense. Elite groups are seen to distance themselves from lower-status speakers by resisting 'natural' simplifying phonetic changes, and by using forms which require greater effort, or cultural capital to which they have exclusive access. From the sixteenth century onwards, variable liaison has consistently borne out Kroch's predictions, serving as a social marker for a privileged elite able to master its complexities. Resistance to change, as was seen in Part II, initially takes the form of purist opposition to word-final consonant deletion, and more generally a preference among high-status speakers for pronunciations which signal mastery of a complex, Latinate written norm. By the nineteenth century, however, a change in tone is evident: in the context of widening access to education, the currency of literacy becomes devalued, and 'overuse' of liaison starts to draw condemnation from grammarians, who now express nostalgia for the measured and modest usage of the eighteenth-century *homme du monde*.

We saw in Part III that the link between liaison and the written word remains strong in contemporary French, with consistently higher rates observed in scripted than in unscripted styles: overall liaison rates for the PFC were 59% for the former and 43% for the latter; variable liaison

D. Hornsby, *Norm and Ideology in Spoken French*,
https://doi.org/10.1007/978-3-030-49300-4_9

figures for the Four Cities corpus were 33% and 20% respectively. In most other respects, however, liaison proves puzzling from a variationist perspective. For Encrevé liaison is an 'inverted' sociolinguistic phenomenon in that it shows greatest variability in the formal speech of high-status speakers rather than in the relaxed vernacular usage of low-status speakers, as was the case in New York and Norwich. Liaison also fails consistently to display the regular patterns of correlation with key extra-linguistic factors which have been observed in urban surveys over the last fifty years. Findings from studies of liaison and class or gender in Chap. 6 presented a confusing and often contradictory picture, and even for age, for which most apparent time studies have reported lower incidence of liaison among younger speakers, there were outliers which obtained the opposite result.[1]

Findings for intraspeaker variation were no less surprising, and appeared to challenge a tenet of variationist theory. While increased use of liaison was regularly reported in scripted styles, there was no consistent correlation otherwise with formality as measured by Labov's criterion of attention to speech. Labov's department store informants produced more prestige /r/ variants in the 'careful' style of a repetition; the Four Cities informants by contrast were as likely on rereading (see Sect. 7.2.3) to avoid prestige liaison forms as to realise them. Similarly, Durand et al. (2011: 126) report no significant difference between liaison rates observed in the *conversation guidée* and *conversation libre* sections of the PFC interviews. In the Four Cities corpus, a number of liaisons which were made in RS (notably after *beaucoup*, *-er* infinitive forms and plural nouns) were categorically absent or all but absent in unscripted IS, which would appear to make liaison a 'hyper-style' variable, for which variation on the style dimension exceeds that observed on the social dimension. According to Bell (1984: 152–54), hyper-style variables are a theoretical impossibility, because the stylistic range of any individual speaker can only be an imperfect mirror of variation in society.

[1] For Meinschaeffer et al. (2015: 372) in particular, this was a surprising but statistically significant finding, though it remains unclear precisely what 'statistically significant' might actually mean in this context.

9.2 Liaison and 'hyper-style'

The behaviour of variable liaison is by no means the first example of French data failing to fit an established variationist mould, and indeed the failure of quantitative sociolinguistics in its Labovian guise to make a significant impact in France (though not in francophone Canada) is well documented (for discussion see Hornsby and Jones 2013). We saw in Chap. 6 how this particular *exception française* had left more than one researcher struggling to offer *ad hoc* explanations for findings which defy the expectations of the paradigm. Generally, however, the apparently erratic behaviour of liaison from a variationist perspective receives surprisingly little comment in the literature. We would suggest that this silence stems from a failure to address two essentially flawed assumptions.

Firstly, it is noteworthy that Encrevé describes liaison as *un* phénomène *sociolinguistique inversé* (my emphasis), not *une variable*, and we presume his terminological selection is not accidental. There are certainly good reasons why liaison cannot be treated as a conventional sociolinguistic variable like New York (r), in spite of the fact that it meets Chambers' (1995: 17) essential criterion that 'In order for something to be a linguistic variable, it must occur in variant forms'. As we have seen repeatedly, liaison is not one variable, but many, and proves atomised to a quite exceptional degree. Much of the statistical inconsistency and indeterminacy we saw in Part III could be attributed to mixing of data from variable and non-variable liaison contexts, with the result that like was rarely compared strictly with like. But even where variable contexts—however defined—could be isolated, these were found to be subject to very different constraints and probabilities. Breaking down the variable liaison contexts only revealed significant variation in frequencies within individual grammatical categories (see e.g. Table 7.4 above for Adj + N sequences), and even for individual lexical items, as in the case of *pas*. Liaison therefore presents the researcher with a frustrating 'Catch 22': to ensure strict comparability it is necessary to focus on individual constructions, but in doing so the analyst risks obtaining too few data for meaningful conclusions to be drawn.

The second difficulty lies with a core assumption underpinning the audio-monitoring hypothesis in New York and Norwich in particular, namely that scripted styles can be ranged at the formal end of a single style continuum. This assumption, challenged notably by Bell,[2] proves especially problematic for French, where the scripted/unscripted and formal/informal dimensions must be kept separate.

A comparison between liaison and the variably deleted negative particle *ne* is instructive in this regard. As we noted above, Ågren found low levels of liaison after *pas* where *ne* was deleted, and high levels of liaison where it was not. It would be simplistic, however, to conclude that the two variable phenomena operate in tandem: Ashby (1976) finds high *ne* retention in Malécot's (1975a and b) data, but relatively low incidence of variable liaison, leading Armstrong (2001: 190) to conclude that liaison is 'more tied to style than to social class'. A slightly more nuanced position would be that speakers exploit two kinds of variability in different ways. As a binary variable with a standard and non-standard variant to which most speakers will be exposed early in life, variable (ne) behaves similarly to New York (r) and Norwich (ng), for which use of the standard variant increases with social status and formality of style. The more idiosyncratic behaviour of variable liaison, by contrast, reflects its role not as a style marker in Labov's sense, but as resource available to speakers, in particular those possessed of what Bourdieu would term educational or cultural capital, to signal written or prepared discourse through realisation of orthographic consonants in a restricted range of environments.[3]

[2] Bell (1984: 198 fn):

> we cannot a priori assume ad lib speech and reading are on the same dimension. At least in some communities, they appear to be two different types of speech behaviour.

[3] Cf. Armstrong (2001: 195), commenting on a higher than expected incidence of variable liaison from one of his Dieuze informants, SM:

> This tantalising glimpse into the communicative competence of an individual emphasises that variable liaison is part of a supralectal overlay whose mastery seems quite highly dependent on individual competence.

Less advantaged speakers, of course, may not acquire this 'supralectal overlay' at all, or may feel uncomfortable using variable liaison forms, in the manner of Labiche's Caboussat (see Sect. 1.3).

The findings of Chaps. 6 and 7 in particular bear out Gadet's (2007: 84) observation that:

> Le rôle de la liaison dans la parole publique, jusqu'à la liaison sans enchaînement et la liaison consonantique, va aussi dans le sens d'un attachement des Français à la valorisation d'une culture de l'écrit.

For Koch and Oesterreicher (1985), the written-oral dimension in French is best understood in terms of the distance-proximity model outlined in Sect. 8.6, where written language features were seen to mark distance in the timeless fairy tales of children's audiobooks examined by Pustka (2017), while features associated with the spoken language marked proximity and were accordingly more common in modern tales and in dialogue between characters. The distance-proximity model reflects the fact that writing is designed for communication across time and space, while for most of human existence speech has only been available for immediate interpersonal communication. But in the conditions of modern mass communication which make new rhetorical demands of *professionnels de la parole publique*, a distance-proximity model will only get us so far: as we will see below, the particular demands of a speech event may include mixing of spoken and written language elements. To understand how variable liaison is used, therefore, we need first to consider the different ways in which speakers engage with the written word. To this end, we can envisage a new version of Delattre's style typology (Sect. 2.2), updated for the modern media age.

9.3 Liaison and Style in the Twenty-First Century

It will be recalled from Sect. 2.2 that Delattre (1966) offers a four-term style hierarchy, consisting (in descending order of liaison frequency) of *la récitation des vers*, *la conférence*, *la conversation soignée* and *la conversation familière*, but beyond the four potential liaisons of his example sentence (*Des hommes illustres ont attendu*), he offers little guidance as to where the boundaries between styles lie. The implication is that differences between them are not merely quantitative (more liaisons across the board as one ascends the scale), but also qualitative (low-frequency liaison forms are acceptable only in higher placed styles), and that acceptability of different variable liaison categories is cumulative, that is a form acceptable in *conversation soignée* for example is also acceptable in the two higher ranked styles, but not necessarily in the lower ranked *conversation familière*. Delattre, like Labov, places his two scripted styles (*récitation des vers, conférence*) at the formal end of a single style spectrum. An alternative approach for liaison, adopted here, is to view style in terms of positions adopted by the speaker in relation to written discourse, following the example of Encrevé's *style faussement parlé*.

At one end of the spectrum, we would expect incidence of variable liaison to be greatest where the speaker's engagement with the written word is clear and unambiguous: a style we might label ***style lu***. This style would be most natural in poetry recital (Delattre's *récitation des vers*), or in the more contemporary case of audiobooks, but it would also encompass prepared speeches in which the status of the office demands the authority of the written word—a paradigm example being Jacques Chirac's first New Year presidential address on 31st December 1995, in which the variable liaison rate was close to 100% (see Armstrong 2001: 188). Use of highly marked or archaic liaisons in this style (see Sect. 8.6) may additionally evoke a past temporal setting for a classic work of literature, in much the same way as sets or period costumes would in a visual medium.

A different kind of engagement with written discourse is seen in ***style faussement parlé***, in which the scripted nature of the content is disguised, at least nominally, by autocue or similar device. Now an established feature of modern newsreading and political conference speeches, Encrevé saw it in 1988 as as a relatively new style to which *professionnels de la parole publique* were still adapting. The label itself, however, implies a contradiction: *faussement parlé* rather than simply *parlé* suggests either a failed attempt to imitate spoken language or, more likely, an attempt which the speaker does not actually intend to be successful. While aiming to fail may seem perverse, it does neatly resolve for the speaker a tension between two contradictory imperatives. On the one hand, modern mass media project *professionnels de la parole publique* directly into viewers' homes (and even onto their mobile phone screens), and require a style which suggests closeness and empathy with the viewer. On the other, speakers are required to demonstrate authority and perhaps policy expertise in the case of a politician, or veracity and credibility in the case of a newsreader: in both cases a scripted style conveys the appropriate message. Accordingly we find high rates of variable liaison and some highly marked liaison forms even when *professionnels de la parole publique* mask the fact that they are reading aloud. A surprising example of *style faussement parlé* is seen in singer Renaud Séchan's 1986 hit single 'Miss Maggie', cited by Hornsby (2019: 591), which juxtaposes non-standard or vulgar spoken language features and highly marked liaison forms, including two instances of liaison after *-er* infinitives (*pour astiquer* [ʁ] *un revolver*; *pour l'employer* [ʁ] *à tour de bras*), which are 'très rares' for Delattre and 'extrêmement rares' for Laks and Peuvergne (2017). In the absence of any other distance markers in Koch and Oesterreicher's terms, it seems unlikely that this was a conscious clashing of styles for comic effect,[4] but equally unlikely that an artist as stylistically accomplished as Renaud would have been unaware of the associations of highly marked liaisons in a pop music context. These liaisons serve as a gentle reminder to the listener that, for all its earthy vocabulary and sentiments, this remains a carefully crafted piece of art, to be admired for its stylistic dexterity and wit. Pustka et al.'s (2017) findings, like those of Encrevé (1988) and Laks and Peuvergne (2017), suggest overall rates of liaison are higher for *professionnels de la parole publique* in *style lu* than in *style faussement parlé*, and significantly higher again than in unscripted speech events.

'Unscripted' public speech events may not, however, be as spontaneous as they appear (see Laks and Peuvergne 2017: 58). Politicians in particular must strike a balance between projecting the authority which comes with leadership, and at the same time demonstrating an ability to respond quickly to events as they unfold, in the unforgiving context of a twenty-four-hour news cycle which allows little time to prepare a considered response. Where spontaneity trumps authority, for example in

[4] A stylistic clash of this kind is provided by Battye et al. (2000: 307), who cite Alain Schifrès (*Le Nouvel Observateur*, 23–29.1.1990: 76): 'La grammaire fut inventée pour servir l'humanité en général et faire chier les mômes en France'.

televised debates or interviews, and an ability to think on one's feet is required, we would expect, and find, a lower rate of liaison than when the material is unambiguously pre-prepared. Nonetheless, a speaker may exploit the written language associations of a few carefully realised variable liaisons, in order to suggest that he or she is a serious candidate for office, who has taken time to reflect upon the issue in question. In this style, which we might label ***style faussement spontané***, the speaker treads a fine line between judicious use of variable liaison and overuse, the latter having the potential to be politically damaging, either by suggesting an inability to depart from a carefully prepared policy script, or by emphasising the gulf between a candidate and his or her electors, who generally use few variable liaisons. Engagement with the written code, finally, is weakest in what we might term ***style spontané***, which for a *professionnel de la parole publique* in particular may well be rather more formal than *français courant* in Delattre's typology. A style appropriate for discourse which is neither prepared nor scripted would show lowest incidence of variable liaison and befit speech events in which neither the speaker's authority nor his or her professional expertise are at issue. Hornsby (2019: 595) offers as possible examples a news journalist talking at home about his or her family, or a politician expressing support for the constituency football team during a good run in the Coupe de France, but it is legitimate to wonder whether *professionnels de la parole publique* are ever truly 'off the record'.

We leave open the question raised above of whether differences between styles are qualitative, quantitative, or both. Encrevé appears to see them as purely quantitative, a position which finds some support in Laks and Peuvergne's data, but Pustka's (2017) findings certainly raise the possibility of qualitative differences between styles, at least between *style lu* and *style faussement parlé*. The relationship between the two middle styles is probably the least well understood, as the difference between them—the one scripted, but superficially disguised; the other superficially spontaneous but with some prepared if not actually scripted elements—is quite a subtle one. We might suggest that liaisons of the kind isolated by Pustka in classic audiobooks—for example after *tu es* or following singular nouns—would be out of place in any style but *style lu*, and that liaison with /r/ after *-er* infinitive forms would be expected—at least until recently—in *style faussement parlé* but not in *style faussement spontané*. But as Pustka herself points out the current dearth of liaison studies involving *professionnels de la parole publique* makes any conclusions in this area tentative.

9.4 The Future of Liaison

The role of liaison as a subtle marker of scripted speech derives from the peculiar conditions under which French was codified. As we saw in Chap. 4, these notably included fetishisation of the written code and exaggerated reverence for its Latin forbear in the seventeenth century, since when a phalanx of conservative normative institutions, most notably the Académie Française, have dedicated themselves to the preservation in writing of forms which are moribund in spoken French. This raises the question of whether variable liaison itself may in time go the way of the imperfect subjunctive, the past anterior, or first-person interrogative inversion (*donné-je?*) in being lost altogether from the spoken language. This is an area in which it is dangerous to make predictions: the demise of liaison, like that of the negative particle *ne*, has been prematurely forecast in the past (see e.g. Langlard 1928; Ashby 1981). But evidence from *professionnels de la parole publique* suggests that while overall incidence of liaison (variable and non-variable environments combined) has remained fairly stable over the last century, the last two decades have seen a significant fall in use of liaison in variable environments. A number of apparent time studies of *non-professionnels de la parole publique*, moreover, seem to point in a similar direction, though as with *ne* the possibility of age-grading cannot entirely be ruled out. Armstrong refers to the historical 'ebb and flow' of liaison (2001: 206) and it is too early to state with confidence whether or not these findings are indicative of a long-term trend. But if, as we have good reason to suspect, skilled speakers use variable liaison to invoke the authority of the written language, then any change in society's relationship with writing will inevitably have important consequences for liaison. The rapid evolution of the contemporary media landscape, in particular, would certainly appear to be challenging the traditional status of the written word in francophone societies.

One important consequence of technological change is that writing has long since lost its monopoly of communication across time and distance. Facetime, video-conferencing, video-messaging and voicemail, all relatively recent developments which have become commonplace, provide readily accessible channels of oral communication with an interlocutor who is not physically present. Writing, moreover, is now a medium of immediate interpersonal communication rather than one reserved for more considered, delayed interaction: email, Twitter, and particularly SMS texting all favour a proximate style of communication incorporating features which mimic the spoken language (*fingierte Mündlichkeit* in Koch and Oesterreicher's terms) rather than those of formal writing: few texters check their preceding direct object agreements before pressing the 'send' button. The new media landscape favours a more 'democratic' and less top-down communication, in which authority is questioned rather than passively deferred to. Expert reporting from trained journalists competes with (and is sometimes informed by) immediate popular reaction to events on Twitter, or from mobile phone uploads to YouTube and other platforms, while a New Year's Eve presidential address, in a multi-channel, Netflix age can no longer command the undivided attention of the nation. The twenty-four-hour news cycle in a multi-media world favours the immediate ('breaking news') over the authoritative: being first to lead with a story is often more important than checking its veracity. In the age of the sound bite, the TWIT,[5] and the presidential tweet, it is only to be expected that, in Laks and Peuvergne's (2017: 67) words 'pour ce qui concerne la liaison au moins, la distinction stylistique et le style oratoire du grand discours régressent massivement'. If, as is likely, the authority ascribed to the written language has been weakened, the symbolic value of variable liaison may well have peaked as, it appears, did the rhetorical power of *liaison sans enchaînement* in the late 1970s and early

[5]TWIT: 'Three-Word Inspirational Treatise', by which a candidate, movement or party attempts to sum up its values or philosophy, e.g. 'Yes we can!', 'Britain deserves better', or more recently 'Take Back Control' and 'Get Brexit Done'. At the time of writing there was no accepted French translation for this Anglo-Saxon political marketing concept, but the power of a three- (or four-) word slogan has not been lost on candidates for high office in the francophone world: cf. 'La France Présidente'; 'Au nom du peuple !' 'Place au peuple', 'La France forte'.

1980s, when politicians in particular were still experimenting with styles for a burgeoning but still relatively uncomplicated audiovisual world.

In Morrison's (1968: 208) summary of a century and a half of scholarship, one senses something akin to a note of despair: 'Perhaps the principal accomplishment of the 200 studies of liaison made in the last 150 years has been the discovery of the true complexity of the problem'. Five decades later, the availability of searchable speech corpora in particular has broadened our knowledge considerably, but many questions remain unanswered. The advent of new media in particular is blurring the traditional boundaries between spoken and written language, and to understand the consequences of this for liaison, a much larger corpus of data from different types of *professionnel de la parole publique*, in a range of styles, is needed to complement that available for the wider francophone public via the PFC project. While we cannot predict the future with any certainty, we can be sure that this most enigmatic of linguistic phenomena will continue to excite, inspire and frustrate linguists in equal measure for some time to come.

References

Armstrong, N. (2001). *Social and Stylistic Variation in Spoken French: A Comparative Approach*. Amsterdam, Netherlands: John Benjamins.

Ashby, W. J. (1976). The Loss of the Negative Morpheme *Ne* in Parisian French. *Lingua, 39*, 119–137.

Ashby, W. J. (1981). French Liaison as a Sociolinguistic Phenomenon. In W. W. Cressey & D. J. Napoli (Eds.), *Linguistic Symposium on Romance Languages 9* (pp. 46–57). Washington, DC: Georgetown University Press.

Battye, A., Rowlett, P., & Hintze, M.-A. (2000). *The French Language Today: A Linguistic Introduction* (2nd ed.). London: Routledge.

Bell, A. (1984). Language Style as Audience Design. *Language in Society, 13*(2), 145–204.

Chambers, J. (1995). *Sociolinguistic Theory*. Oxford: Blackwell.

Delattre, P. (1966 [1947]). La liaison en français, tendances et classifications. In P. Delattre (Ed.), *Studies in French and Comparative Phonetics: Selected Papers in French and English* (pp. 39–48). The Hague: Mouton. First Published in *French Review, 21*(2), 148–157.

Durand, J., Laks, B., Calderone, B., & Tchobanov, A. (2011). Que savons-nous de la liaison aujourd'hui? *Langue française, 169*, 103–135.

Gadet, F. (2007). *La variation sociale en français* (2nd ed.). Paris: Ophrys.

Hornsby, D. (2019). Variable Liaison, Diglossia, and the Style Dimension in Spoken French. *French Studies, 73*(4), 578–597.

Hornsby, D., & Jones, M. (2013). *Exception française*? Levelling, Exclusion and Urban Social Structure in France. In M. Jones & D. C. Hornsby (Eds.), *Language and Social Structure in Urban France* (pp. 94–109). Oxford: Legenda.

Koch, P., & Oesterreicher, W. (1985). Sprache der Nähe – Sprache der Distanz. Mündlichkeit und Schriftlichkeit im Spannungsfeld von Sprachtheorie und Sprachgeschichte. *Romanistisches Jahrbuch, 36*, 15–43.

Laks, B., & Peuvergne, C. (2017). La liaison en français contemporain dans la parole publique (1999–2015). *Journal of French Language Studies, 27*(1), 55–72.

Langlard, H. (1928). *La Liaison dans le français*. Paris: Champion.

Malécot, A. (1975a). The Glottal Stop in French. *Phonetica, 29*, 51–63.

Malécot, A. (1975b). French Liaison as a Function of Grammatical, Phonetic and Paralinguistic Variables. *Phonetica, 32*, 161–179.

Meinschaeffer, J., Bonifer, S., & Frisch, C. (2015). Variable and Invariable Liaison in a Corpus of Spoken French. *Journal of French Language Studies, 25*, 367–396.

Morrison, A. S. (1968). *A Critical Bibliography of Studies of Liaison in French Speech Since 1800*. Unpublished PhD thesis, Columbia University.

Pustka, E. (2017). *Liaisons 'interdites': infractions à la norme dans un style de parole hautement contrôlé*. Paper Presented at AFLS Annual Conference, Glendon College of York University, Toronto, August 8–10. Published Abstract.

Pustka, E., Chalier, M., & Jansen, L. (2017). A la recherche d'une norme de prononciation: le modèle des présentateurs de télévision. *Journal of French Language Studies, 27*, 101–115.

References

Académie Française. (1935). *Dictionnaire de l'Académie Française de 1932–35* (8th ed.). Paris: Firmin Didot.

Ackernecht, J. (1895). Die binding in franzöischen unterricht. *Die Neueren Sprachen, III*, 393–408.

Ågren, J. (1973). *Etude sur quelques liaisons facultatives dans le français de conversation radiophonique: Fréquences et facteurs*. Uppsala: Acta Universitatis Upsaliensis.

Alemand, L. (1968 [1688]). *Nouvelles observations ou guerre civile des Français sur la langue*. Geneva: Slatkine Reprints.

van Ameringen, A. (1977). *La liaison en français de Montréal*. Unpublished Masters dissertation, Université du Québec à Montréal, Montreal.

van Ameringen, A., & Cedergren, H. (1981). Observations sur la liaison en français de Montréal. In D. Sankoff & H. Cedergren (Eds.), *Variation Omnibus* (pp. 141–149). Edmonton, Alberta: Linguistic Research.

Andersen, H. (1988). Center and Periphery: Adoption, Diffusion, and Spread. In J. Fisiak (Ed.), *Historical Dialectology: Regional and Social* (pp. 39–84). Berlin: Mouton de Gruyter.

Anderson, R. (1982). New Light on French Secondary Education in the Nineteenth Century. *Social History, 7*(2), 147–165.

D. Hornsby, *Norm and Ideology in Spoken French*,
https://doi.org/10.1007/978-3-030-49300-4

Anderwald, L. (2011). Are Non-Standard Dialects More 'Natural' Than the Standard? A Test Case from English Verb Morphology. *Journal of Linguistics, 47*, 251–274.

Anonymous. (1624). *Eclogue præcipuarum legum gallicæ pronunciationis*. Mons.

Anonymous. (1669). *La veritable orthographe françoise opposée à l'orthographe imaginaire du sieur Lesclache*. Paris: Jacques Bottin.

Anonymous. (1696). *Dissertation sur la prononciation de la langue française*. The Hague: Van Dole.

Armstrong, L. (1932). *The Phonetics of French: A Practical Handbook*. London: Bell.

Armstrong, N. (2001). *Social and Stylistic Variation in Spoken French: A Comparative Approach*. Amsterdam, Netherlands: John Benjamins.

Armstrong, N., & Mackenzie, I. (2012). *Standardization, Ideology and Linguistics*. Basingstoke: Palgrave Macmillan.

Ashby, W. J. (1975). The Rhythmic Group, Liaison, Nouns and Verbs of French. *Studia Linguistica, 29*, 110–116.

Ashby, W. J. (1976). The Loss of the Negative Morpheme *Ne* in Parisian French. *Lingua, 39*, 119–137.

Ashby, W. J. (1981a). The Loss of the Negative Particle *Ne* in French: A Syntactic Change in Progress. *Language, 57*, 674–687.

Ashby, W. J. (1981b). French Liaison as a Sociolinguistic Phenomenon. In W. W. Cressey & D. J. Napoli (Eds.), *Linguistic Symposium on Romance Languages 9* (pp. 46–57). Washington, DC: Georgetown University Press.

Ayres-Bennett, W. (1994). Elaboration and Codification: The French Language. In W. Davies, M. Mair Perry, & R. Temple (Eds.), *The Changing Voices of Europe: Social and Political Change and Their Linguistic Repercussions, Past, Present and Future: Papers in Honour of Professor Glanville Price* (pp. 53–73). Cardiff: University of Wales Press.

Ayres-Bennett, W. (1996). *A History of the French Language Through Texts*. London: Routledge.

Ayres-Bennett, W. (2004). *Sociolinguistic Variation in Seventeenth-Century French: Methodology and Case Studies*. Cambridge: Cambridge University Press.

Baddeley, S. (1993). *L'Orthographe française au temps de la réforme*. Geneva: Droz.

Ball, R. (1997). *The French-Speaking World: An Introduction to Sociolinguistic Issues*. London; New York: Routledge.

Bally, C. (1932). *Linguistique générale et linguistique française* (4th ed.). Bern: Francke.

Barclay, A. (1521). *Here Begynneth the Introductory to Write and to Pronounce Frenche*. London: Coplande.

Barreca, G. (2015). *L'acquisition de la liaison chez des apprenants italophones. Des atouts d'un corpus de natifs pour l'étude de la liaison en français langue étrangère (FLE)*. Unpublished doctoral dissertation, Université Paris Ouest Nanterre La Défense/Università Cattolica del Sacro Cuore di Milano.

Bascan, L. (1912). *Manuel pratique de prononciation et de lecture française*. Rambouillet: Institut de Phonétique Française.

Battye, A., Rowlett, P., & Hintze, M.-A. (2000). *The French Language Today: A Linguistic Introduction* (2nd ed.). London: Routledge.

Bauche, H. (1920). *Le langage populaire: Grammaire, syntaxe et dictionnaire du français tel qu'on le parle dans le peuple de Paris*. Paris: Payot.

Bell, A. (1984). Language Style as Audience Design. *Language in Society, 13*(2), 145–204.

Bell, A. (2001). Back in Style: Reworking Audience Design. In P. Eckert & J. R. Rickford (Eds.), *Style and Sociolinguistic Variation* (pp. 139–169). New York: Cambridge University Press.

Beyer, F. (1888). *Französische Phonetik für Lehrer und Studierende. 3. Auflage in Auftrage des Verfassers neu bearbeitet von H. Klinghardt*. Cöthen: Schulze.

Beyer, F., & Passy, P. (1893). *Elementarbuch des gesprochenen Französisch*. Cöthen: Schulze.

de Bèze, T. (1584). *De francicæ linguæ recta pronuntiatione*. Geneva: Vignon.

Blainey, D. (2013). *First to Come, Last to Go: Phonological Change and Resilience in Louisiana Regional French*. Unpublished doctoral thesis, Tulane University.

Blanc, M., & Biggs, P. (1971). L'enquête socio-linguistique sur le français parlé à Orléans. *Le Français dans le monde, 85*, 16–25.

Blanche-Benveniste, C., & Jeanjean, C. (1987). *Le français parlé: transcription et édition*. Paris: Didier.

Block, J. (1892). Zur Aussprache des Französischen. *Zeitschrift für französische Sprache und Litteratur, XIV*, 236–265.

Bloomfield, L. (1964 [1927]). Literate and Illiterate Speech. *American Speech, 2*(10), 432–439. Reprinted in D. Hymes (Ed.), *Language in Culture and Society* (pp. 391–396). New York: Harper and Row.

Boersma, P., & Weenink, D. (2016). Praat: Doing Phonetics by Computer. Retrieved from http://www.fon.hum.uva.nl/praat/ [Computer Program. Version 6.0.10].

Bollack, L. (1903). La Langue française en l'an 2003. *La Revue, 15 July*, 5–24.

Bonnard, G. (1927). *Manuel de phonétique française*. Lausanne: Payot.

Bordal, G. (2012). A Phonological Study of French Spoken by Multilingual Speakers from Bangui, the Capital of the Central African Republic. In R. Gess, C. Lyche, & T. Meisenburg (Eds.), *Phonological Variation in French: Illustrations from Three Continents* (pp. 23–44). Amsterdam; Philadelphia: John Benjamins.

Bordal, G., & Lyche, C. (2008). La liaison en terre africaine. In *Colloque international 'Phonologie du français contemporain: variation, interfaces, cognition' (11–13 décembre 2008)*. Paris: MSH.

Bourciez, E., & Bourciez, J. (1967). *Phonetique Française: étude historique*. Paris: Klincksieck.

Bourdieu, P. (1979). *La Distinction*. Paris: Minuit.

Bourdieu, P. (1982). *Ce que parler veut dire: L'Economie des échanges linguistiques*. Paris: Fayard.

Boutin, B. A. (2014). Liaisons en français et terrains africains. In J. Durand, G. Kristoffersen, & B. Laks, avec la collaboration de J. Peuvergne (Eds.), *La phonologie du français: normes, périphéries, modélisation* (pp. 153–172). Nanterre: Presses Universitaires de Paris Ouest.

Boutin, B. A., & Lyche, C. (2014). Ce que nous apprenent des locuteurs francophones non-lecteurs sur la liaison. In C. Soum-Favaro, A. Coquillon, & J.-P. Chevrot (Eds.), *La liaison: approches contemporaines* (pp. 283–310). Bern: Peter Lang.

Boutin, B. A., & Turcsan, G. (2009). La prononciation du français en Afrique: la Côte d'Ivoire. In J. Durand, B. Laks, & C. Lyche (Eds.), *Phonologie, variation et accents du français* (pp. 131–152). Paris, France: Hermès.

Boutin, B. A., Gess, R., & Guèye, G. M. (2012). French in Senegal After Three Centuries: A Phonological Study of Wolof Speakers' French. In R. Gess, C. Lyche, & T. Meisenburg (Eds.), *Phonological Variation in French: Illustrations from Three Continents* (pp. 45–71). Amsterdam; Philadelphia: John Benjamins.

Bovelles, C. de (1973 [1533]). *Liber de differentia vulgarium linguarum et Gallici sermonis varietate* (C. Demaizière, Trans.). Paris: Klincsieck.

Britain, D., & Fox, S. (2008). Vernacular Universals and the Regularisation of Hiatus Resolution. *Essex Research Reports in Linguistics, 57*(3).

Brown, R., & Gilman, A. (1960). The Pronouns of Power and Solidarity. In T. A. Sebeok (Ed.), *Style in Language* (pp. 253–276). Cambridge, MA: MIT Press.

Brown, K., & Miller, J. (2013). *The Cambridge Dictionary of Linguistics*. Cambridge: Cambridge University Press.

Brun, A. (1931). *Le français de Marseille: Étude de parler régional.* Marseille: Institut historique de Provence.

Bruneau, C. (1927). *Manuel de phonétique pratique.* Paris: Berger-Levrault.

Brunot, F. (1907). La Langue du Palais et la formation du « bel usage ». In *Mélanges Chabaneau, 1973* (pp. 677–685). Erlangen: Slatkine Reprints.

Brunot, F. (1966). *Histoire de la langue française: des origines à 1900* (13 Vols.). Paris: Colin.

Buben, V. (1935). *Influence de l'orthographe sur la prononciation du français moderne.* Bratislava: Faculty of Humanities, University of Bratislava.

Bybee, J. (2005). La liaison: effets de fréquence et constructions. *Langages, 158*, 24–37.

Carton, F. (1995). La Prononciation du Français. In G. Antoine & R. Martin (Eds.), *Histoire de la Langue Française 1914–1945* (pp. 27–59). Paris: CNRS-Éditions.

Carton, F. (2000). La prononciation. In G. Antoine & B. Cerquiglini (Eds.), *Histoire de la langue française 1945–2000* (pp. 25–60). Paris: CNRS Editions.

Catach, N. (1997). Orthographe de la Renaissance: Perspectives d'ensemble. *L'information grammaticale, 74*, 34–38.

Catach, N. (1998). *L'Orthographe (Que sais-je?).* Paris: Presses Universitaires de France.

Chambers, J. (1995). *Sociolinguistic Theory.* Oxford: Blackwell.

Chambers, J. (2000). Universal Sources of the Vernacular. In U. Ammon, K. Mattheier, & P. Nelde (Eds.), *The Future of European Sociolinguistics* (Special Issue of *Sociolinguistica: International Yearbook of European Sociolinguistics* 14) (pp. 11–15). Tübingen: Niemeyer.

Chambers, J. (2004). Dynamic Typology and Vernacular Universals. In B. Kortmann (Ed.), *Dialectology Meets Typology* (pp. 127–145). Berlin; New York: Mouton de Gruyter.

Chervel, A. (2006). *Histoire de l'enseignement du français du XVIIe au XXe siècle.* Paris: Retz.

Cheshire, J. (1982). *Variation in an English Dialect: A Sociolinguistic Study.* Cambridge: Cambridge University Press.

Chevrot, J.-P., & Malderez, I. (1999). L'effet Buben de la linguistique diachronique à l'approche cognitive (et retour). *Langue Française, 124*, 104–125.

Chevrot, J.-P., Dugua, C., & Fayol, M. (2005). Liaison et formation des mots en français: un scénario développemental. *Langages, 158*, 38–52.

Chevrot, J.-P., Chabanal, D., & Dugua, C. (2007). Pour un modèle de l'acquisition des liaisons basé sur l'usage: trois études de cas. *Journal of French Language Studies, 17*, 103–128.

Chifflet, L. (1659). *Essai d'une parfaite grammaire de la langue française*. Brussels: Lambert Marchand.

Christen, A. (1893). *Vade-Mecum of French Pronunciation*. London: Hachette.

Cichocki, W. (2012). An Overview of the Phonetics and Phonology of Acadian French Spoken in Northeastern New Brunswick (Canada). In R. Gess, C. Lyche, & T. Meisenburg (Eds.), *Phonological Variation in French: Illustrations from Three Continents* (pp. 211–234). Amsterdam; Philadelphia: John Benjamins.

Clédat, L. (1917). *Manuel de phonétique et de morphologie historique du français*. Paris: Hachette.

Cohen, M. (1947). *Histoire d'une langue: le français*. Paris: Editions Hier et Aujourd'hui.

Coquillon, A., Durand, J., Lyche, C., & Eychenne, J. (2010). French Liaison: From Global Results to Local Varieties. In *Colloque International PHONLEX*. Université de Toulouse II–Le Mirail (8–10 septembre 2010).

Côté, M.-H. (2005). Le statut lexical des consonnes de liaison. *Langages, 158*, 66–78.

Côté, M.-H. (2012). Laurentian French (Québec): Extra Vowels, Missing Schwas and Surprising Liaison Consonants. In R. Gess, C. Lyche, & T. Meisenburg (Eds.), *Phonological Variation in French: Illustrations from Three Continents* (pp. 235–274). Amsterdam: John Benjamins.

Côté, M.-H. (2017). La liaison en diatopie: esquisse d'une typologie. *Journal of French Language Studies, 27*, 13–25.

Coupland, N. (1980). Style Shifting in a Cardiff Work Setting. *Language in Society, 9*, 1–12.

Coutenson, G. (forthcoming 2021). La liaison dans un corpus de hits francophones (1956–2017). In E. Pustka, A. Dufter, & D. Hornsby (Eds.), L'Oralité mise en scène; *Special Issue of Journal of French Language Studies*.

Coveney, A. (2002). *Variability in Spoken French: A Sociolinguistic Study of Interrogation and Negation*. Bristol: Elm Bank Publications.

Coveney, A. (2011). A Language Divided Against Itself? Diglossia, Code-Switching and Variation in French. In F. Martineau & T. Nadasdi (Eds.), *Le français en contact: Hommages à Raymond Mougeon* (pp. 51–85). Québec: Presses de l'Université Laval.

D'Aisy, F. (1674). *Nouvelle méthode de la langue française*. Paris.

D'Olivet, P.-J. (1736). *Traité de la prosodie françoise*. Paris: Gandouin.

Damourette, J., & Pichon, E. (1911–1927). *Des mots à la pensée. Essai de grammaire de la langue française*. Paris: D'Artrey.

Damourette, J., & Pichon, E. (1936). Questions de liaisons. *Le Français Moderne, IV*, 347–353.

Dangeau. (1694). *Premiere lettre d'un academicien à un autre sur le sujet des voyelles*. Paris: Coignard.

Dante Aligheri. (1996 [1305]). *De volgari eloquentia* (S. Botterill, Ed.). Cambridge: Cambridge University Press.

Darmesteter, A. (1910). *Cours de Grammaire historique de la langue française* (2 Vols.). Paris: Delagrave.

Dauzat, A. (1930). *Histoire de la langue française*. Paris: Payot.

De Jong, D. (1988). *Sociolinguistic Aspects of French Liaison*. Unpublished PhD thesis, University of Amsterdam.

De Jong, D. (1993). Sociolinguistic Aspects of Montreal French Liaison. In W. Ashby, W. Mithun, G. Perisonotto, & E. Raposo (Eds.), *Linguistic Perspectives on the Romance Languages* (pp. 127–138). Amsterdam: Benjamins.

De Jong, D. (1994). La sociophonologie de la liaison orléanaise. In C. Lyche (Ed.), *French Generative Phonology: Retrospective and Perspectives* (pp. 95–130). Salford: European Studies Research Institute.

De la Faye, A. (1613). *Institutiones linguæ gallicaæ oder Gründliche Unterweising der frantzösischen Sprachen*. Jehna: Beithmann.

Delamothe, G. (1592). *The French Alphabet Teaching in a Very Short Time by a Most Easie Way to Pronounce French Naturally, to Read It Perfectly, to Write It Truly and to Speak It Accordingly*. London: Jillier.

Delattre, P. (1966a [1947]). La liaison en français, tendances et classifications. In P. Delattre (Ed.), *Studies in French and Comparative Phonetics: Selected Papers in French and English* (pp. 39–48). The Hague: Mouton. First Published in *French Review, 21*(2), 148–157.

Delattre, P. (1966b [1955]). Les facteurs de la liaison facultative en français. In P. Delattre (Ed.), *Studies in French and Comparative Phonetics: Selected Papers in French and English* (pp. 55–62). The Hague: Mouton. First Published in *French Review, 29*(1), 42–49.

Delattre, P. (1966c [1956]). La fréquence des liaisons facultatives en français. In P. Delattre (Ed.), *Studies in French and Comparative Phonetics: Selected Papers in French and English* (pp. 49–54). The Hague: Mouton. First Published in *French Review, 30*(1), 48–54.

Dell, F. (1973). *Les règles et les sons: introduction à la phonologie générative*. Paris: Hermann.

DEPP. (2015). *Filles et garçons sur le chemin de l'égalité de l'école à l'enseignement supérieur*. Paris: Ministry of National Education, Division for Evaluation, Forecasting and Performance.

Désirat, C., & Hordé, T. (1976). *La Langue française au 20ᵉ siècle*. Paris: Bordas.

Detey, S., Lyche, C., Racine, I., Schwab, S., & Le Gac, D. (2016). The Notion of Norm in Spoken French: Production and Perception. In S. Detey, J. Durand, B. Laks, & C. Lyche (Eds.), *Varieties of Spoken French*. Oxford: Oxford University Press.

Domergue, U. (1805). *Manuel des étrangers amateurs de la langue française*. Paris: Pillet Ainé.

Drosai, J. (1544). *Grammaticae quadrilinguis partitiones*. Paris: Perler.

Du Bellay, J. (1549). *Defense et illustration de la langue françoise*. Paris: Arnoul l'Angelier.

Du Val, J.-B. (1973 [1604]). *L'Eschole françoyse: pour apprendre à bien parler et escrire selon l'usage de ce temps et pratique des bons auteurs*. Geneva: Slatkine Reprints.

Dubois, J. [J. Sylvius]. (1531). *In Linguam gallicam isagoge, una cum eiusdem grammatica Latino-Gallica*. Paris: R. Estienne.

Dubois, C. G. (1970). *Mythe et langage qu XVIᵉ siècle*. Paris: Ducros.

Dubroca, L. (1824). *Traité de la prononciation des consonnes et des voyelles finales des mots français dans leur rapport avec les consonnes et les voyelles initiales des mots suivants*. Paris: Author.

Duez, N. (1973 [1639]). *Le vray guidon de la langue françoise*. Leiden: Elsevier. (Geneva: Slatkine Reprints).

Duhamel, G. (1944). *Civilisation Française*. Paris: Hachette.

Dumville, B. (1904). *Elements of French Pronunciation and Diction*. London: Dent.

Dupuis, S. (1836). *Traité de prononciation, ou nouvelle prosodie française*. Paris: Hachette.

Durand, J., & Lyche, C. (2003). Le projet « Phonologie du français contemporain » (PFC) et sa méthodologie. In E. Delais & J. Durand (Eds.), *Corpus et variation en phonologie du français: méthodes et analyses* (pp. 212–276). Toulouse: Presses Universitaires du Mirail.

Durand, J., & Lyche, C. (2008). French Liaison in the Light of Corpus Data. *Journal of French Language Studies, 18*, 33–66.

Durand, J., Laks, B., & Lyche, C. (2009). Le projet PFC (Phonologie du Français Contemporain): une source de données primaires structurées. In J. Durand, B. Laks, & C. Lyche (Eds.), *Phonologie, variation et accents du français* (pp. 19–61). Paris: Hermès.

Durand, J., Laks, B., Calderone, B., & Tchobanov, A. (2011). Que savons-nous de la liaison aujourd'hui? *Langue française, 169*, 103–135.

Encrevé, P. (1983). La Liaison sans enchaînement. *Actes de la Recherche en Sciences Sociales, 46*, 39–66.

Encrevé, P. (1988). *La Liaison avec et sans enchaînement: phonologie tridimensionnelle et usages du français*. Paris: Seuil.

Erasmus, D. (1528). *De recta latini græcique sermonis pronuntiatone*. Basel: Froben.

Estienne, R. (1549). *Dictionnaire François-latin, contenant les motz et manieres de parler Français, tournez en Latin*. Paris: R. Etienne.

Estienne, H. (1565). *Traité de conformité du langage françois avec le grec*. Paris: Delalain.

Estienne, H. (1578a). *Deux Dialogues du nouveau langage françois*. Paris: Mamert Patisson.

Estienne, H. (1578b). *La Précellence du langage françois*. Paris: Mamert Patisson.

Étiemble, R. (1964). *Parlez-vous franglais?* Paris: Gallimard.

Ewert, A. (1966). *The French Language* (2nd ed.). London: Faber & Faber.

Eychenne, J. (2009). Une variété de français conservatrice en Languedoc. In J. Durand, B. Laks, & C. Lyche (Eds.), *Phonologie, variation et accents du français* (pp. 265–290). Paris: Hermès.

Eychenne, J., & Paternostro, R. (2016). Analyzing Transcribed Speech with Dolmen. In S. Detey, J. Durand, B. Laks, & C. Lyche (Eds.), *Varieties of Spoken French: A Source Book* (pp. D35–D52). Oxford: Oxford University Press.

Eychenne, J., & Walker, D. (2010). Le français en Amérique du Nord: éléments de synthèse. In S. Detey, J. Durand, B. Laks, & C. Lyche (Eds.), *Les variétés du français parlé dans l'espace francophone: Ressources pour l'enseignement* (pp. 249–264). Paris: Ophrys.

Eychenne, J., Lyche, C., Durand, J., & Coquillon, A. (2014). Quelles données pour la liaison en français: la question des corpus. In C. Soum-Favaro, A. Coquillon, & J.-P. Chevrot (Eds.), *La liaison: approches contemporaines*. Bern: Peter Lang.

Fagyal, Z., Kibbee, D., & Jenkins, F. (2006). *French: A Linguistic Introduction*. Cambridge: Cambridge University Press.

Fénelon, F. (1934 [1714]). *Lettre à l'Académie*. Paris: Classiques Larousse.

Ferguson, C. (1959). Diglossia. *Word, 15*, 324–340.

Feugère, L. (1849). *Œuvres choisies d'Etienne Pasquier accompagnées de notes et d'une étude sur sa vie et sur ses ouvrages*. Paris: Firmin Didot.

Fischer, J. (1964 [1958]). Social Influences on the Choice of a Linguistic Variant. *Word, 14*, 47–56. Reprinted in D. Hymes (Ed.), *Language in Culture and Society* (pp. 483–489). New York: Harper and Row.

Fouché, P. (1934). L'Évolution phonétique du français du XVIe siècle à nos jours. *Le Français Moderne, II*, 217–236.
Fouché, P. (1936). Les diverses sortes de français au point de vue phonétique. *Le Français Moderne, IV*, 199–216.
Fouché, P. (1952). *Phonétique historique du français*. Paris: Klincksieck.
Fouché, P. (1959). *Traité de prononciation française* (2nd ed.). Paris: Klincksieck.
Frei, H. (1993 [1929]). *La Grammaire des Fautes*. Geneva, Paris: Slatkine Reprints.
Gaatone, D. (1979). Liaison et structure syllabique en français. *Français Moderne, 47*(4), 312–334.
Gadet, F. (1992). *Le Français populaire (Que sais-je?)*. Paris: Presses Universitaires de France.
Gadet, F. (2007). *La variation sociale en français* (2nd ed.). Paris: Ophrys.
Garnier, P. (1607). *Præcepta gallici sermonis ad pleniorem perfectioremque eius linguæ cognitionem necessaria tum breussima, tum facillima*. Bacot.
Gauchat, L. (1905). L'unité phonétique dans le patois d'une commune. In *Aus Romanischen Sprachen und Literaturen: Festschrift H. Mort* (pp. 175–232). Halle: Max Niemeyer.
Genévrier, P. (1927). *Précis de phonétique comparée française et anglaise et manuel de prononciation française à l'usage des étudiants anglo-saxons*. Paris: Didier.
Génin, F. (1845). *Des variations du langage français depuis le XIIe siècle, ou recherche des principes qui devraient régler l'orthographe et la prononciation*. Paris: Didot.
Giles, H. (1973). Accent Mobility: A Model and Some Data. *Anthropological Linguistics, 15*, 87–105.
Girault-Duvivier, C. P. (1811). *Grammaire des Grammaires, ou Analyse raisonnée des meilleurs traités sur la langue française*. Brussels: Tircher.
Goémans, L., & Antoine, G. (1919). *Traité de prononciation française*. Liège: Bénard.
Goosse, A. (Ed.). (1986). *Le Bon Usage*. Paris: Duculot.
Grammont, M. (1914). *Traité pratique de prononciation française*. Paris: Delagrave.
Green, J., & Hintze, M.-A. (1990). Variation and Change in French Linking Phenomena. In M.-A. Hintze & J. N. Green (Eds.), *Variation and Change in French: Essays Presented to Rebecca Posner on the Occasion of Her Sixtieth Birthday* (pp. 61–88). London: Routledge.
Green, J., & Hintze, A.-M. (2001). The Maintenance of Liaison in a Family Network. In M.-A. Hintze, T. Pooley, & A. Judge (Eds.), *French Accents: Phonological and Sociological Perspectives*. London: AFLS/CILT.

Grevisse, M. (1936). *Le Bon Usage. Grammaire française avec des remarques sur la langue française d'aujourd'hui* (7th ed.). Gembloux: Duculot.

Gueunier, N., Genouvrier, E., Khomsi, A., Carayol, M., & Chaudenson, R. (1978). *Les Français devant la norme*. Paris: Champion.

Guiraud. (1965). *Le Français populaire (Que sais-je?)*. Paris: Presses Universitaires de France.

Hambye, P., & Simon, A.-C. (2012). The Variation of Pronunciation in Belgian French: From Segmental Phonology to Prosody. In R. Gess, C. Lyche, & T. Meisenburg (Eds.), *Phonological Variation in French: Illustrations from Three Continents* (pp. 129–150). Amsterdam; Philadelphia: John Benjamins.

Hamlaoui, F. (2011). On the Role of Phonology and Discourse in Francilian French Wh-Questions. *Journal of Linguistics, 47*(1), 129–162.

Hansen, A.-B. (2012). A Study of Young Parisian Speech: Some Trends in Pronunciation. In R. Gess, C. Lyche, & T. Meisenburg (Eds.), *Phonological Variation in French: Illustrations from Three Continents* (pp. 151–172). Amsterdam; Philadelphia: John Benjamins.

Harmer, L. C. (1954). *The French Language Today: Its Characteristics and Tendencies*. London: Hutchinson.

Harris, R. (1972). Words and Word Criteria in French. In F. Barnett et al. (Eds.), *History and Structure of French. Essays in the Honour of Professor T.B.W. Reid* (pp. 117–133). Oxford: Blackwell.

Haugen, E. (1966). Dialect, Language, Nation. *American Anthropologist, 68*, 922–935. Reprinted in J. B. Pride, & J. Holmes (Eds.), *Sociolinguistics* (pp. 99–111). Harmondsworth: Penguin.

Heselwood, B. (2006). *Final Schwa and R-Sandhi in RP English*. Leeds Working Papers in Linguistics and Phonetics.

Hindret, J. (1659). *L'Art de bien prononcer et de bien parler la langue françoise*. Paris: Laurent D'Houry.

Hornsby, D. (1998). Patriotism and Linguistic Purism in France: *Deux dialogues dans le nouveau langage françois* and *Parlez-vous Franglais? Journal of European Studies, 28/4*(112), 331–354.

Hornsby, D. (2009). *Liaison and Reading Styles in French*. Paper to Cambridge University Linguistics Society, 2.4.2009.

Hornsby, D. (2011). Getting It Wrong: Liaison, *Pataquès* and Repair in Contemporary French. In D. Lagorgette & T. Pooley (Eds.), *On Linguistic Change in French: Studies in Honour of R. Anthony Lodge* (pp. 69–83). Chambéry: Presses Universitaires de Savoie.

Hornsby, D. (2019). Variable Liaison, Diglossia, and the Style Dimension in Spoken French. *French Studies, 73*(4), 578–597.

Hornsby, D., & Jones, M. (2006). Blue-Sky Thinking? Léon Bollack and 'La Langue française en l'an 2003'. *Language Planning and Language Issues, 30*(3), 215–238.

Hornsby, D., & Jones, M. (2013). *Exception française*? Levelling, Exclusion and Urban Social Structure in France. In M. Jones & D. C. Hornsby (Eds.), *Language and Social Structure in Urban France* (pp. 94–109). Oxford: Legenda.

Huchon, M. (1981). *Rabelais grammairien: de l'histoire du texte aux problèmes d'authenticité*. Geneva: Droz.

Johnson, S., & Johnson, R. (2016). *Literacy in France: Country Report. Children and Adolescents*. European Literacy Policy Network (ELINET).

Joos, M. (1952). The Medieval Sibilants. *Language, 28*, 222–231.

Joos, M. (1962). *The Five Clocks*. New York: Harcourt.

Juillland. (1965). *Dictionnaire inverse de la langue française*. The Hague: Mouton.

Kammans, L.-P. (1956). *La Prononciation française d'aujourd'hui. Manuel à 1'usage des étudiants, des comédiens, des speakers*. Brussels: Bauds.

Kaye, J., & Lowenstrum, J. (1984). De la syllabicité. In F. Dell, D. Hirst, & J.-R. Vergnaud (Eds.), *La Forme sonore du langage* (pp. 123–155). Paris: Hermann.

Klingler, T., & Lyche, C. (2012). "Cajun" French in a Non-Acadian Community: A Phonological Study of the French of Ville Platte, Louisiana. In R. Gess, C. Lyche, & T. Meisenburg (Eds.), *Phonological Variation in French: Illustrations from Three Continents* (pp. 275–312). Amsterdam; Philadelphia: John Benjamins.

Klinkenberg, J.-M. (1992). Le français, une langue en crise? In M. Wilmet, J.-M. Klinkenberg, B. Cerquiglini, & R. Dehaybe (Eds.), *Le français en débat* (pp. 25–44). Brussels: Duculot.

Koch, P., & Oesterreicher, W. (1985). Sprache der Nähe – Sprache der Distanz. Mündlichkeit und Schriftlichkeit im Spannungsfeld von Sprachtheorie und Sprachgeschichte. *Romanistisches Jahrbuch, 36*, 15–43.

Koschwitz, E. (1893). *Les Parlers parisiens, d'après les témoignages de MM. de Bornier, Coppé, A. Daudet, P. Desjardins, Got, Mgr d'Hulst, le P. Hyacinthe, Leconte de Lisle, G. Paris, Renan, Rod, Sully-Prudhomme, Zola, et autres. Anthologie phonétique*. Marburg: Elvert.

Kroch, A. (1978). Toward a Theory of Social Dialect Variation. *Language in Society, 7*, 17–36.

de L'Esclaches, L. (1668). *Les véritables règles de l'ortografe franceze*. Paris: Laurent Rondet.

Labiche, E. (1867). *La Grammaire*. Retrieved from http://www.corpusetampois.com/cle-19-labiche1867lagrammaire.html.

Labov, W. (1966). *The Social Stratification of English in New York City*. Washington, DC: Center for Applied Linguistics.

Labov, W. (1972). *Sociolinguistic Patterns*. Philadelphia: University of Pennsylvania Press.

Labov, W. (2001). *Principles of Linguistic Change, Vol. 2: Social Factors*. Malden, MA: Blackwell Publishers.

Labov, W. (2006). *The Social Stratification of English in New York City* (2nd ed.). Cambridge: Cambridge University Press.

Labov, W., Weinreich, U., & Herzog, M. (1968). Empirical Foundations for a Theory of Language Change. In W. P. Lehmann & Y. Malkeil (Eds.), *Directions for Historical Linguistics: A Symposium* (pp. 95–188). Austin: University of Texas Press.

Laks, B. (1983). Langage et pratiques sociales: étude sociolinguistique d'un groupe d'adolescents. *Actes de la recherche en sciences sociales, 46*, 73–97.

Laks, B. (2009). Les hommes politiques et la liaison (1908–1998). In L. Baronian & F. Martineau (Eds.), *Le français d'un continent à l'autre: mélanges offerts à Yves-Charles Morin* (pp. 237–269). Quebec: Presses Universitaires de Laval.

Laks, B. (2014). Diachronie de la liaison en français contemporain: le cas de la parole publique (1999–2011). In J. Durand, G. Kristofersen, & B. Laks (Eds.), *La phonologie du français: normes, périphéries, modélisation* (pp. 333–375). Paris: Presses Universitaires de Paris Ouest.

Laks, B., & Calderone, B. (2014). La liaison en français contemporain: approches lexicales et exemplaristes. In C. Soum-Favaro, A. Coquillon, & J.-P. Chevrot (Eds.), *La liaison: approches contemporaines* (pp. 61–89). Bern: Peter Lang.

Laks, B., & Peuvergne, C. (2017). La liaison en français contemporain dans la parole publique (1999–2015). *Journal of French Language Studies, 27*(1), 55–72.

Landais, N. (1835). *Dictionnaire Général et Grammatical des Dictionnaires Français*. Paris: Didier.

Langlard, H. (1928). *La Liaison dans le français*. Paris: Champion.

Lartigaut, A. (1669). *Les progres de la véritable ortografe, ou l'ortografe francèze fondée sur ses principes, confirmée par démonstrations*. Paris: Laurent Ravenau.

Lavandera, B. (1978). Where Does the Sociolinguistic Variable Stop? *Language in Society, 7*(2), 171–182.

Le Mare, P. (1819). *Cours de langue française*. Paris.
Le Page, R., & Tabouret-Keller, A. (1985). *Acts of Identity: Creole-Based Approaches to Language and Ethnicity*. Cambridge: Cambridge University Press.
Le Roy, G. (1911). *La Diction française par les textes*. Paris: Mellottée.
Léon, P. (1971). *Essai de phonostylistique*. Paris: Didier.
Léon, P. (1978). *La Prononciation du français standard* (4th ed.). Paris: Didier.
Léon, P. (1992). *Phonétisme et prononciations du français avec des travaux d'application et leurs corrigés*. Paris: Nathan.
Léon, P. (1993). *Précis de phonostylistique: Parole et expressivité*. Paris, France: Fernand Nathan.
Léon, P., & Tennant, J. (1990). "Bad French" and Nice Guys: A Morphophonetic Study. *French Review, 63*, 763–778.
Lesaint. (1850). *Traité complet de la prononciation française dans la seconde moitié du XIXe siècle*. Halle: Gesenius.
Littré, E. (1863–1869). *Dictionnaire de la langue française* (4 Vols.). Paris: Hachette.
Lodge, R. A. (1993). *French: From Dialect to Standard*. London: Routledge.
Lodge, R. A. (2004). *A Sociolinguistic History of Parisian French*. Cambridge: Cambridge University Press.
Lombardi, L. (2002). Coronal Epenthesis and Markedness. *Phonology, 19*, 219–251.
Lopez, J. S. (2009). Langue française et éducation des élites. *Synergies Espagne, 2*, 81–97.
Lyche, C. (2007). Constructing a Large Oral Corpus for French. In Y. Kawaguchi, T. Takagaki, N. Tomimori, & Y. Tsuruga (Eds.), *Corpus Based Perspectives in Linguistics* (pp. 91–113). Amsterdam: John Benjamins.
Lyche, C., & Østby, K. (2009). Le français de la haute bourgeoisie parisienne: une variété conservatrice? In J. Durand, B. Laks, & C. Lyche (Eds.), *Phonologie, variation et accents du français* (pp. 203–230). Paris, France: Hermès.
Lyche, C., & Skattum, I. (2012). The Phonological Characteristics of French in Bamako, Mali: A Sociolinguistic Approach. In R. Gess, C. Lyche, & T. Meisenburg (Eds.), *Phonological Variation in French: Illustrations from Three Continents* (pp. 73–101). Amsterdam, Philadelphia: John Benjamins.
Lyche, C., Meisenberg, T., & Gess, R. (2012). Phonological Variation in French: Unity and Diversity Across Continents. In R. Gess, C. Lyche, & T. Meisenburg (Eds.), *Phonological Variation in French: Illustrations from Three Continents* (pp. 369–388). Amsterdam; Philadelphia: John Benjamins.

Malécot, A. (1972). New Procedures for Descriptive Phonetics. In *Papers in Linguistics and Phonetics to the Memory of Pierre Delattre* (pp. 345–355). The Hague: Mouton.

Malécot, A. (1975a). The Glottal Stop in French. *Phonetica, 29*, 51–63.

Malécot, A. (1975b). French Liaison as a Function of Grammatical, Phonetic and Paralinguistic Variables. *Phonetica, 32*, 161–179.

Mallet, G.-M. (2008). *La liaison en français: descriptions et analyses dans le corpus PFC*. Doctoral thesis, Université Paris Ouest Nanterre la Défense, Paris, France. Retrieved from http://www.projet-pfc.net.

de Malvin-Cazal, J. (1846). *Prononciation de la langue française au XIXe siècle, tant dans le langage soutenu que dans la conversation*. Paris: Imprimerie Royale.

Marceau, S. (1977). *Class and Status in France: Economic Change and Social Immobility 1945–75*. Oxford: Clarendon Press.

Marouzeau, J. (1963). *Précis de stylistique française* (5th ed.). Paris: Masson.

Martinet, A. (1945). *La Prononciation du français contemporain*. Paris: Droz.

Martinet, A. (1947). Notes sur la phonologie du français vers 1700. *Bulletin de la Société de linguistique de Paris, XLIII*(1), 13–23.

Martinon, P. (1913). *Comment on prononce le français. Traité complet de prononciation pratique avec les noms propres et les mots étrangers*. Paris: Larousse.

Martinon, P. (1927). *Comment on parle en français. La langue parlée correcte comparée avec la langue littéraire et la langue familière*. Paris: Larousse.

Massot, B. (2005). *Français et diglossie: Décrire la situation linguistique française contemporaine comme une diglossie: arguments morphosyntactiques*. Thèse de doctorat, Université de Paris 8. Retrieved from http://inferno.philosophie.uni-stuttgart.de/~benjamin/pdf/these-benjamin-massot-version-soutenance.pdf.

Massot, B. (2006). *Corpus-Based Ungrammaticality in French: A Pilot-Study*. Unpublished paper. Retrieved from http://inferno.philosophie.uni-stuttgart.de/~benjamin/recherche.html.

Matzke, J. (1897). *A Primer of Prench Pronunciation* (Revised 3rd ed.). New York: Holt.

Maupas, C. (1625). *Grammaire et syntaxe françoise*. Paris. Jacques Cailloué.

McMahon, A. (2002). *An Introduction to English Phonology*. Edinburgh: Edinburgh University Press.

Meigret, L. (1972 [1550]). *Traité touchant le commun usage de l'écriture françoise*. Republications Genève: Slatkine.

Meinschaeffer, J., Bonifer, S., & Frisch, C. (2015). Variable and Invariable Liaison in a Corpus of Spoken French. *Journal of French Language Studies, 25*, 367–396.

Miller, P. (1972). Vowel Neutralization and Vowel Reduction. In P. Petanteau, J. Levi, & G. Phares (Eds.), *Papers from the Eighth Regional Meeting of the Chicago Linguistic Society* (pp. 482–489). Chicago: Chicago Linguistic Society.
Milroy, L. (1980). *Language and Social Networks*. Oxford: Blackwell.
Milroy, L. (2003). Social and Linguistic Dimensions of Phonological Change. Fitting the Pieces of the Puzzle Together. In D. Britain & J. Cheshire (Eds.), *Social Dialectology: In Honour of Peter Trudgill* (pp. 155–172). Amsterdam: John Benjamins.
Milroy, L., & Margrain, S. (1980). Vernacular Language Loyalty and Social Network. *Language in Society, 9*, 43–70.
Milroy, J., & Milroy, L. (1985). Linguistic Change: Social Networks and Speaker Innovation. *Journal of Linguistics, 21*, 339–384.
Milroy, J., & Milroy, L. (2012). *Authority in Language: Investigating Standard English* (4th ed.). London: Routledge.
Milroy, J., Milroy, L., Hartley, S., & Walshaw, D. (1994). Glottal Stops and Tyneside Glottalization: Competing Patterns of Variation and Change in British English. *Language Variation and Change, 6*, 327–357.
Montaigne, M. de (1967 [1580]). *Essais* (R. Barral, Ed.). Paris: Seuil.
Morrison, A. S. (1968). *A Critical Bibliography of Studies of Liaison in French Speech Since 1800*. Unpublished PhD thesis, Columbia University.
Mugglestone, L. (2003). *Talking Proper: The Rise of Accent as Social Symbol* (2nd ed.). Oxford: Oxford University Press.
Müller, K. (1904). Die Bindung sonst stummer Endkonsonanten in französischen Sprachunterricht. In *Festschrift zum elften deutschen Neuphlologentage* (pp. 149–199). Coin: Neubner.
Mullineaux, A., & Blanc, M. (1982). The Problems of Classifying the Population Sample in the Sociolinguistic Survey of Orléans in Terms of Socio-Economic, Social and Educational Categories. *Review of Applied Linguistics, 55*, 3–37.
Myers-Scotton, C. (1976). Strategies of Neutrality: Language Choice in Uncertain Situations. *Language, 52*(4), 919–941.
Nicholson, G. (1909). *A Practical Introduction to French Phonetics for the Use of English-Speaking Students and Teachers*. London: Macmillan.
Nyrop, K. (1935). *Grammaire historique de la langue française* (Vol. 1, 4th ed.). Copenhagen: Nordisk Forlag.
Pagnol, M. (2004 [1928]). *Topaze: pièce en quatre actes*. Paris: De Fallois.
Palmer, R. (1985). *The Improvement of Humanity: Education and the French Revolution*. Princeton: Princeton University Press.

Palsgrave, J. (2003 [1530]). *L'esclarcissement de la langue françoyse, composé par maistre Jehan Palsgrave, Angloys, natyf de Londres et gradué de Paris*. Paris: Honoré Champion.

Pasquier, E. (1560). *Les Recherches de la France*. Paris: Mettayer & L'Huillier.

Passy, P. (1906). *Les Sons du Français: leur formation, leur combinaison, leur représentation*. Paris: Firmin-Didot.

Peletier Du Mans, J. (1550). *Dialogue de l'ortografe é prononciacion françoese*. Poitiers: J. & E. de Marnef.

Peyrollaz, M., & Bara de Tovar, M.-L. (1954). *Manuel de phonétique et de diction françaises à l'usage des étrangers*. Paris: Larousse.

Pichon, E. (1938). Genre et questions connexes (sur les pas de Mlle Durand). *Le Français Moderne, 6*, 107–126.

Picoche, J., & Marchello-Nizia, C. (1989). *Histoire de la langue française*. Paris: Nathan.

Pleasants, J. (1933). *Pronunciation of French: Articulation and Intonation*. Ann Arbor: Edwards.

Ploetz, K. (1873). *Systematische Darstellung der französischen Aussprache*. Berlin: Herbig.

Pope, M. K. (1952). *From Latin to Modern French with Especial Consideration of Anglo-Norman. Phonology and Morphology* (2nd ed.). Manchester: Manchester University Press.

Poplack, S., Jarmasz, L.-G., Dion, N., & Rosen, N. (2015). Searching for Standard French: The Construction and Mining of the *Recueil historique des grammaires du français*. *Journal of Historical Sociolinguistics, 1*(1), 13–55.

Portebois, Y. (2006). *Les Arrhes de la Douairière: Histoire de la dictée de Mérimée ou l'orthographe sous le Second Empire*. Geneva; Paris: Droz.

Posner, R. (1997). *Linguistic Change in French*. Oxford: Clarendon Press.

Price, G. (1971). *The French Language: Present and Past*. London: Edward Arnold.

Pustka, E. (2009). PFC et la phonologie du français en Vendée. In J. Durand, B. Laks, & C. Lyche (Eds.), *Phonologie, variation et accents du français* (pp. 307–335). Paris, France: Hermès.

Pustka, E. (2016). *Einführung in die Phonetik und Phonologie des Französischen* (2nd ed.). Berlin: Erich Schmidt Verlag.

Pustka, E. (2017a). L'écrit avant l'écriture: la liaison dans les livres audio pour enfants. *Journal of French Language Studies, 27*, 187–214.

Pustka, E. (2017b). *Liaisons 'interdites': infractions à la norme dans un style de parole hautement contrôlé*. Paper Presented at AFLS Annual Conference, Glendon College of York University, Toronto, August 8–10. Published Abstract.

Pustka, E., Chalier, M., & Jansen, L. (2017). A la recherche d'une norme de prononciation: le modèle des présentateurs de télévision. *Journal of French Language Studies, 27*, 101–115.

Quiehl, K. (1906). *Französischen Aussprache und Sprachfertigkeit. Ein Hilfsbuch zur Einführung in die Phonetik und Methodik des Französischen*. Marburg: Elvert.

Racine, I., & Andreasson, H. (2012). A Phonological Study of a Swiss French Variety: Data from the Canton of Neuchâtel. In R. Gess, C. Lyche, & T. Meisenburg (Eds.), *Phonological Variation in French: Illustrations from Three Continents* (pp. 173–206). Amsterdam; Philadelphia: John Benjamins.

Rambaud, H. (1578). *La declaration des abus que l'on commet en escrivant et le moyen de les eviter, et representer nayvement les paroles: ce que jamais homme n'a faict*. Lyon: Jean de Tournes.

de la Ramée, P. (Ramus). (1562). *Gramère*. Paris: Wéchel.

Ranson, D. (2008). La liaison variable dans un corpus du français méridional: l'importance relative de la fonction grammaticale. In J. Durand, B. Habert, & B. Laks (Eds.), *Congrès mondial de linguistique française. Recueil des résumés et CD-ROM des actes*. Paris: Institut de Linguistique Française & EDP Sciences, 1657–1671.

Régnier-Desmarets, F.-S. (1973 [1706]). *Traité de la Grammaire française*. Geneva: Slatkine Reprints.

Richelet, P. (1680). *Nouveau Dictionnaire François*. Geneva: J.-H. Widerhold.

Rickard, P. (1989). *A History of the French Language* (2nd ed.). London: Routledge.

Rickford, J. R., & McNair-Knox, F. (1994). Addressee- and Topic-Influenced Style Shift: A Quantitative Sociolinguistic Study. In D. Biber & E. Finegan (Eds.), *Sociolinguistic Perspectives on Register* (pp. 235–276). New York: Oxford University Press.

Rousselot, J.-P. (1911). Dictionnaire de la prononciation française. *Revue de phonétique, I*, 169–180.

Rousselot, J.-P., & Laclotte, F. (1902). *Précis de prononciation française*. Paris: Velter.

Roux, S. (1694). *Méthode nouvelle pour apprendre aux enfants à lire parfaitement bien le latin et le françois*. Paris: Warin.

Sampson, R. (2001). Liaison, Nasal Vowels and Productivity. *Journal of French Language Studies, 11*, 241–258.

Sankoff, D., & Laberge, S. (1978). The Linguistic Market and the Statistical Explanation of Variability. In D. Sankoff (Ed.), *Linguistic Variation: Models and Methods* (pp. 239–250). New York: Academic Press.

Sankoff, D., Sankoff, G., Laberge, S., & Topham, M. (1976). Méthodes d'échantillonage et utilisation de l'ordinateur dans l'étude de la variation grammaticale. *Cahiers de Linguistique de l'Université du Québec, 6*, 85–125. Montréal: Presses de l'Université du Québec.

Schane, S. (1965). The Phonological and Morphological Structure of French. Unpublished PhD thesis, MIT.

Scherm, C. (1909). *Französische Lautschule*. Nürnberg: Koch.

Schmidt, H. (1909). *Französische Schulphonetik. Praktische Anleitung für den Unterricht in der französischen Anssprache*. Cöthen: Schulse.

Schogt, H. G. (1961). La notion de loi dans la phonétique historique. *Lingua, 10*, 72–92.

Selkirk, E. (1972). *The Phrase Phonology of English and French*. Unpublished PhD dissertation, MIT.

Smith, A. (1998). French Variable Liaison: A Proposed Simplification. *Francophonie, 17*, 11–14.

Smith, A. (1999). *Linguistic Change on British and French Public Service Radio*. Unpublished PhD thesis, University of Newcastle-Upon-Tyne.

Stampe, D. (1972). On the Natural History of Diphthongs. In P. Petanteau, J. Levi, & G. Phares (Eds.), *Papers from the Eighth Regional Meeting of the Chicago Linguistic Society* (pp. 578–590). Chicago: Chicago Linguistic Society.

Stubelius, S. (1943). *Le Manuel phonétique de Nyrop à la lumière de recherches plus récentes sur le phonétisme français* (pp. 6–22). Gothenburg: Wettergren & Kerber.

Tabourot, E. (1603). *Les Bigarrures et touches du seigneur des Accords avec les apophthegmes du sieur Goulard et les escraignes dijonnoises*. Paris: Jean Richer.

Tappolet, E. (1932). Hiatusfurcht und Wohllauttheorie in Französischen. *Die Neueren Sprachen, XL*, 385–398.

Thibault, P., & Vincent, D. (1990). *Un corpus de français parlé. Montréal 84: historique, méthodes, et perspectives de recherche*. Quebec: Department of Languages and Linguistics, Laval University.

Thurot, C. (1881). *De la prononciation française depuis le commencement du XVIe siècle, d'après les témoignages des grammairiens* (Vol. 2). Paris: Imprimerie Nationale.

Tory. (1529). *Champfleury* (facsimile ed., 1931). Paris: Bosse.

Tranel, B. (1987). *The Sounds of French*. Cambridge: Cambridge University Press.

Trudeau, D. (1992). *Les inventeurs du bon usage (1529–1647)*. Paris: Minuit.

Trudgill, P. (1974a). *The Social Differentiation of English in Norwich*. Cambridge: Cambridge University Press.

Trudgill, P. (1974b). *Sociolinguistics: An Introduction to Language and Society*. Harmondsworth: Penguin.

Trudgill, P. (1983). Acts of Conflicting Identity: The Sociolinguistics of British Pop-Song Pronunciation. In P. Trudgill (Ed.), *On Dialect: Social and Geographical Perspectives* (pp. 141–160). Oxford: Blackwell.

Trudgill, P. (1986). *Dialects in Contact*. Oxford: Blackwell.

Trudgill, P. (1988). Norwich Revisited: Recent Changes in an English Urban Dialect. *English World-Wide, 9*, 33–49.

Trudgill, P. (1992). Dialect Typology and Social Structure. In E. Jahr (Ed.), *Language Contact and Language Change* (pp. 195–212). Berlin: Mouton de Gruyter.

Trudgill, P. (2011). *Sociolinguistic Typology: Social Determinants of Linguistic Complexity*. Oxford: Oxford University Press.

Van der Aa, J. (1622). *Grammatica Gallica*. Louvain.

Vandaele, H. (1909). *Phonétique du français moderne*. Besançon: Dodivers.

Vaugelas, C. F. de (1970 [1647]). *Remarques sur la langue françoise* (J. Streicher, Ed.). Geneva: Slatkine Reprints.

Vossler, K. (1913). *Frankreichs Kultur und Sprache. Geschichte der französischen Schriftsprache von den Anfängen bis zur Gegenwart*. Heidelberg: Vinter.

Wagner, R. L. (1951). Contribution à la préhistoire du romanisme. *Conférences de l'Institut de Paris, X*, 101–124.

Walker, D. (2012). Albertan French Phonology: French in an Anglophone Context. In R. Gess, C. Lyche, & T. Meisenburg (Eds.), *Phonological Variation in French: Illustrations from Three Continents* (pp. 341–368). Amsterdam; Philadelphia: John Benjamins.

von Wartburg, W. (1934). *Évolution et structure de la langue française*. Bern: Francke.

Wey, F. (1845). *Remarques sur la langue française au dix-neuvième siècle, sur le style et la composition littéraire* (2 Vols.). Paris: Didot.

Zink, G. (1986). *Phonétique historique du français*. Paris: Presses Universitaires de France.

Zribi-Hertz, A. (2006). Français standard et francilien commun: conséquences du phénomène diglossique pour la description et l'enseignement du français. Retrieved from www.soc.nii.ac.jp/sjllf/archives/taikai/2006a/2006a.conference.hertz.pdf.

Zribi-Hertz, A. (2011). Pour un modèle diglossique de description du français: quelques implications théoriques, didactiques et méthodologiques. *Journal of French Language Studies, 21*, 231–256.

Index[1]

[1] Note: Page numbers followed by 'n' refer to notes.

D. Hornsby, *Norm and Ideology in Spoken French*,
https://doi.org/10.1007/978-3-030-49300-4

	OBLIGATOIRES	FACULTATIVES	INTERDITES
NOM	*déterminatif* + {*nom* / *nopronom* / *adjectif*}	*nom pluriel* +	*nom singulier* +
		des soldats anglais	un soldat anglais
		ses plans ont réussi	son plan a réussi
	vos enfants		
	deux autres		
	un ancien ami		
VERBE	*pronom personnel* + *verbe*	*verbe* +	
	ils ont compris	je vais essayer	
	nous en avons	j'avais entendu dire	
	verbe + *pronom personnel*	vous êtes invité	
	ont-ils compris	il commençait à lire	
	allons-y		
INVARIABLES	*invariables monosyllabiques* +	*invariables polysyllabiques* +	*et* +
	en une journée	pendant un jour	et on l'a fait
	très intéressant	toujours utile	
SPÉCIALES	*formes figées*		*h aspiré*
	comment allez-vous		des héros
	les Etats-Unis		en haut
	accent aigu		+ *un, huit, onze et dérivés*
	tout à coup		la cent huitième
	de temps en temps		en onze jours

The manufacturer's authorised representative in the EU is Springer Nature Customer Service Centre GmbH, Europaplatz 3, 69115 Heidelberg, Germany. If you have any concerns regarding our products, please contact ProductSafety@springernature.com

Printed and bound by CPI Group (UK) Ltd, Croydon, CR0 4YY

30/09/2026

02225495-0001